TRANSACTIONS
of
AMERICAN PHILO.
Held at Pl
For Promoting U
Volume 9

PARADOXES OF FREE WILL

Gunther S. Stent

American Philosophical Society
Philadelphia • 2002

ISBN: 0-87169-926-5
US ISSN: 0065-9746

Library of Congress Cataloging-in-Publication Data

Stent, Gunther S. (Gunther Siegmund), 1924–
    Paradoxes of free will / Gunther S. Stent.
      p.   cm. — (Transactions of the American Philosophical Society, ISSN 0065-9746 ;
    v. 92, pt. 6)
    Includes bibliographical references and index.
    ISBN 0-87169-926-5 (pbk.)
    1. Free will and determinism.   I. Title.   II. Series.

BJ1461 .S69 2002
123'.5–dc21   2002038602

To Judith Martin

Contents

CONTENTS

Chapter Four
Theodicy

Chapter Five
Personhood

Chapter Six
Responsibility

Chapter Seven
Determinism

CONTENTS

Chapter Eight
Freedom

Chapter Nine
Mind-Body Problem

Chapter Ten
Critical Idealism

CONTENTS

Chapter Eleven
Etiquette

Chapter Twelve
Evolutionary and Genetic Epistemology

CONTENTS

Chapter Thirteen
Scientism

Chapter Fourteen
Complementarity

I thank Gonzalo Munevar for critical discussions and helpful advice and gratefully acknowledge the financial support of this project provided by the Committee on Research of the Berkeley Division of the Academic Senate of the University of California.

IMMANUEL KANT (1724–1804)

Engraving by Döbler (1791)

Chapter One

Prologue

Limits of Rationality. Immanuel Kant, the eighteenth century German philosopher, and Niels Bohr, the twentieth century Danish physicist, both noted that driving human reason too far in the analysis of deep problems often leads to irresolvable contradictions. Kant (1784) epitomized his insight into this fundamental limitation of our—on the whole admirably serviceable—reason with his aphorism "Out of timber so crooked as that from which man is made nothing entirely straight can be built." And Bohr (1949) drew attention to the limits of human reason by citing what he referred to as an 'old saying,' according to which there are two kinds of truths: "To the one kind belong statements so simple and clear that the opposite assertion obviously could not be defended. The other kind, the so-called '*deep truths*,' are statements whose opposite also contains deep truth." Most likely, the 'old saying' was Bohr's paraphrase of an epigram by his Danish philosopher-compatriot, Søren Kierkegaard, who asserted that "in the end, every truth is true only up to a certain degree. Once it transcends that degree, the truth meets its negation and turns into a falsehood." (Heiberg, P.A., V. Kuhr, and E. Torsting, 1909)

Free Will. Following Kant, we shall consider free will as our principal (but not sole) example of a deep truth that reflects the ultimate limits of human reason. The notion of free will attributes to persons the capacity to choose *autonomously* among possible alternative actions. This presumed autonomy of the will does not imply that a person's volition is totally immune to influence by other persons or by the natural world. What it does imply is that such *heteronomous* influences on a person's will not withstanding, there remains a substantial residue of independence of them, by virtue of which her rational faculty remains the final arbiter of what she actually wills. The outcome of this *autonomous* arbitration process is not capricious or random, but determined by the person's *soul*.

1

Soul. Despite the virtual disappearance of the old-fashioned term 'soul' from contemporary moral discourse held in secular rather than religious contexts, in this essay we shall continue to speak of 'soul' as well as of 'self,' the latter-day psychological term that has largely replaced 'soul.' For as Sigmund Freud's most brilliant disciple and eventual critic and adversary, Otto Rank (1930), pointed out, the principal goal of psychology is, and has always been, the elucidation of the soul, a concept that has been passed on to us from times immemorial by popular belief, religion and mythology. And yet, psychology has done its best to deny the existence of the soul, the very agency of which its practitioners are actually in search.

We *will* make a verbal distinction, however, between the quasi-synonyms of 'soul' and 'mind.' Both terms refer to the seat of consciousness, thought volition, emotions, and feelings, with the choice of one or the other word depending on the historical or disciplinary context of our discussion. We are going to speak of 'mind' when dealing with these mental phenomena in a *natural* (that is, amoral or secular) context. But we will speak of these same mental phenomena as 'soul' when dealing with them in, what Kant referred to as a '*non-natural*' (that is, moral or religious) context.

Moral Responsibility. Free will presents us with one of the oldest and most vexatious philosophical problems, dating back to the very beginnings of moral philosophy in ancient Greece. This problem is well nigh unavoidable within that tradition, because free will provides the basis for one of its central concerns, namely *moral responsibility*. This term refers to the human intuition that persons can be judged as *praiseworthy* or *blameworthy* for the volitions that motivated their actions. These judgments are based on established ethical criteria, such as those found in the Ten Commandments of Book 2 (*Exodus*) of the Israelite Torah.

Determinism. One necessary condition for holding persons morally responsible for their actions is to presume that they willed them freely, although just what is, or ought to be meant by 'freely' has been, as we shall see, subject to considerable controversy. Yet, whatever reasonable meaning we may attribute to the phrase 'willed them freely,' the concept of free will cannot help but contradict another human intuition. This is the belief, to which philosophers refer as '*determinism,*' according to which a seamless web of causal connections governs whatever happens in the world. Thus the free will of morally responsible persons and the causation of all of the world's happenings by the inexorable forces of determinism jointly exemplify the kind of *deep truths* of which Bohr had said that their opposites are deep truths as well. Moreover, according to Kant, the failure of philosophers to find an acceptable resolution of this contradictory aspect of such pairs of deep truths is attributable to the timber from which man is made being so crooked that nothing entirely straight can be built from it.

Metaphysics. The branch of philosophy that deals with the troublesome conceptual relations between free will, moral responsibility, and determinism is known as *metaphysics*. The term 'metaphysics' was coined by Andronikos of Rhodes, an editor of Aristotle's manuscripts, 300 years after Aristotle's death in 322 BCE, to designate the part of Aristotle's writings that Andronikos placed after (*meta*) the part that dealt with natural or physical things (*ta physika*). Upon the rise of Christian Philosophy in the early Middle Ages, 'metaphysics' took on a more general meaning than that intended by Andronikos, although, as is the case also for other terms of central importance for philosophical discourse, there is no general agreement on what that meaning actually is. For the purpose of our discussions we shall adopt the definition of metaphysics provided by the third edition of the *Shorter Oxford English Dictionary*. "*It is the branch of speculation which deals with the first principles of things, including such concepts as being, substance, essence, time, space, cause, identity, etc; theoretical philosophy as the ultimate science of being and knowing.*"

A derogatory connotation came to be attached to 'metaphysics' in the eighteenth century, especially by French and British philosophers of the Enlightenment. They laid the groundwork for such disciplines as psychology and psychiatry that were meant to provide a scientific account of morally relevant human behavior, and they relegated free will to the category of subjective metaphysical illusions. So by the first half of the twentieth century, scientifically sophisticated people had come to believe that the more we learn about someone's personal history, the less we can hold that person morally responsible for his behavior, and the very concept of moral responsibility would be vacuous. (Hook, 1981) Thus upon my first exposure to philosophy as an undergraduate at the University of Illinois in the early 1940s, my teachers left me with the impression that metaphysics is mainly hot air about how many angels can dance on the head of a pin.

In the wake of the Second World War, however, and the existential problems raised by the unprecedented scale of the crimes against mankind then recently perpetrated by Nazi Germany and other totalitarian states, metaphysics regained respectability. The problem of moral responsibility now loomed larger than ever. It would have taken a lunatic to forgive Hitler or Stalin for their voluntarily committed crimes, on the scientific grounds that poor Adolph and poor Joseph started their lives as babies who had inherited the genes (causally) responsible for the complexes and obsessions that turned them into world-class monsters. Thus, in our present, postmodern era, metaphysics came to be widely appreciated as the most interesting, and, in New-Age California-speak, the most *relevant* branch of philosophy.

Morals and Ethics. Two other key philosophical terms on which there is no general agreement regarding their proper usage are '*morals*' and '*ethics*,' except that it is widely admitted that the two terms—the former of Latin and the latter of Greek origin—do not refer to the same thing. Bernard Williams (1985), one of the foremost contemporary moral philosophers, wants "morals to be understood as a particular development of the ethical." This definition, however, matches none of the several definitions of 'ethics' offered by the third edition of the *Shorter Oxford English Dictionary* and seems to have a direct inverse relation to 'morals' as that implied by at least one of them. For the purpose of our discussions, we shall adopt as the meaning of 'morals' the principles of right and wrong that we are about to identify with the set of value-laden, tacitly held human intuitions designated by Immanuel Kant as *categories of pure practical reason*. This set of categories includes good and evil, free will, duty, compassion, and sacredness of the person. And as the meaning of 'ethics' we shall adopt the set of rules, or laws, that are intended to regulate social behavior in conformance with those principles of right and wrong.

In metaphysical discourse, the principles of right and wrong are said to be *transcendental*, an adjective that Kant used to refer to ideas or concepts that we apply to rather than derive from experience. We will elucidate in Chapter 12 how it is possible for us to understand words whose meaning does not arise from experience, and merely note for the time

4

being that 'God' and 'soul,' are further examples of such transcendental concepts.

Origins of Morals and Moral Philosophy. How did the belief arise that humans are moral beings who know the difference between good and evil and can tell right from wrong? Some suggestive clues regarding the high antiquity of moral beliefs of prehistoric people are provided by archeological finds, such as burial plots, clay statuettes, and cave paintings. But the earliest available explicit information about ancient moral beliefs dates back about 5000 years, to the long-dead civilizations of ancient Egypt and Sumer. (McNeil, 1963). All these ancient beliefs had in common that, though they may acknowledge an anatomical and behavioral affinity between humans and animals, they set humans apart from animals as uniquely moral beings. [Unless stated explicitly otherwise, in this essay the meaning of the term "animal" does not include the species *Homo sapiens*, which from a biological point of view is, of course, a member of the animal kingdom.]

These beliefs hold that humans are partly animal and partly divine, that humans live in nature, as do the animals, and that humans also live outside of nature, as does Divinity but as the animals do not. This hybrid theory of human nature was eventually reformulated in terms of the concept of the human being as a moral person, comprised of a body and a soul. The human body was considered as being endowed with the *natural* attributes that it shares with the bodies of animals, such as its anatomy and physiology, and which are amenable to study by physical methods. The human soul, on the other hand, was thought to be endowed with *non-natural* attributes, which it shares with Divinity, such as uniqueness, irreplaceability and being an end in itself, and which are amenable to study only by metaphysical methods.

Secular (rather than religion-based) moral philosophy arose as an identifiable subject of intellectual inquiry independently in Greece, as well as in India and China, during the sixth and fifth centuries BCE. In Greece this development was set off by Socrates, Plato and Aristotle and in East Asia by the 'Three Teachings' of Buddha, Confucius and Lao-Tzu.

Socrates was the first Western philosopher to recognize the importance of making a rational analysis of the meaning of such moral concepts as 'the Good,' 'right,' 'just,' and 'virtuous,' and of detailing the criteria for ascribing them to people. He was Plato's teacher, and Plato, in turn, was Aristotle's teacher. All three agreed in identifying the individual Good with the social Good and in defining moral categories, such as justice and virtue, in terms of their role in achieving the Good. Moreover, they used similar terminology and shared many principles and attitudes expressive of the rationality of Hellenic culture.

Nevertheless, Plato's method of inquiry and his conception of the role of moral principles in human affairs were different enough from Aristotle's that teacher and student founded two everlasting rival metaphysical approaches to the world, namely 'materialism' and 'idealism.' Neither of these terms means the same thing in philosophical discourse as it does in ordinary, everyday conversation. In the street, 'materialism' and 'idealism' refer to alternative personal attitudes towards life, with materialism denoting a preoccupation with material goods, such as BMW convertibles or jewelry, and idealism denoting a preoccupation with ideals, such as democracy or environmentalism. In the philosophers' ivory tower, however, the paired opposites refer to alternative conceptions of the nature of reality. There, materialism denotes the doctrine that physical matter is the only essential reality of the world and that all beings, processes and phenomena can be explained as manifestations or results of matter. And idealism is the philosophers' opposite of materialism, denoting the doctrine that the essential reality of the world is transcendental and exists only in our consciousness and reason.

Plato was an idealist. He believed in the independent reality of ideas, or 'Forms,' while he considered the reality of the material world as being merely relative to that of the ideal world of the Forms. The fundamental moral Form, according to Plato, is that of the Good—an ideal model of virtue that serves as a standard for moral judgments. Actions are right, laws are just, and people are virtuous insofar as they conform to that ideal model. And the only possible way for people to recognize the Good when they encounter it is that they are born into the world with an innate, transcendental knowledge of its Form. According to Plato, the Form of the Good, as well the Forms of all other moral categories, such as Justice, is stored in the soul rather than in the body. He asserted that the soul is immaterial, imperceptible, and immortal, while the body is material, perceptible, and mortal. Thus Plato charted an idealistic direction for fathoming the meanings of moral categories in a realm of timeless, universal, and transcendental Forms.

Aristotle was a materialist and rejected Plato's theory of the independent existence of Forms. He thought that all Forms are merely immanent in matter and have no independent existence, especially not moral Forms such as the Good. According to Aristotle, the highest Good for mankind is the balanced satisfaction of its desires, which he called *eudaemonia*—meaning 'happiness' or material and spiritual well being. So *eudaemonia* ought to be attainable by the exercise of our most precious, specifically human endowment, namely our reason. Aristotle sought an understanding of the principles of eudaemonia through the study of scientific disciplines such as biology, psychology, and physics.

Paradoxes. Kant's, Bohr's, and Kierkegaard's statements regarding the ultimate bounds of human reason reflect their perception of *paradoxes* generated by our rational faculty. According to the original Greek sense of the term, a 'paradox' is a statement that is seemingly self-contradictory or goes against generally accepted opinion, as did the paradoxical claim of Aristarchus of Samos in the third century BCE that our obviously stationary Earth rotates about the obviously moving sun. This paradox was eventually resolved by observational evidence indicating that the generally accepted opinion was wrong.

Earlier, in the fifth century BCE, the philosopher Zeno of Elea had developed some paradoxes that were meant to show the impossibility of dividing up space or motion. The best known of these is 'Achilles and the Tortoise,' whose conclusion is that if in a race between the two the tortoise has a head start, Achilles cannot overtake the tortoise, no matter how fast he runs. For, according to Zeno, after speedy Achilles has cut down the distance between himself and the slow tortoise by half, he can cut down the remaining distance by half again. But since he always has to cut in half whatever distance still remains between them, he can never reach the tortoise. Today, we know that this is not a genuine paradox because it was based on Zeno's lack of knowledge about convergent infinite mathematical series.

However, the 'Liar's Paradox' devised in the fourth century BCE by Eubulides of Miletus, which asks "does a man who says he is now lying speak the truth?" is still of interest today because, as we shall see, its resolution is not all that obvious.

In modern times, the term 'paradox' took on a more precise meaning. A paradox may consist of an, on first sight reasonable proposition, but which, on second sight, turns out to be self-contradictory. Or it may consist of two paired propositions, either of which, when considered alone, is supported by apparently sound arguments but which, when they are considered together, turn out to be mutually contradictory.

Thus the incompatibility of our intuitive (and unavoidable) concepts of free will and determinism qualifies as a paradox, to which we will refer henceforth as *The Paradox of Moral Responsibility*.

Theodicy Paradox. A new era began in the history of Western moral philosophy, as Christian philosophy arose in the fourth century CE as a fusion of secular Greek philosophy with Jewish monotheism. Of these, the former grounded morals in rational principles and the latter in God's commandments revealed in the Torah. [Strictly speaking, this Hebrew term designates the Five Books of Moses, or speaking more loosely, all of those parts of the Bible that Christians call *The Old Testament*.] These doubly-based, Judeo-Greco morals confronted Christians with the baffling paradox eventually called 'Theodicy,' according to which our one-and-only, all-powerful, righteous, and benign God rules over a world that abounds in evil and misery.

St. Augustine, the first philosopher among the Christian church fathers, offered a resolution of the Theodicy paradox by focusing on the concept of evil. As we will consider in Chapter 4, Augustine argued that what *appears* to be evil turns out to be a necessary element in the perception of the Good. God *has* to allow the existence of evil to provide mankind with a contrasting background that makes the Good shine more brightly and thus more easily perceptible to the dim-witted mortals.

Divine Foreknowledge. Augustine addressed also another paradox inherent in the free will concept, which is entailed by the all but universal belief, shared also by Christianity, that God has foreknowledge of the future. How can our will be free if God knew how we were going to act long before we actually *did* will freely how to act? Such divine foreknowledge does not seem to allow for the kind of free will that would provide a rational basis for moral responsibility in the first place. How can God be just in rewarding us for our good deeds and punishing us for our evil deeds, if these had all been foreordained by Him? Augustine's answer was that God's foreknowledge of movements of the human will does not create their necessity. The will He gave us could not be a will unless it remained in our power rather than in His. According to Augustine, God's foreknowledge of how we are going to use that power does not take away its freedom.

Utopia. The sixteenth century Italian statesman and political theorist Niccolo Machiavelli published a most disturbing insight that no visionary ideologue could accept, namely that the ensemble of our utopian aspirations for a perfect society is paradoxical. Utopian writers, from Plato (the inventor of the genre) with his *Republic*, through St. Augustine with his *City of God*, Thomas More (the inventor of the *name* of the genre) with his '*Utopia,*' and Francis Bacon with his *New Atlantis*, to one of the final utopists, Edward Bellamy (1888), with his socialist vision *Looking Backward, 2000–1887*, all differed in their vision of a perfect society and/or in how to go about achieving it. Yet, they all shared the same fervent belief that such a thing as a perfect society is possible. (Schaer, Clayes, and Sargent, 2000). As Machiavelli was the first to point out, however, this fervent belief is mistaken, since all these visions include two mutually incompatible aims and values. (Berlin, 1971). They are freedom and justice for the individual, on the one hand, and law and order for the society, on the other. From this Machiavellian discovery it followed that the belief that the correct, objectively valid solution to the question of how men should live can in principle be discovered is itself, in principle, not true. Utopia cannot be achieved on Earth, not because of the frailties and imperfections of mankind, but because every conceivable ideal society is meant to satisfy mutually incompatible, that is, paradoxical, goals.

Self-referential Paradoxes. Moral responsibility, Theodicy, and utopian social goals are only three of the many metaphysical paradoxes with which our, on the whole reasonably functional reason has saddled us.

Upon the revival of the study of formal logic at the turn of the twentieth century, the attention of modern logicians was drawn to *self-referential* paradoxes, of which the 'Liar's Paradox' of Eubulides was an early example. A modern example is Kurt Grelling's paradox about *autological* words, words whose meaning applies to themselves (such as 'short' and 'polysyllabic'), and *heterological* words, that is, words for which this is not the case (such as 'French' and 'monosyllabic'). So, is the word 'heterological' heterological? If it were, then it would be autological. But if it were autological, then it would be heterological.

Another self-referential paradox is Bertrand Russell's story about the Barber of Seville, who shaves all those men of Seville, and only those men, who do not shave themselves. So does the Barber shave himself? If the Barber is a man of Seville, the conclusion is that if he shaves himself, he does not, and if he does not shave himself, he does.

The easy way to resolve such self-referential paradoxes is to point out that their premises are impossible. There can be no lexical categories such as 'liar,' 'autology/heterology,' or 'Barber of Seville' with their stipulated attributes, *because* they engender paradoxes. This eliminative procedure may be acceptable in cases where, as in these examples, the premises are of no existential importance for us. But it is not acceptable in cases where our intuition tells us that the premises *have* to be true. Admittedly, some paradoxes were explained out of existence as breaches of one or another rule of logic, and others were at least tamed by the development of the mathematical doctrine of sets. But paradoxes still remained a source of concern for logicians and mathematicians, and dealing with paradoxes exerted a profound influence on thought about the validity of the foundations of their disciplines.

It seemed especially urgent to demonstrate that mathematics is free of inconsistencies and genuine paradoxes because it provides the principal medium for the rigorous description and rational analysis of complex scientific data. Thus any inadequacy of the descriptive and analytical powers of mathematics would place a limit on the depth of our ultimate understanding of nature. To eliminate that dire possibility, the eminent mathematician David Hilbert set out in the early years of the twentieth century to demonstrate the descriptive and analytical adequacy of mathematics. He hoped to prove that it is *consistent* (that is, free of paradoxes) and *complete* (that is, free of propositions whose truth is undecidable). By mid-century, Hilbert's project had failed spectacularly, when Kurt Gödel showed that arithmetic is neither consistent nor complete. On first thought, it seemed inconceivable that nature herself is inconsistent and incomplete, even if mathematics should turn out to embody some annoying rational deficits. But as the development of quantum physics that we will consider in our last chapter soon showed, this is not only conceivable but it also happens to be the case.

Bohr, who played a crucial role in these ominous scientific developments, was led by them to state his paradoxical proposition about deep truths, which I conjectured to be his paraphrase of Kierkegaards' epigram. Like Bohr and many other Danes, Kierkegaard was a devotee of paradoxes, about which he said that they are "a passion of thought; and the thinker who is without paradox is like a lover without passion—an inconsiderable fellow. . . . Take away the paradox from the thinker and you have the professor." (Gates, 1960)

SØREN KIERKEGAARD (1813–1855)
Drawing made by Søren's cousin
Niels Christian Kierkegaard in 1840.

This Danish love of paradoxes was not shared by hard-nosed, mainly British and American twentieth century, 'analytical' philosophers, who regarded the logical analysis of language as the way to settle many of the unsolved philosophical problems. One of them, D. J. O'Connor (1971), asserted in his essay entitled *Free Will* that "the existence of such paradoxes [as that of freedom vs. determinism] is proof that we are in an intellectual muddle, and such muddles can be cleared up in one of two ways. Either we must show that at least one of the offending propositions is false, or we must show that each does not really, despite of first appearances, entail the negation of the other." But it is O'Connor who was muddled, not Kant, Kierkegaard, or Bohr.

Mind-Body Problem. To find a place for mankind as free-willed creatures in a world, whose events are governed by determinism, that is, to resolve the Paradox of Moral Responsibility, the Ancient Greeks saddled us with another existential headache, namely the evergreen philosophical chestnut known as the '*mind-body problem.*' It poses the question whether there is not some basic difference between the human body—the target of nature's forces of determinism—and the human mind—the seat of an autonomous free will.

The Greeks noted that the *physicalist* statements we make about peoples' bodies are different in kind from the *mentalist* statements we make about their thoughts and feelings. But that difference does not necessarily imply that mentalist statements do not refer to some special kind of bodily functions. If mental phenomena, including willing, were nothing other than ordinary bodily functions, a view that came to be known as *monism*, they would be governed by determinism, and the Paradox of Moral Responsibility could not be resolved. But if mental phenomena were more than, or basically different from ordinary bodily functions, a view that came to be known as *dualism*, some mental phenomena, especially willing, might *not* be governed by determinism. In that case, the will *could* enjoy the freedom, or autonomy of choice, required for the resolution of the Paradox of Moral Responsibility. We will examine in Chapter 9 how some philosophers since Greek Antiquity have tried to deal with the mind-body problem and in the meanwhile merely note that Plato favored dualism and Aristotle monism.

Brain Science. Where are the choices made—or the acts of willing done—which are the manifestations of free will? Ever since the great Alexandrine physician, Galen, had shown in the second century CE that the brain is the seat of consciousness, it has been known that this is where willing is done. So it ought to be feasible to ascertain by neurobiological studies of the human brain whether peoples' will is subject to the natural laws of causal determination, or whether, by any chance, it happens to be independent of them. Thus far, neurobiological studies of the brain leave no doubt that its overall function, just as the overall function of the rest of the human body, is governed by the laws of physics and chemistry. But these studies have not yet managed to fathom in detail the mechanisms of many important mental phenomena (including willing). So it could be argued that the belief in free will is still an option not yet ruled out by scientific evidence.

12

This last-ditch proviso notwithstanding, contemporary investigators of the human brain generally consider the question of the existence of free will as a pseudo-problem and its discussion as a waste of time. Most of them are confident that the recent great advances in brain research will soon allow us to account for all mental processes in neurobiological terms, and they regard the dualism doctrine as a crackpot idea that is—or ought to be—dead and gone.

The philosopher Patricia Churchland became a prominent exponent of that view when she published a book in the 1980s entitled *Neurophilosophy* (Churchland, 1986). What is 'Neurophilosophy'? Its subject is what Churchland called the "mind-brain," and its agenda is to produce, by means of an interdisciplinary interaction among philosophers, psychologists, and neuroscientists a unified monist theory that explains the mind-brain.

Thus far, Churchland's Neurophilosophy has failed to make any striking progress towards producing the unified mind-brain theory. Its only achievement thus far, in my opinion at least, is to have put forward a convincing theoretical refutation of the claims by some philosophers and psychologists that a reductionist explanation of mental processes—of thoughts and feelings—in terms of neurobiological brain processes is impossible in principle. (Stent, 1990)

The neurophilosophical obituary notices of dualism are premature, reflecting merely the failure of devotees of monism to fathom the moral depth of the mind-body problem. For the deep question to be resolved in connection with that problem, at least as it pertains to the Paradox of Moral Responsibility, is not the empirical question whether the mind is in possession of a free will, which—from the human subjective perspective—it obviously is. Rather it is the transcendental question whether our notions about the natural world can accommodate creatures exercising free will. As we will see, the answer to that question is 'negative.'

However incisive and illuminating may have been the neurobiological progress made in recent years in the study of the brain, monism remains the existentially unsatisfactory solution of the mind-body problem that it has always been. While monism may be an adequate, or maybe even the only way to deal with mind as a natural phenomenon, it cannot give a satisfactory account of mind as a moral phenomenon. For such an existentially satisfying account, dualism has to be invoked, which is why dualism turns out to be alive and well and likely to be with us as long as there are people who live as social beings.

Critical Idealism. In mid-seventeenth century, the French philosopher René Descartes (1637, 1650) proposed a dualist solution of the mind-body problem, according to which human beings are comprised of two distinct substances. One of them he supposed to be the substance of the body, which, being material, is subject to determinism. The other he supposed to be the substance of the mind, which, being non-material, is not subject to determinism and from which we derive our free will and the responsibility for our actions. By the latter part of the eighteenth century, however, the explanatory success of Isaac Newton's physics in the natural world of material substances had discredited Descartes' concept of a non-material mind substance.

Rather than abandoning dualism, Immanuel Kant, put forward a radically different dualist resolution to the mind-body problem, to which I will refer as '*epistemic dualism*' (Stent, 1998, 2002), and which we will consider in more detail in Chapter 10. Kant's epistemic dualist resolution of the mind-body problem and of the Paradox of Moral Responsibility is based on his revolutionary epistemological theory of *critical idealism*. (Kant, 1934) The point of departure of Kant's *critical idealism* is Plato's insight that our direct contact with things is limited to their *appearances* in a *sensible* world of *phenomena*, which we perceive via our sensory faculties, such as sight, smell, hearing, and touch. According to Kant, we manage to make sense of these phenomena by interpreting their sources as real things-in-themselves, or '*noumena,*' of an '*intelligible*' (that is, understandable) world. For this interpretative process we resort to transcendental concepts, or *categories*, that arise *a priori* in our rational faculty rather than being inferred *a posteriori* from our experience.

Thus Kantian critical idealism is a blend of Aristotelian materialism and Platonic idealism. It is *materialist* in the sense that it posits the existence of a real external source—the noumena—of the phenomena we perceive in the phenomenal world. However, it is *idealist* as well, in that the intelligible world is of our own mental construction, based on our application of transcendental categories (or Platonic Forms) to the perceived phenomena, and in that the true nature of the noumenal source of the phenomena is, in principle, unknowable.

The gist of Kant's epistemic dualism is that it envisages two metaphysically distinct sets of *transcendental* categories, by use of which we construct two metaphysically distinct realms of the intelligible world. One realm, the *natural/amoral realm*, we construct by use of one set of transcendental categories, such as space, time and causality, to which Kant referred as *pure theoretical reason*. The noumena of that realm are material objects. The other realm, the *non-natural/moral realm*, we construct by use of another set of transcendental categories, such as good/evil, sacredness and free will, to which Kant referred as *pure practical reason*. The noumena of that other realm are human subjects. (Kant, 1949) According to Kant, to be human means to live as a dualist in both realms of the intelligible world and struggle with the paradoxes that arise from their incompatibility.

Evolutionary Epistemology. How can it be that if our mind brings its transcendental categories of Kantian *critical idealism to* the sensible world of phenomena *a priori*, they happen to fit that world so well? The answer was provided in mid-twentieth century by the Austrian student of animal behavior (or *'ethologist'*) Konrad Lorenz (1944), on the basis of the evolutionary history of biological species. According to Lorenz, what is *a priori* for individual animals is *a posteriori* for their species. Thus experience has as little to do with the matching of the Kantian categories with reality, as has the matching of the fin structure of a fish with the properties of water. Lorenz pointed out that the success of the brain of *Homo sapiens* in constructing an intelligible world that is well matched with the phenomenal world is simply another product of the Darwinian natural selection process that guided the development of the human brain in the course of mankind's evolution. Any early hominids who happened to think that before is after, or that near is far, or who failed to apprehend that phenomenon A is the cause of phenomenon B, left few descendants. Lorenz' evolutionary explanations of the origins of the Kantian categories gave rise to a discipline at the interface between biology and philosophy called *'evolutionary epistemology.'* (Campbell, 1974)

Characterization of the Kantian categories as *a priori* for the individual does not mean, however, that they are present already full-blown at a person's birth. Instead, as the cognitive developmental studies that Jean Piaget (1971) initiated in the 1920s and designated by him as *'genetic epistemology'* have shown, the Kantian categories arise in our mind postnatally. They are the result of a reciprocal interaction between the genome-controlled development of the infantile nervous system and the sensible world.

15

Complementarity. In putting forward his epistemic dualism in the latter part of the eighteenth century, Kant anticipated the epistemic dualism of 'complementarity' of quantum physics put forward by Niels Bohr (1928) in the first part of the twentieth century. In his use of 'complementarity,' Bohr did not refer to its ordinary, everyday meaning, namely the aspects of two different parts of a thing that make them a whole. Rather, under Bohr's meaning, complementary aspects of the world give rise to rationally irreconcilable concepts, whose inconsistency can never be demonstrated empirically.

As we will consider in more detail in our final Chapter 14, Bohr introduced his complementarity concept upon the advent of quantum mechanics and its epistemological paradoxes, such as the incoherent description of the electron in terms of a wave as well as a particle. According to Bohr, the wave-like mode of electron propagation, on the one hand, and the particulate nature of electron effects, on the other, each expresses an important feature of the phenomena associated with electrons. These features are 'complementary' aspects of reality because, although they are irreconcilable from a conceptual point of view, there are no observational setups under which they can be shown to be in direct contradiction. For mutually exclusive observational setups are required for demonstrating *either* the wave *or* the particle nature of the electron.

Bohr's lesson of the need for mutually exclusive observational setups for the analysis of the complementary aspects of the electron revealed that Kant's principle of epistemic dualism is not restricted to metaphysics, which is widely regarded as a soft discipline in which anything goes. Bohr showed that epistemic dualism applies also to physics, which is widely regarded as the hardest of disciplines, which brooks no irrational inconsistencies.

Coda. Our intuitive attribution of free will to the person is incompatible with our attribution of causal necessity to nature. Yet as rational beings, we cannot abandon the idea of non-natural moral autonomy any more than we can abandon the idea of natural causal necessity. Indeed, those rare individuals who *have* abandoned either of these ideas are usually diagnosed as irrational psychopaths, and most of them live in prisons or mental institutions. It seems unlikely that philosophers will be able to develop a solution to the mind body problem that is much of an im-

16

provement over Kant's plausible, albeit intrinsically incoherent epistemic dualism.

Being the bizarre creatures that we are, we have no choice other than to consider the beastly and the divine—the natural and the non-natural—as complementary aspects of the person. That is the essence of the deeply paradoxical nature of the mind that *Homo sapiens* drew in the lottery of organic evolution.

MOSES IS SHOWING THE TABLES
OF THE LAW TO THE PEOPLE.

Painting by Rembrandt (1659)

Chapter Two

———⊰◈⊱———

Civilization

Ancient peoples were no more and no less rational in the *existential*—especially moral—aspects of their religious beliefs than are we moderns, and many of those olden beliefs have been essentially conserved over the ages. (Eliade, 1978; Ferm, 1950). They were conserved because the human mind tends to deal with the metaphysical problems of existence in terms of Platonic Forms, which, being innate, and hence inherited, we still share with our—on an evolutionary time scale—not very remote ancestors living at the beginning of recorded history. Moreover, as we briefly noted in Chapter 1 and will discuss in more detail in later chapters, there is another reason for this lack of philosophical progress across the ages: Application of in-depth logical analyses to Platonic Forms in the moral realm leads, more often than not, to irresolvable paradoxes.

Fortunately, this troublesome rational limitation in dealing with existential problems does not apply to *epistemological*—especially cosmological and scientific—problems (aside from a few exceptions, such as those that we will consider in our final Chapter 14). That is why it was possible to make such great scientific progress in recent centuries in our understanding of the natural world and in making it do our bidding. Because of that progress many of the beliefs about the natural world embedded not only in ancient but also in not-so-ancient religions are no longer credible, indeed strike us moderns as ludicrous.

Prehistoric Mankind

Chronology (BCE)

50,000	Graves
30,000–9,000	Painting
8,000	Agriculture
4,000	Statuettes
3,000	Writing

It is a not uncommon surmise that in the course of the intellectual evolution of mankind its beliefs have progressed from the simple and uncomplicated concepts of our distant ancestors to the ever more complex ideas of modern people. The history of religion shows otherwise, however, in that over the millennia, the fantastically complex religious beliefs of our ancestors became ever simpler.

The earliest indications about mankind's metaphysical beliefs date back to about 50,000 years, provided by graves, rock paintings and statuettes. These ancient artifacts show that Early Stone Age people living on all five continents went to some trouble to dispose of their deceased in a ritual manner, rather than letting the human cadavers be eaten by scavengers or simply rot wherever they happened to fall dead. One well-nigh-universal funerary ritual was the dusting of corpses with red ocher, generally interpreted by paleoanthropologists as a token of blood and as an indication of a belief in life after death. Such a belief may envisage either the survival of an immortal, disembodied soul leaving the cadaver or the bodily resurrection of the deceased in a transcendental land of the dead. The prevalence of the latter belief is supported by the discovery of two widespread ancient customs: burying the corpse in a bent-over, fetal position to facilitate its rebirth and providing the grave with food, tools or adornments that will be helpful to the deceased in after-life.

Rock paintings provide the most important figurative testimonials of prehistoric human beliefs. Many of these treasures of Early Stone Age art were found in decorated caves dispersed over the European Continent, from the Atlantic Ocean to the Ural Mountains. One striking aspect of these paintings is their uniformity of style and content over time and geographical location. They changed very little in the period from 30,000 BCE to 9,000 BCE, and, for any given era, they are virtually the same at sites ranging from Northern Spain to the River Don. Since the paintings are mostly located at barely accessible sites at considerable distances from the entrances of mostly uninhabitable caves, there is a strong presumption that they were meant to serve some ritualistic or occult rather than practical purpose. That the depicted bears, lions, and other wild animals are often riddled with arrows has been interpreted in terms of the hunters' sympathetic magic, as have been some dancing human figures clad in animal skins.

The statuettes are representations of women, carved in stone, bone or ivory, ranging from two to ten inches in height. They date back to about

4,000 BCE, the time of the last Ice Age, and have been found over a wide area of Eurasia, extending from southwestern France to Lake Baikal in Siberia. These female figures lack the realism of the rock paintings. Their abdomens are exaggerated in size, their heads have no facial features, and their bodies are decorated with diverse geometric designs, among them the swastika. Paleoanthropologists are generally agreed that these statuettes had some religious or magical function, but they disagree about what this function might have been. Some scholars conjecture that the statuettes represent feminine sacredness and hence the magico-religious powers of goddesses. Others hold that they were portable mini-sanctuaries with the same symbolic structure and magical powers as the decorated caves.

The Rise of Civilization. A dramatic change in the human condition, known as the 'agricultural-urban revolution,' took place in the Late Stone Age, in about 8,000 BCE. It was set off by the domestication and breeding of wild animals and plants and by the resulting substantial increases in the food supply over that previously available to the roving bands of hunter-gatherers. These first regular food surpluses in human history brought about by this Mother of All Biotechnological Revolutions meant that it was no longer necessary for all of the people to spend all of their time looking for their next meal. A professional specialization of labor now became possible, which resulted in the differentiation of the social roles of various members of the society, such as king, priest, soldier, or artisan, who rendered expert services to their fellow citizens and, in return, were provided with food by the farmers. In this way there arose the civilizations and their large settlements in the part of southwestern Asia extending from the Persian Gulf northward to the mountains of Armenia, southward to North Africa, and westward to the Mediterranean Sea.

No doubt, there existed some rules that regulated the social relations between people even prior to the rise of civilizations. But as long as the horizon of human social life did not reach beyond the narrowly circumscribed group of the hunter-gatherer family or clan, any rules needed for the regulation of social relations would be known to and understood by every member of the clan. In contrast to a life lived wholly within family and clan, however, civilized life in large urban settlements now required codified imperatives of social behavior. To that end, the first explicit laws were devised as systems of rules for dealing with strangers and fellow citizens belonging to a wide range of social types, from slave to priest and king. Such laws had to consist of easily intelligible and ecumenical formulations of the rules of conduct, to provide for predictability, coherence, peace and harmony in the lives of the citizenry, by demanding that each person surrenders some of her freedom of action for the common Good. It is no coincidence, therefore, that the appearance of formal religion, with its professional priesthood and religious precepts, and of jurisprudence, with its professional judges and secular law, accompanied the rise of civilization.

Egypt

Chronology (BCE)

Ca. 3000	Hieroglyphic script.
3100–2258	Old Kingdom.
2500–2300	Pyramid Texts
2258–2000	First Interregnum
2000–1786	Middle Kingdom
1786–1570	Second Interregnum, Hyksos occupation
1570–332	New Kingdom
1419–1402	Amenhotep IV; Atonist Monotheism
332	Conquest of Egypt by Alexander
30	Roman province
642 CE	Invasion by Arabs. End of Roman province.

Once upon a time, the North African plateau had plentiful rains. It supported rich vegetation, teemed with wild animals, and provided an ideal habitat for Stone Age hunters. Then, about 40,000 years ago, rain fall declined, bringing on a drought that transformed this fertile region into the vast desert that we now call 'Sahara.' However, there did remain the narrow fertile corridor of the lower Nile Valley, irrigated by the water brought northward by the Nile from the mountains of tropical Central Africa. This corridor, which came to be called 'Egypt,' offered the displaced hunters a refuge with inexhaustible natural resources, protected from invaders by impenetrable deserts to the East, South, and West, and by the Mediterranean Sea to the North.

By the thirty-first century BCE, an Egyptian state—the 'Old Kingdom,' ruled by a pharaoh—had arisen, the earliest known national organization of people in history. This date roughly corresponds to the beginning of Egypt's historic period, since hieroglyphic writing was invented at just about the same time. The Nile Valley's uniquely favorable geography turned it into an isolated social laboratory in which the world's first great civilization could develop for two millennia, undisturbed by the waves of rapacious invading barbarians to which most other civilizations emerging elsewhere at that time were periodically subject.

The political and social structure of the first Egyptian state became a theological model for understanding how the natural world works. It evoked the conception of a kingdom-like, divinely ruled nature, with an important god being called 'pharaoh,' that shaped Egyptian religion for the next two millennia. Under a stable government ruling by standards of justice, there arose in Egypt the earliest known conception of a moral order, with the first explicit articulation of moral values, as we know them. Much of our knowledge about Egyptian theology is derived from the world's oldest and still extant collection of literature, the *Pyramid Texts*. They were inscribed on the stone walls of some pyramids built during the latter part of the Old Kingdom and had been compiled by scholarly priests.

The Egyptian religion was polytheistic, in that it held that many divinities rule the world. Some of them are benign (and worshipped) and others malign (called 'demons' and abhorred). The highest gods in the Egyptian Pantheon were those identified with the most important phenomena of nature. The sky was the goddess Nut, while the sun was the god Re. Other deities were identified with important attributes of phenomena. For instance, fertility was identified with the god Osiris, marital fidelity with Osiris' sister-wife Isis, and truth with the goddess Maat. Some deities were represented as animal-human chimeras, such as Horus, the son of Osiris and Isis, who was depicted as a falcon-headed man. But in whatever form they appeared, the Egyptian gods were endowed with a human personality. They suffered, took revenge, and even died. (Mercer, 1950)

The Egyptians developed a multifaceted existential doctrine of human nature, according to which, in addition to the body, many other elements go into making up a person. The most important of these elements is the *ka*, a ghostly double given to each person at birth. As long as persons are alive, they are masters of their *ka*. But as soon as they die, their *ka* begins a separate existence, resembling the body to which they had been formerly attached and needing food for their subsistence. The *ka* became the center of the cult of the dead. In addition to the *ka*, there is the *ba*, or soul, which upon a person's death leaves the body in the form of a human-headed bird. The person's name (*ren*), which has an independent existence, is the person's permanent essence. In addition to these distinctive elements of personhood, there is the *khu* (intelligence), the *ab*, (heart), the *sakhem* (ruling power), and the *khaybet* (shadow). This ancient Egyptian doctrine of personhood provides a dramatic example of the general trend of initially very complex religious beliefs becoming simpler rather than ever more complex in the course of social evolution.

No ancient people believed in a life after death more fervently than did the Egyptians. Although the body obviously becomes inert upon death, it does not vanish. Death consists merely of a changed relationship between a person's *ka* and her *ba*. To insure the post-mortem persistence of the *ka* as a home for the deceased's immortal *ba*, the Egyptians took great care to preserve the dead body. It was embalmed and mummified and laid in a coffin on its side like a sleeper, and all the utensils that a living person might possibly need, along with vessels for food and water, weapons and toilet articles, were placed in the grave. The most important ceremony connected with burial was the opening of the eyes, mouth, ears, and nose of the deceased. This ceremony guaranteed the continued existence the *ka* and made it possible as the home of the *ba*.

After death came the judgment of the moral rectitude of the life of the deceased. Each case was heard by a panel of forty-two judges in the presence of Osiris, sitting upon his throne. If the judges found the person guilty of having led a life lacking in virtue, her *ka* was devoured on the spot by a large beast also present at the hearing. If the panel found in favor of the person, her *ka and ba* whereas ferried on board the divine bark to the fields of eternal afterlife, to enjoy an ever-lasting companionship with the gods.

The intense concern of the Egyptians with the immortality of the soul addressed an existential paradox that is not resolved by simply declaring the belief in a life-after-death to be nonsense or self-serving priestly lies, as we will consider in more detail in Chapter 9. Since death evidently annihilates saints and sinners alike, the paradoxical conclusion would follow that, in the end, it makes no difference whether a person's moral behavior—from the cradle to the grave—was good or evil. So the paradox is resolved by the belief that the account is settled with deceased person's immortal soul during an eternal afterlife in heaven or in hell.

If the morals of a people may be defined by their conception of virtue, purity, faithfulness, truth and justice and of evil, impurity, faithlessness, falsehood and injustice, the Egyptian would stand high morally among the peoples of the ancient past. Thus the Egyptologist, James H. Breasted (1933) had good reasons to name his account of the rise of Egyptian civilization *The Dawn of Conscience*. That is not to say, of course, that by our modern standards the religion and laws of ancient Egypt did not have many defects. The Egyptians' idea of a deity was very anthropomorphic. The gods were created and died; married and suffered; they intrigued and could be coerced. They accepted human sacrifices, and magic words could control them. In family life, polygamy was permissible, concubinage was common; in social life punishments were very severe; slavery and forced labor were legal; and in international affairs, cruelty to captives was common. Yet, the Egyptians were devoted to their gods and sure of their love, righteousness, truth, and justice.

The Old Kingdom lasted for nearly a thousand years, towards the end of which the centralized, initially highly efficient administrative machinery run by a small number of bureaucrats and presided over by the pharaoh began to fall apart, because of excessive nepotism and cronyism in the national government. Local princelings and regional barons assumed sovereign power, several of them even claiming supreme royal authority. Before long, the Old Kingdom disintegrated, and there began a period of disorder which historians call 'First Interregnum.'

The collapse of the Old Kingdom was perceived a national catastrophe. The formerly happy-go-lucky outlook on life of the Egyptians was replaced by the earliest known period of national pessimism and disillusionment. It was during those troubled times that there arose in Egypt the first known instance of Messianism, that is, of the belief in a righteous ruler yet to come who would set things aright and usher in a Golden Age of Justice for all mankind.

In the middle of the twenty-first century, a local lord from Thebes gained military ascendancy over other would-be pharaohs and united Egypt once more. This ended the First Interregnum and inaugurated the Middle Kingdom. Although some of the centralized rule of the Old Kingdom was restored, the authority of the pharaohs of the Middle Kingdom was less exalted and absolute than it had been in the Old Kingdom. But by the beginning of the eighteenth century BCE, the country had lost once more its political cohesion, and the Egyptians were unable to ward off a threat they had never-before-faced in their history: They were invaded and conquered in 1786 BCE by the Hyksos, foreign barbarians from Southwestern Asia. The Hyksos were a Semitic people, who had crossed the Sinai desert and overwhelmed the Egyptian infantry by use of a novel war engine, the horse-drawn chariot. Thus ended the Middle Kingdom and began the Second Interregnum.

At the times of the Old and Middle Kingdoms, geographical barriers to foreign contacts had allowed the inhabitants of the Nile Valley to regard themselves as infinitely superior to all other peoples. The Hyksos conquest rudely challenged this chauvinistic belief. But after the Hyksos were finally expelled in 1570 BCE and the New Kingdom had been established, Egypt became a colonial power in Southwestern Asia, lording it over the Semitic natives. This imperial adventure made it impossible for the traditionally isolationist Egyptians to ignore foreign ideas and practices. With the expansion of trade under the empire, new cities attracted nests of foreigners to the soil of Egypt itself, while the imperial Egyptian armies were recruited largely from neighboring barbarian peoples. Thus as conqueror and defender of strange lands, and as Commander-in-Chief of an army composed largely of foreign mercenaries, the pharaoh was constantly exposed to foreign customs. Therefore there was a real danger of his turning away from established Egyptian mores.

A young pharaoh, who ascended the throne in about 1380 BCE under the name Amenhotep IV, did in fact become a royal revolutionary of the most radical sort. He forced a new religion—Atonism—on his subjects. In contrast to the traditional polytheistic Egyptian worship of many gods—some major and others minor—Atonism was monotheistic, devoted to the worship of a single, all-powerful deity, the sun god Aton, an upgraded version of the sun god, Re, of Old Kingdom polytheism. Atonism was the first known strictly monotheistic religion in history. Its advent in Egypt brought on a novel ideology that was previously unknown to the ancient world, namely religious intolerance. Amenhotep IV suppressed all extant polytheistic faiths devoted to the worship of other gods and made the worship of Aton—and of himself as the self-proclaimed son of Aton—the sole religion of the Egyptian Empire. He renamed himself 'Ikhnaton,' which means 'Aton is pleased.'

Atonist doctrine conceived the power of the deified sun disk as extending equally to all peoples, whether within or without the borders of the Egyptian empire. Such universalism may have reflected a radically rational reaction to the religious diversity of mankind—a diversity which had come to Egyptian attention with all the force of a new revelation when their imperial armies and officials had begun to move in distant lands and among alien people. Pious and devout souls, disturbed by such religious variety, the Egyptians may well have been struck by the undoubted presence of the sun in every part of the world, shining with majesty and overwhelming brightness upon all men. Here was clearly a true God, manifest and indubitable, unique, universal and beneficent. By comparison, other so-called deities appeared to be false, distorted, manmade. Yet only a minority of Egyptians embraced Atonism, and it seems unlikely that the movement would have attained any importance at all without the support of the pharaoh's power. Amenhotep's backers seem to have been mainly social upstarts and soldiers, so that it is possible to interpret the Atonist movement as a struggle between army and priesthood for primacy in the state.

Atonism collapsed upon Amenhotep's death. And once the fanaticism of Atonist reform had been abandoned, the Egyptian priests and nobles whose privileges Amenhotep had abrogated saw to it that all traces of what they regarded as barbarian religious subversion were eradicated. Amenhotep's palaces and temples were razed, and his new capital at Amarna was abandoned, never to be reoccupied. Amenhotep's Atonist creed left few traces, except that, as we shall soon consider, it possibly gave rise to the Mosaic religion of the Israelites.

The ancient Egyptian national way of life began to disappear upon the conquest of the country by Alexander the Great in 330 BCE, even though Alexander did not seek to annex Egypt. On the contrary, he wanted to rule it as an Egyptian pharaoh and had himself deified. Alexander's successors, the Ptolemies, actively encouraged the preservation of Egyptian life and religion. For the Greeks generally admired the Egyptians and learned much from them. Thus during the Ptolomaic period, the deities of Egypt remained mainly the same. The great triad of Osiris, Isis and their son Horus, remained supreme, but they came to be called by their Greek equivalents, Zeus, Hera and Ares. When Egypt became a Roman province in 30 BCE, there was no essential change in religion and worship, except that some new deities were introduced from

Rome, such as the Jupiter, Juno and Mars triad, chiefly for the benefit and comfort of Roman officials and soldiers. The passion of Osiris and mysteries of Isis became very popular with the Romans, and the religion of Ancient Egypt spread over the highways of the Roman Empire, even as far as France, the Rhineland and England. Its definitive end came in 642 CE, when the Arabs invaded the Valley of the Nile and put an end to the Roman Empire in Egypt.

Sumer

Chronology (BCE)

3000	Rise of Sumerian culture; development of cuneiform script.
2350	Conquest of Sumer by Sargon of Akkad
2000	Sumerian language ceases to be spoken but is retained in liturgy.
1792–1750	Hammurabi, Amorite sovereign of Babylon,
1500	End of the creative period of Sumerian thought.

In a historical context, the whole part of southwestern Asia designated as the 'Fertile Crescent' (that is, modern Turkish Anatolia, Iraq, Iran, and Palestine) can be considered as a single cultural region. Its ancient Greek name was 'Mesopotamia,' although, strictly speaking, that name (meaning 'between rivers') denotes only to the territory lying in present-day Iraq between the two great rivers, Tigris and Euphrates. Just as is the case for Egypt, the earliest archeological indications of a civilized Mesopotamian state date back to the fourth millennium BCE. By that time, artificially irrigated agriculture had been developed and permanent settlements established in the plain of Sumer in southern Mesopotamia, whose people are known as 'Sumerians.' Despite the known presence of other ethnic groups in that region, it is usual to refer to the earliest Mesopotamian civilization as *'Sumerian.'*

The development of the main lines of Sumerian civilization took place during the pre-historic period, i.e. before the invention of cuneiform script in about 3000 BCE. This is evident from Sumerian works of art, whose major forms, motifs and styles had already been developed before the earliest appearance of written records. Similarly, as shown by the archeological record, the development of Sumerian technology, whose cluster of great inventions—irrigation, wheeled vehicles, sailing ships, metallurgy, and oven-baked and wheel-turned pottery—also dates back to the pre-historic period.

The problem of who the Sumerians were and whence they came has not been solved. Their language seems unrelated to any other known tongue, and their skeletons provide no definitive morphological clues regarding their racial origins. Sumerian religion and art gave special prominence to animals, suggesting that its background was pastoral. Unlike ancient Egyptian society, which developed for millennia in the isolated Lower Nile Valley by the undisturbed descendants of the original settlers, barbarian invaders from all sides periodically inundated the easily accessible plains of Mesopotamia. Thus by the beginnings of recorded history, a mixture of peoples were already populating the Fertile Crescent. The earliest available records show Sumerians living side by side with speakers of Semitic languages. Though Sumerians predominated in the south and Semites in the north, there was extensive ethnic intermingling in many areas.

The Sumerian religion, like that of ancient Egypt, was polytheistic, embracing a panoply of local deities. As in Egypt, the high gods of the land were conceived in human form, each personifying an important phenomenon of nature—sky, sun, earth, water and wind. The rounds of the seasons were accounted for by a myth of an annual life-death cycle of a God of Vegetation. His disappearance into the underworld in the fall causes plant life to wither, until his springtime return to the living world revives it.

The Sumerian myth of the creation of mankind by divine agency has an important feature in common with the Torah's story of Genesis 1 (of which it is likely to be the source); namely that mankind is partly animal and partly divine. This implied that there is no impassable distance between the divine mode of being and the human condition. Although mankind was created to serve the gods, who, their great supernatural powers notwithstanding, need to be fed and clothed, humans are not merely servants but also imitators of the gods, and hence their coworkers rather than their slaves.

Since the gods are responsible for the cosmic order, people must obey the divine decrees that insure the well-being of the world. These decrees determine the destiny of every being, of every form of life, of every divine and human enterprise. Yet, the cosmic order established by the gods is continually troubled by mankind's crimes, faults, and errors, which must be expiated and purged by means of various rites. Thus the Sumerians anticipated the Paradox of Moral Responsibility, by holding people morally responsible for their actions which, being determined or foreordained by the gods, they could not have chosen freely.

The myth of the Flood—which was common to several ancient religions and undoubtedly reached the Torah from a Sumerian source as well—is another early example of the Paradox of Moral Responsibility. Although the details of the myth as told by different traditions vary, the Flood stories generally agree in attributing the cause of the Flood to divine displeasure over the sins of the morally decrepit mankind in a world that the gods (or God) created. Thus by drowning the whole lot in the waters of the Flood, they (or He) make room for morally superior folks to populate a new and better world after their (or His) having another try at Creation. The myth of the Flood is also an early version of *theodicy*, the baffling theological paradox of a God who is omnipotent and omniscient and yet can make mistakes and fail to foresee the regrettable results of his handiwork. The paradox is sharper, of course, in the context of an uncompromisingly monotheistic faith, such as that of the Israelites with its one-and-only almighty God. It is less acute in the context of polytheistic pagan religions, such as the Sumerian, and the Greco-Roman, with their Pantheons of many gods, none of whom is wholly devoid of human frailties. Whereas the attribution to God of having made a mistake in creating Adam and Eve would be sacrilegious, the tales of pagan deities, such as Marduk and Zeus/Jupiter and their consorts, abound in errors and foibles of their divine personages.

The Sumerians divided the irrigated land into large agricultural estates, tended by many serf-like resident farmers. Ownership of an individual estate was nominally vested in a local god residing in an on-site temple, whose priests provided the visible members of the divine household. The priests looked after the wants of their divine squire through ceremonies and sacrifices. They also acted as mediators between the god and the temple's work force. An agglomeration of several such temple communities constituted a Sumerian city.

As the agricultural temple estates flourished in Sumer, they too produced more food than was needed to feed their farmers. This surplus allowed the priestly managers to withhold a substantial part of the harvest from the farmers, for storage in the temple granaries. Far from being entirely parasitic on the farmers, however, the priests performed vital managerial functions without which Sumerian civilization could not have come into existence in the first place or long survived. The priests supervised the allocation of land, maintained boundary markers, and directed the gangs of laborers who maintained the irrigation canals and strengthened the dikes. Moreover, only the priests had the skills needed for reckoning the seasonal calendar, laying out the canals and keeping accounts. More important still for the legitimization of the priests' power was their role as the chosen communication channel linking the immortal gods and their mortal people.

Priestly management of the agricultural surplus led to the emergence of a class of workers who rendered services that were no longer directly connected with the production of food but provided the farmers with technical support, such as administrators, craftsmen, or soldiers. Thus the Sumerian temple-estate community with its agricultural surpluses provided the first institution in human history at which non-agricultural specialists could make a living. These people became the city dwellers whose relief from backbreaking labor allowed them to become the creators, sustainers, and organizers of civilized life.

The Sumerian city-temples were unified in the twenty-fourth century BCE upon the conquest of Sumer by a Semitic king, Sargon, of Akkad in northern Mesopotamia. He transformed the ancient pattern of Sumerian political life by changing the agglomeration of city-states of essentially equal standing into an empire administered from a newly built capital city and reaching beyond the limits of Sumer. The Sumerian language ceased to be a spoken tongue, but retained its function as a liturgical language in religious ceremony, as was the case later also for Sanskrit, Hebrew, Latin, and Old Slavic.

In contrast to the millennia-long political stability of Egypt as a nation-state, Mesopotamia was in constant turmoil, with no state able to defend itself for long against invasion and takeover by fierce barbarian hordes. No sooner had one of the barbarian invaders settled down to found a new state and assimilated the civilized Sumerian way of life than another barbarian horde turned up at the gates for the next conquest-assimilation-cycle. Among the ancient successor states to Sumer, Babylonia is the one whose name remained better known in the Western

World than that of any of the others, long after southwestern Asia had ceased to be a focal point of the civilized world. No doubt, the reason for this preferential remembrance is Babylonia's prominent mention in the Torah as the country where the Israelites were held captive in the sixth century BCE.

Babylon, an ancient town located on the River Euphrates not far downstream from modern Baghdad, became the most important city in Sumer when Hammurabi, king of the Barbarian Amorite invaders, made it the capital of his empire in 1750 BCE. Hammurabi was of vital importance for the development of formal ethics because, as far as is known, he was the first sovereign in the history of mankind to promulgate an explicit code of laws for the regulation of social behavior. Its text came down to us in 3,600 lines of cuneiform script carved on a stone column found in the ancient Persian city of Susa. (Hammurabi's code anticipated by about 500 years the meanwhile better known code that Moses brought down to the Israelites from Mount Sinai). Hammurabi's code provides for some cruel and unusual punishments meanwhile outlawed by the U.S. Constitution, such as the precursor of Moses' 'eye for eye' principle mentioned in Exodus 21:24. But, on the whole and for its time, it was reasonably humane.

The polytheistic Babylonian religion was derived from an elder Sumerian theology. As were the gods of both Egypt and Sumer, so were also the gods of Babylon regarded as divine sovereigns responsible for the world's being orderly rather than chaotic. During Hammurabi's reign there began a trend towards monotheism, in that Marduk, the patron god of Babylon, became the omniscient, all-powerful deity of the Babylonian Pantheon—the creator of mankind and the God of Light and Life. Moreover, by way of a conceptual extension of Hammurabi's creation of social order out of chaos in human affairs by the promulgation of his moral code, the idea arose in Babylon that Marduk legislated explicit natural laws whose obeisance by nature generated cosmic order out of chaos. Thus the metaphysical concept of universally valid 'laws of nature' promulgated by superlunary divinity, whose discovery is the Holy Grail of modern science, turns out to be a metaphorical extension of the laws of human affairs promulgated by sublunary legislators.

Israel

Chronology (BCE), according to the Torah

1800	Patriarch Abraham. Israelites from the city of Ur settle in northwestern Mesopotamia.
1700	Jacob leads southward migration of Israelites to Canaan (Palestine).
1600	Israelites migrate to and are enslaved in Egypt.
1300–1250	Exodus from Egypt. Adoption of Yahwistic monotheism.
1200	Israelites return to Canaan (Palestine) under leadership of Joshua.
1000	Saul, first king of the Israelites.
900–300	First five books of the Torah written.

Many of the moral and religious traditions that are characteristic for the modern Western world are rooted in ideas that came down to us from the IsraeliteTorah. Its earliest version was written as late as the ninth century BCE, or some five hundred years after the Israelite Exodus from Egypt, as told in the Torah. Our *direct* knowledge of these ancient traditions was greatly extended, however, once Egyptian hieroglyphic as well as Sumerian cuneiform script had finally been deciphered in the first part of the nineteenth century CE. Then it transpired from documents dating back to the *thirtieth* century BCE that many elements of the Mosaic religion of the Israelites were derived from the much older traditions of Egypt and Sumer, the two main cradles of Western civilization. (McNeil, 1963). Despite the doubtful authenticity of the Torah's account of early Israelite history, it does provide a deep perspective of the source of some of the beliefs and metaphysical views in which contemporary (Western) moral philosophy is rooted.

In about 1800 BCE—according to the Torah—the Israelites, a peripatetic Semitic tribe hailing from the city of Ur in the southernmost part of Mesopotamia, migrated to its northwestern part under the leadership of the Patriarch Abraham. Two generations later, Abraham's grandson, Jacob, led the Israelites in a southwestward migration to Palestine, then populated by the Canaanite people. It was from Jacob, who was later called, 'Israel' [srah+el = fight+God], that the Israelites derived their name.

To escape the consequences of a famine in Palestine in about 1600 BCE, some Israelites migrated southward to Egypt. After making themselves at home in the fertile Nile delta, then only recently liberated from the occupation by the Semitic Hyksos invaders, the Israelites were enslaved by the first pharaohs of the New Kingdom and remained enslaved for nearly three centuries. Finally, in about 1300 BCE, the Israelites found a dynamic leader in Moses. He freed them from bondage, by leading their flight from Egypt to the Sinai desert. Once safely in the desert, Moses persuaded his Israelite followers to adopt a monotheistic religion, which entailed the worship of the one and only, all-powerful, ecumenical God, nicknamed 'Yahweh' because his (unknown) real name was too holy to be uttered.

One reason why many modern scholars doubt the authenticity of this account of Israelite history provided by the Torah is the absence of any archeological evidence that a substantial number of Israelites ever *were* enslaved in Egypt. In view of written records of Egyptian history dating back to 2000 BCE, it seems unlikely that—had they really happened—the three-century-long presence of Israelites in Egypt and the dramatic events connected with their eventual escape would have gone unrecorded.

Moses and Monotheism. Who was Moses, if he indeed existed? According to the Torah's chapter Exodus 2:5-10, an Egyptian princess saved Baby Moses from the waters of the Nile, where he had been abandoned by his Israelite parents. She gave him his name, which was supposedly derived from a Hebrew phrase meaning 'he who was pulled from the water.' Even among those historians, however, who believe that Moses was a historical person, few accept this Biblical story, not least because it seems highly improbable that an Egyptian princess would have given the foundling a Hebrew name. According to J.H. Breasted's history of Egypt, the name 'Moses' is derived from the Egyptian word 'mos' meaning 'child.'

In his fascinating but much-maligned book, *Moses and Monotheism*, Sigmund Freud (1939) (who believed that Moses *was* a historical person) addressed the mystery of Moses' origins. In accord with Otto Rank's (1914) psychoanalytic interpretation of the ubiquitous theme of the hero as a foundling in mythic biographies, Freud concluded that Moses was not a child abandoned on the Nile by his Israelite parents. Rather—so

Freud conjectured—Moses was a highborn Egyptian, perhaps a prince or priest.

But what could have motivated a highborn Egyptian to make himself the leader of a crowd of down-and-out Israelite slaves and leave his native Egypt with them. Freud finds it noteworthy that Moses not only became the Israelites' political leader but that he also foisted a novel religion on them, which is called 'Mosaic' to this day. But how likely is it that Moses, however highborn, would have created a new religion from scratch? Would it not have been much more probable that Moses simply converted the downtrodden Israelites, who undoubtedly had some kind of religion when they arrived in Egypt three centuries earlier, to the traditional Egyptian religion?

No, this could not have been the case, since there are profound differences between the Mosaic and the Egyptian faiths. The Mosaic religion is as purely monotheistic as a religion can get. There is only one God—unique, omnipotent, unapproachable. The sight of His countenance cannot be borne; one must not make any image of Him, nor even breathe His name. The traditional Egyptian religion, by contrast, acknowledged a bewildering diversity of deities, differing in their origin, importance, and special competence. As we noted previously, some of these deities were personifications of concrete natural phenomena, such as heaven and earth, sun and moon. Others personified abstractions, such as justice and truth. The shape of Egyptian deities is often that of an animal, as if the gods had not yet overcome their origin in the totem animals of the Old Stone Age. Moreover, the dominion of most traditional Egyptian deities was local rather than global, dating back to the time when the Egyptian state was split into many provinces.

There is yet another difference between the Mosaic and the Egyptian faiths. No other people of antiquity did so much to deny death as the Egyptians. They made elaborate provisions for an after-life and worshipped Osiris, the god of death and ruler of the netherworld, as their most popular deity. The Mosaic faith, on the other hand, does not believe in immortality and does not mention the possibility of a life after death. This is all the more remarkable in that the later rise of Christianity showed that a belief in a life-after-death *is* compatible with monotheism.

Thus the faith to which Moses allegedly converted his Israelite followers was not the traditional polytheistic Egyptian religion. Instead, it would have had to be the short-lived, revolutionary monotheistic Atonism that briefly held sway in Egypt under Amenhotep IV, alias 'Ikhnaton,' a few decades before the Israelite's Exodus from Egypt under Moses' leadership. Admittedly, there are some striking differences between Atonism and the Mosaic faith (in addition to God's different name), one of them being that Mosaic monotheism is even more uncompromising than that of Atonism. The Mosaic faith forbids all visual representations of God and abandoned His Atonist identification with the sun.

In considering why Moses, if he was indeed an Egyptian, was motivated to convert the downtrodden Israelites to Atonism and lead them out of Egypt, Freud suggests the following, highly speculative but not implausible scenario. Suppose that Moses was a noble and distinguished Egyptian, perhaps a member of the royal household, as the Torah has it. Highly intelligent, ambitious and energetic, he saw himself as a future leader of his people, a governor of the Empire. Inspired by pharaoh Amenhotep/Ikhnaton, Moses became a devout convert to Atonism, whose basic principles he made his own. However, upon the suppression of Atonism and restoration of Amonism following Amenhotep/Ikhnaton's early death, Moses saw all his hopes and prospects destroyed. He realized that he had no political future in Egypt if he were not to recant the new Atonist faith. So Moses sought to found his own empire, by looking for a hapless group of people whom he could convert to the monotheistic religion that his fellow Egyptians had rejected and lead them to settle outside of Egypt. The people who turned out to be willing to follow Moses were the enslaved Israelites.

For all its plausibility, there inheres at least one obvious defect in Freud's *Moses and Monotheism* story: Freud does not mention what kind of religion he thinks the Israelites had at the time they *came* to Egypt and were enslaved. According to the Torah, the Israelites not only had been monotheists for at least 200 years *before* they ever migrated to Egypt, but they were even partners with the one-and-only God in a covenant made on their behalf by the Patriarch Abraham. That covenant established the Israelites as His chosen people. So they wouldn't have needed Moses to tell them about Yahweh (alias Aton).

One might have expected the Israelites to assimilate the traditional Egyptian and Sumerian modes of thought, since these were supported by such vast prestige. But assimilation was not a characteristic Israelite trait. On the contrary, the Israelites held out with a peculiar stubbornness against the religions of their neighbors. Admittedly, one can detect many reflections of Egyptian and Sumerian myths and beliefs in the Torah. Yet for the student of comparative religion the Torah evokes more an impression of originality than of derivation.

The outstanding tenet of Mosaic theology is the absolute transcendence of God. He is not in nature. Neither earth, nor sun, nor heaven is divine; even the most powerful natural phenomena are merely reflections of His greatness. It is not even possible to name Him properly. The God of Israel is pure holiness, which means that all spiritual values are ultimately attributes of Him alone and that all concrete values are devaluated. It may be true that under Israelite belief mankind and nature are not necessarily corrupt; but both are valueless before God. Such a conception of God led the Israelites to their iconoclasm vis-à-vis the ancient nature-based Gentile religions. An effort of the imagination is needed to appreciate the shattering boldness of Israelite contempt for the dominant theological imagery of their particular time and historical setting. Southwestern Asian religious fervor not only inspired verse and rite but also sought expression in sculpture and painting. But the Israelites were not of the party. They eschewed 'graven images' of God because the boundless cannot be rendered in a finite form. He could not be other than offended by any representation of Himself, whatever the skill and the devotion that went into its making. Every finite reality shrivels into nothingness before God's absolute value.

And it was this God whose will the Israelites believed was focused on them as His chosen people. According to Exodus 19:6, He said to them in Sinai: "Ye shall be unto me a kingdom of priests and a holy nation." This myth of a chosen people, of a divine promise made, imposed a terrifying moral burden on the Israelites. They were not merely the servants of divinity, as were the Sumerians; nor were they placed, as were the Egyptians, at a pre-ordained station in a static universe that could not be questioned. Rather, the Israelites thought of themselves as the interpreters and persons of God, honored by the assignment of seeing to it that God's will be done. Thus the Israelites were bound to unending efforts that were doomed to fail because of their own shortcomings. In the Torah one finds the Israelites endowed with a novel kind of freedom and a novel burden of responsibility.

According to the Egyptian and Sumerian traditions, people were dominated, but also supported, by the great rhythm of nature. If in their dark moments they felt caught and held in the net of unfathomable decisions, their involvement with nature had, on the whole, a soothing character. They were gently carried along on the perennial cosmic tides of the seasons. The depth and intimacy of peoples' relations with nature found expression in the ancient pagan symbol of the nurturing mother-goddess. But Israelite thought ignored this pagan symbol entirely. It only recognized God-the-stern-Father.

Mankind in God's Image. Some of the passages in the Torah that are most relevant for appreciating the robustness of the ancient Western tradition of mind-body dualism occur in the first Book of Moses in the description of God's final acts of creation of the animals and mankind on the sixth day. Thus, according to Genesis 1:26-31:

> "After God had filled the sea and the air with fish and birds on the fifth day of creation, he made land animals on the sixth. Later on the sixth day, God said: 'Let us make mankind in Our image, after Our likeness. Mankind shall rule the fish of the sea, the birds of the sky, the cattle, the whole earth, and all the creatures that creep on the earth.' And God created mankind in His image, the image of God. He created them, male and female. God blessed them and said to them, "Be fertile and increase, fill the earth and master it, and rule the fish of the sea, the birds of the sky, and all the living things that creep upon the earth."

What is this creation in God's image supposed to consist of? It can hardly be mankind's bodily form, which is obviously that of an animal. And what's more, the Israelite God isn't supposed to have a bodily form in the first place! No, God made mankind in His image by virtue of its spiritual form, by virtue of endowing mankind with a transcendental soul that He breathed into them. Thus the Torah passed on to us an ancient, albeit paradoxical doctrine of human nature, which holds that we are both beastly as well as divine, that we live both in as well as out of nature.

The centerpiece of that paradoxical doctrine of human nature is the person, who is comprised of both a body and a soul. The person's body is endowed with natural properties, which it shares with the bodies of animals and which are amenable to study by the scientific methods of biology. The person's soul is endowed with a set of *non-natural* properties, such as uniqueness, irreplaceability, and sacredness or being an end in itself and, above all, a free will. The soul shares these *non-natural* properties, which are beyond the reach of scientific study, with God rather than with the animals. It is because of the difficulty of rejecting that ancient theory out of hand that, since the time of the Ancients, philosophers and theologians have struggled with the semi-divine, semi-animal paradox of human nature and put forward dualist solutions to the mind-body problem.

The Fall of Man. How did mankind turn into moral beings who know good and evil, right and wrong? Genesis 2:7 to 3:24 provides a not wholly coherent answer with its account of Adam and Eve's expulsion from the paradise of the Garden of Eden. In the middle of the Garden, which is occupied by the animals as well as the first two humans God created, stands a magical 'Tree of Knowledge.' Eating the fruit of this tree brings the knowledge of good and evil, which is a *non-natural* attribute and divine prerogative that animals lack. God forbids Adam and Eve to partake of the tree's fruit, but they do so anyhow and illicitly achieve moral standing. It was God, of course, who empowered them to defy Him in the first place, by having created them in His image, and endowed them with non-natural free will. Thus He had personally seen to it that, unlike their fellow animals in the Garden, Adam and Eve were capable of committing sin. Adam and Eve's awareness of their freely willed, sinful disobedience resulted in their shame and guilt and expulsion from Eden.

Biblical scholars argue that this story was foreign to Egyptian moral theology and has to stem from that part of Israel's inheritance of Southwestern Asian mythology that was either passed on directly from Sumer to Israelite ancestors during the Middle Bronze Age or indirectly via Canaanite culture. Most scholars reject the eighteenth century Enlightenment's Promethean interpretation of the myth, namely that the Tree of Knowledge provided mankind with secular knowledge, culture and reason, by means of which humans can rival God's power in the management of secular affairs.

Coda. The deep psychological insight provided by the bottom line of the Southwest-Asian myth of the Tree of Knowledge seems to be that only sinners, but neither morally innocent animals nor morally perfect angels can be truly human.

SYMPOSION

Painting by Anselm Feuerbach (1866)

Left to right: Agathon (standing), Socrates (seated, turning his back on

Agathon), Aristophanes (seated, facing Socrates)

Chapter Three

———❖———

Moral Philosophy

In the sixth century BCE, the seafaring Greeks came into contact with all the then leading centers of the Western civilized world, including Egypt and Southwestern Asia. These contacts set off a rapid development of Greek culture. But it is not so easy to pinpoint the Greeks' cultural indebtedness to specific elder civilizations, because most of what the Greeks borrowed from other peoples they transmuted and improved. And this uncertainty regarding its pre-Hellenic roots applies also to philosophy (meaning 'love of wisdom'), whose practice as an identifiable intellectual discipline emerged in Greece at that time. As conceived by the Greeks, who founded the world's first philosophical school in the harbor city of Miletus on the Eastern shore of the Aegean Sea, one branch of philosophy seeks to provide insights into the nature of existence (*ontology*) and of our knowledge about the world (*epistemology*). Two further branches of philosophy seek to provide criteria for artistic judgment (*aesthetics*) and for valid reasoning (*logic*). The distinctly novel feature of Greek philosophy was that its inquiries were undertaken in a wholly secular context, independently of the religious beliefs and theological dogmas that had provided earlier approaches to these problems in Egypt and Southwestern Asia.

Socrates. Greek society was changing from an agrarian monarchy to a commercial and industrial democracy in the century following the birth of philosophy in Miletus. The archaic religious and secular traditions governing social transactions that had been handed down from one generation to the next came to be disdained by the uncouth commercial class of *nouveaux riches*, scornful of the ancestral way of life. A novel metaphysical basis was therefore needed for justifying rules of moral conduct for a democratic market society, in which wealth counted for more than noble birth, and people—the buyers and sellers—had to be considered as social equals. Socrates, a secular rather than religious prophet, who was born in

41

Athens in 469 BCE, met that need. His self-appointed mission was to awaken mankind to the need for rational criticism of its moral beliefs and rules of conduct, and to find an answer to the central existential question: 'How should one live?'

Socrates held that by use of reason, mankind can devise a universal moral code that reconciles personal self-interest with the Common Good and applies to all people at all times. Thus he sought a rational rather than divinely ordained justification of morals. Rejecting the self-validating claims of religious tradition, Socrates searched for rational answers to questions such as 'What is justice?' 'What is piety?' 'What is courage?' and 'What is virtue?' In this search, he rejected all attempts to explicate concepts laden with moral value, such as justice, piety, courage, and virtue, in terms of morally neutral facts. Indeed, he wondered how a question such as 'What is justice?' could be answered at all, because our understanding of the meaning of 'justice' cannot be based on our personal experience, since no two actual instances of justice in the world are exactly alike. So a wholly unambiguous statement about what constitutes moral perfection is no more possible than is moral perfection itself. In other words, not knowing exactly what it is, the morally perfect life is an ideal which, at best, we can only approximate. All the same, by virtue of demanding rational grounds for moral judgments and by calling attention to the lack of connection between moral values and morally neutral facts, Socrates became the founder of moral philosophy.

Socrates did not manage to discover the universally valid and self-evident rational basis for a moral code he had set out to find. Yet he proclaimed that, absent such a basis, mankind's actions would lack moral justification. Even though Socrates may be considered the first *moral* philosopher, he neither produced any written philosophical texts nor established a philosophical school. He merely attracted a coterie of disciples, with whom he met regularly at drinking parties, or *symposia*, for philosophical discussions held in the style of the question-and-answer 'Socratic dialogue.'

It is one of the great ironies of history that in 399 BCE, Socrates—who devoted his life to the search for a rational foundation of morality—was tried and condemned to death on a charge of morally corrupting young people and propagating noxious religious heresies. At the time, it was widely believed in Athens, however, that the real reason for Socrates' execution was to punish him for his collaboration with pro-Sparta traitors to the Athenian cause during the Peloponesian War between Athens and Sparta.

Although Socrates' role as the Founding Father of moral philosophy is generally acknowledged, Plato and Aristotle, his two most influential successors laid down the framework of moral philosophy as a coherent rational discipline. It has been said of Plato and Aristotle that all of subsequent (Western) philosophy is merely a commentary on their work.

Plato. A habitué of Socrates' *symposia* and his most renowned disciple, Plato, was born in Athens in 428 BCE. Most of Socrates' philosophical ideas have come down to us via Plato's written accounts of the Socratic dialogues that went on at the *symposia*. After Socrates' death, Plato founded his own philosophical school in Athens, which he called 'Academy,' after the name of the garden in which his house was located. He remained the Academy's head until his death in 347 BCE.

One of Plato's main philosophical preoccupations was the search for answers to such questions as 'What is justice?' 'What is piety?' 'What is courage?' or 'What is virtue?' that had been asked but not answered by Socrates. To resolve Socrates' vexing quandary of how anyone can ever come to know what justice is when no two actual instances to which the concept of justice might apply are ever exactly alike, Plato developed a novel epistemological theory, the 'Theory of Forms.' According to this theory, there exists a perfect, unambiguous and eternal exemplar of justice— its 'Form'—with a dim knowledge of which we are born into the world. This *innate* Form allows us to recognize justice when we encounter it. Plato's Theory of Forms is meant to apply not only to moral categories, such as justice and virtue, but also to all objects of possible knowledge.

Plato divided the objects of possible knowledge into two main sets. One set comprises *sensible* (that is, perceptible to our senses) *concrete* objects. And the other set comprises *imperceptible, abstract* objects, namely the Forms. Our knowledge of sensible, concrete objects is inaccurate and unstable, since the aspects concrete objects present to our senses are in continual flux. Our knowledge of imperceptible abstract Forms, however, is accurate and stable, since Forms, being eternal exemplars, are unchanging.

To support his claim of the unreliability of our knowledge about the true nature of concrete, sensible objects, Plato developed his *Parable of the Cave*. In this tale, he likened persons who believe only what they perceive as concrete objects to prisoners chained since childhood to the floor of an underground cave. All that the prisoners can see, and have ever seen, are the shadows of objects thrown by a fire behind them onto a wall in front of them. According to Plato, our direct knowledge of the real world provided by sensory impressions of sensible objects is as incomplete as would be that of the prisoners. It is only thanks to our capacity to interpret our sensory impressions in terms of imperceptible abstract Forms that we can fathom the world's ultimate realities.

Plato divided the category of abstract Forms into two sub-categories, one consisting of *mathematical*, and the other of *moral* Forms. The philosophically more important of the two categories is that of the moral Forms. And the most important of all moral Forms is that of the Good, because all objects must be defined relative to it if they are to be adequately evaluated. Thus, according to Plato, moral knowledge is the highest and most rigorous kind of knowledge, surpassing even mathematics. Unfortunately, it is also the most difficult knowledge to acquire. Mathematics leads us away from reliance on visual images and sense perception towards reliance on abstract thought. Morality demands an even greater effort of abstraction, because the objects of moral knowledge are even less visualizable than geometrical forms and numbers: Moral knowledge consists of categories and principles ultimately unified under the all-encompassing Form of the Good.

Aristotle. Aristotle was Plato's most renowned disciple, as Plato had been Socrates.' He was born in Macedonia in northern Greece in 384 BCE, socially well connected as the son of the court physician to Amyntas, King of Macedonia, father of Philip II and grandfather of Alexander the Great. Aged 17, Aristotle went down to Athens to study under Plato at the Academy, where he remained for nearly 20 years, until Plato's death in 347 BCE . Failing to be appointed to the directorship of the Academy as Plato's successor, a disgruntled Aristotle left Athens. King Philip II of Macedonia engaged him as the tutor of Prince Alexander, who would presently emerge as the mightiest conqueror of classical antiquity and terminator of the 3000-year-long governance of Egypt by her native dynasties.

After an absence of eight years, Aristotle returned to Athens, where he founded his own philosophical school, the *Lyceum*, named after a nearby temple consecrated to the worship of Apollo. Aristotle's learned interests covered a much wider range than Plato's did. He produced major works on ethics, metaphysics and logic, as well as on subjects as diverse as physics, biology, meteorology, mathematics, psychology, rhetoric, dialectics, aesthetics and politics. The development of Aristotle's philosophical thought continued for most of his life and can be subdivided into three periods.

In the first, or Academy period, lasting until Plato's death and the departure of the 37-year-old Aristotle from Athens, he was an enthusiastic proponent of Platonism and accepted Plato's Theory of Forms. In the second, or Macedonian period, lasting until the return of the 49-year-old Aristotle to Athens, he became increasingly critical of Platonism, above all, of Plato's Theory of Forms. In Aristotle's opinion, asking 'What is a substance?' is *the* central question for the resolution of the mind-body problem. [As we mentioned briefly in Chapter 1, this problem addresses the question whether there is not some basic difference between the human body—the target of nature's forces of determinism—and the human mind—the seat of an autonomous free will.] For Aristotle had come to believe that asking whether some thing is a substance is tantamount to asking whether it exists in the first place. This question is distinct from asking *what* the thing is, since if something does not exist, it cannot *be* anything.

In the third, or Lyceum period, lasting until his death at the age of 62, Aristotle was feeling his way towards a new type of thinking. He drifted towards materialism, moving ever further away from Plato's idealism and stressing the epistemological importance of observation of recurrent patterns in nature. While Plato's paradigm of science had been abstract mathematics, Aristotle's became concrete biology (a discipline which he invented) and physics. And while Plato's goal for moral philosophy was to make human nature conform to an ideal blueprint, Aristotle came to tailor his moral principles to fit the evident demands of human nature.

Aristotle's most influential contribution to the literature of moral philosophy was his treatise *Nicomachean Ethics*. In this work he defined the subject matter of ethics and outlined the methodology for its study, drawing on and revising the moral beliefs of the Greek society of his time (Aristotle, 1999). To explicate the notion of the Good, Aristotle searched for the common feature of all things people consider as good. Plato had taught that there is an abstract Form of the Good that encompasses all good things. But Aristotle held that there are many different senses of 'the Good,' each of which must be defined separately for the circumscribed realm of human experiences to which it applies. Each such sense of 'the Good' is relevant for only one of the diverse practical arts or sciences, such as economics, warfare, medicine, or naval architecture. But the goals of these disparate endeavors can be arranged as a hierarchy of importance, so that the Supreme Good can be identified with the goal of the paramount endeavor to which all the other goals are subordinate. According to Aristotle, that paramount endeavor in the *personal* or *private* sphere is morality, whose goal is happiness, while the paramount endeavor in the *interpersonal* or *social* sphere is politics, whose goal is the general welfare. And since the Good of the whole ranks above the Good of one of its parts, personal morality is subordinate to politics. However, for Aristotle this proposition does not entail that persons must defer their interests to those of the community, except under exceptional conditions, such as war.

Thus, Aristotle identified happiness as the supreme personal Good, which he defined as the exercise of our natural mental functions in accordance with our virtues. 'So what *are* these virtues?' According to Aristotle, a virtue is the skill needed for properly exercising some particular mental function. He distinguished two kinds of virtues—*intellectual* and *moral*. Intellectual virtue comprises the skills needed for intuitive understanding, logical reasoning, practical wisdom, and creating works of art and science. Moral virtue, on the other hand, comprises the skills needed for making felicitous compromises between the extremes of conflicting emotional or rational motivations for action. For instance, the virtue of courage is a compromise between having too much or too little fear. The virtue of temperance is a compromise between wanting to eat or drink too much and too little. And the virtue of justice is a compromise between wanting to reward or punish too much or too little.

So what is the source of these moral virtues? According to Aristotle it is human reason, which he considered as one of mankind's most precious possessions. As social creatures we can attain happiness only through social interactions with other people, because the good life is the common goal of our moral and political striving. These social interactions, which are guided by reason, are optimally realized in the Greek city-state, or *polis*. Aristotle considered the *polis* as the most perfect kind of human society because, while it includes smaller social groups, such as the family or the village, it is large enough to provide within itself everything necessary for the good life. Yet, in contrast to a national state comprising many cities, the *polis* was also small enough so that deliberations could take place and decisions are made in face-to-face discussions among all citizens. These deliberations, in turn, provided the necessary conditions for people to take a critical view of the relation of the individual to the collectivity. Thus, for Aristotle, citizenship was not a matter of passively enjoying rights but of participating actively in the many-sided, rationally guided life of the *polis*.

The bulk of the *Nicomachean Ethics* consists of a detailed list for identifying particular moral virtues. The bottom line of Aristotle's investigation of morals is the definition of happiness and the good life as an activity in accordance with virtue, and thus as the harmonious fulfillment of one's natural tendencies.

This Aristotelian emphasis of happiness and human welfare as the Supreme Good represents a pagan approach to morality, rejected by the austere moral principles of Judaism and of its Christian and Muslim derivatives. Anyone advocating it publicly in Medieval Europe would have risked being burnt on the stake. But upon the advent of the Enlightenment, the eighteenth century English philosopher Jeremy Bentham revived it under the name of '*utilitarianism.*' Bentham held that the greatest happiness for the greatest number is the fundamental and self-evident criterion of morality. Although this criterion may seem self-evident on first sight, on second sight it turns out to provide a license for the majority to trample on the rights of a minority in a complex, heterogeneous society.

Plato had considered the concept of moral responsibility only obliquely. He believed that no one does evil voluntarily. Hence evil actions are always due to intellectual error. Aristotle dealt with responsibility more directly in his *Nicomachean Ethics*, however, although somewhat inconclusively. He noted that since virtue is concerned with actions and passions, praise or blame is conferred only if they were *voluntary*, while pardon (and sometimes also pity) is granted if they were *involuntary*. Hence for fathoming the nature of virtue, as well as for meeting out rewards or punishments, it is necessary to distinguish between the voluntary and the involuntary. Actions and passions that are involuntary arise accidentally or from coercion, meaning that they are brought about by force, dire threat, or authority applied to the agent by other persons or by circumstances beyond the agent's control.

But, so Aristotle pointed out, there are some situations in which it is not obvious whether an action is involuntary or voluntary, such as an evil action undertaken only to avoid an even greater evil, or to achieve some higher purpose. By way of an example he mentioned compliance with an order of a tyrant, who has one's parents or children in his power, to carry out an evil action under the threat that in case of refusal, one's beloved would be put to death. Aristotle thought that the attribution of moral responsibility to a person who is faced with such a dilemma is not all that clear-cut. He judged that an action undertaken in response to a dire threat is actually more voluntary than involuntary. For the agent *was* offered a choice at the time he acted. Hence the distinction between 'voluntary' and 'involuntary' can be made, and the moral justification of the goal of an action can be judged, only by taking into account the entire context of the occasion in which the action occurred. Strictly speaking, all human actions (other than reflexes and movements implemented by the autonomic nervous system) are 'voluntary' (and designated as such by neurophysiologists) in the concrete. An action, therefore, can be regarded as 'coerced' only in the abstract, namely by supposing that the person would never have chosen to carry it out in the absence of the dire threat. [We will return to this argument in Chapter 8, under the rubric of the *Principle of Alternate Possibilities*.]

According to Aristotle, intellectual error has to be distinguished from moral vice, since error, unlike vice, is involuntary. To distinguish culpable evil from innocent mistakes, he explained vice as due to wrong desire as well as to poor judgment. For Aristotle, the will is a rational desire, formed by moral education and training. But since natural tendencies and early training determine even voluntary action, Aristotle searched for an additional factor to account for the freedom (or *autonomy*) of choice necessary for moral responsibility. He thought he found the factor in deliberation, that is, in the consideration of reasons for and against a course of action.

Aristotle did not address the question whether persons actually have any real choice when they deliberate, and consequently bear any responsibility for the outcome of their deliberations. As we will consider in Chapter 7, it remains an unsettled issue, debated by *Determinists* and *Libertarians*. Determinists hold that every action is causally necessitated by prior states of the world and by the laws of nature. Libertarians hold, to the contrary, that despite what happened in the past and given the present state of affairs and ourselves just as they are, we could have chosen or decided differently from what we did choose or decide. Hence we could have made the future different from what it would otherwise have been.

Three East Asian Teachings. At about the same time as secular moral philosophy arose in Greece, there developed in India and China three philosophico-ethical systems (or Godless religions), referred to collectively as the 'Three Teachings' of Buddhism, Confucianism and Taoism, which still govern East Asian social life in large measure today. The defining characteristic of East Asian moral philosophy is the belief that human beings are morally perfectible, by self-effort in ordinary daily life rather than by divine grace. Accordingly, the primary focus of the Three Teachings is *self-knowledge*. None of them even trouble to reject as a possibility the Judeo-Sumerian conception of a divine Creator as the ultimate legislator and guarantor of morals. Rather, the East-Asian approach to personal moral development focuses on learning how to be a righteous human being by self-examination and self-transformation. Moral knowledge so conceived is not a cognitive grasp of a particular ensemble of objective truths but a critical understanding of one's own subjective mental states and feelings. (Tu, 1980)

But how can a critical understanding of one's own *subjective* mental states and inner feelings serve as a guide to *objective*, generally valid moral truths? According to the Three Teachings, this is possible because everybody—simply by virtue of being human—has an innate knowledge of a Sacred Way of Life. This is the *right* Way, the ideal Way of Human Existence, the Way of the Cosmos, or the Generative-Normative Way, which, once it is understood, can guide the adept to righteous social behavior. Buddha referred to this Sacred Way as the *ariya atthangita magga*, or 'Noble Eightfold Path,' while Confucius and Lao Tzu, called it '*Tao*.'

Buddha. The atheistic religion of Buddhism was founded in Northern India by Siddharta Gautama. He was an Indian prince born in 563 BCE, who was later called 'Buddha' (meaning 'Enlightened One'). His main goal was to find an ultimate solution to the problem of the suffering inherent in the human condition. The solution he found was incorporated into the basic Buddhist doctrine of the *dharma*, or 'Four Noble Truths.' They are that existence means suffering; that suffering has a cause, namely craving; that an end to suffering, or *nirvana*, is possible by stopping to crave; and that the way to *nirvana* is provided by the Noble Eightfold Path. The eight stages on that Noble Path are the right world view, the right aspiration, the right speech, the right conduct, the right way of making a living, the right effort, the right mindfulness, and the right contemplation. The moral laws of Buddhism are articulated as 'Five Precepts.' They forbid the taking of life (including animal life), theft, unchaste sex, slander, and imbibing intoxicants.

Buddha rejected the idea of a divine Creator, mainly for the reason (which we will consider in greater detail in Chapter 4 under the rubric of '*theodicy*') that the existence of evil and suffering is an insuperable obstacle

49

to a belief in God. Moreover, Buddha deemed cosmological and metaphysical questions, such as the finitude of the cosmos in space and time or the immortality of the person, as intrinsically unanswerable. According to Buddha, the person is a transient dualist composite of mentalist and physicalist states, and the concept of an inner soul is superfluous as well as false. This is in accord with his doctrine of *impermanence*, which implies that all entities can be resolved into a series of transitory states.

After Buddha's death, his teachings were transmitted, at first by oral tradition and later by texts written in the second and first centuries BCE. Different Buddhist sects eventually arose with varying views on diverse religious and philosophical issues, as Buddhism spread North- and Eastward from India to become one of the world's major religions.

Confucius. The sixth century BCE, during which moral philosophy got its start in China, as it did in Greece, was the era of the waning reign of the Chou dynasty (which dated back to the twelfth century BCE). At that time, China—just as did Greece—consisted of several independent, constantly feuding states. Yet, despite the general political disorder, both China and Greece were then flowering in their classical cultural periods. The most influential of the Chinese philosophers of that era—and probably of *any* Chinese era—was Confucius, who lived in the state of Lu (the modern Chinese province of Shantung) from about 550 to about 480 BCE. As was the case also for the teachings of Socrates, who was born a decade after Confucius died, Confucian philosophy is known to us only second hand, through a collection of his sayings and dialogues recorded by his disciples. In the West, this collection is known as the *Confucian Analects*, (from the Greek *analegein*, to collect).

According to the *Analects*, Confucianism is a set of ethical guidelines for the proper management of society. Its precepts are based on the fundamental premise that people are social creatures and that, therefore, there is virtue in harmonious social relations. The relations are made harmonious, not by obedience to universally valid abstract moral principles, such as freedom and justice, but by exact adherence to a combination of prescribed etiquette and ritual. (We will consider the philosophical distinction between etiquette and ethics in Chapter 11.)

The *Analects* present a thoroughly humanist view of the world, and, accordingly, its Sacred Way of Life, or *Tao*, emphasizes human nature, behavior, and social relationships. The two most important, constantly recurring themes in the *Analects* are ritual (*li*) and virtue (*jen*), with two central components of the *jen* theme being conscientiousness (*chung*) and obligations entailed by familial-social relationships (*shu*). According to the worldly, practical humanism of the *Analects*, one's moral and spiritual accomplishments do not depend on divine grace, good luck or on any other purely external determinants. Instead, they depend on the soul with which one happens to be endowed innately and on the amount and quality of study and good hard work that one puts into shaping it. Thus one has to labor long and hard to learn the *li*, whose root meaning is close to 'holy ritual' or 'sacred ceremony.' It is characteristic of Confucian teaching that the language and the imagery of the *li* is the medium that makes it possible to talk about the entire corpus of human *mores*, or more precisely, about the authentic tradition and reasonable conventions of society. People become truly human as their cravings are shaped by the *li*, because it shows the way to their civilized fulfillment. Rather than being a formalistic dehumanization of personal desires, *li* is a specifically humanizing guide for the dynamics of interpersonal relations.

Confucius did not elaborate on the categories of free will, choice or moral responsibility, no more than did his Indian and Chinese contemporaries. In fact, Confucius did not even have a language in which to express the concepts of 'choice' and 'responsibility,' which were so central for his contemporaries in Greece and Southwestern Asia. Occasionally he used terms roughly akin to them. But he did not develop them in the ways so characteristic of their central import in Western philosophical or religious understanding of mankind.

The language and imagery that is elaborated and that forms the main frame of Confucius' teachings presents a strange yet intelligible and harmonious picture. For Confucius, a human being is not a sovereign person who is innately endowed with an autonomous power of decision to select among real alternatives and thereby to shape a life for himself. Instead Confucius considers people to be born 'raw,' in need of being refined by education to become truly human. To accomplish this, one must learn the Tao, to which one ought to be attracted by virtue of its own nobility and the nobility of those people who walk it. The motivation for following the Tao is not conceived as an enhancement of personal power over the social or physical environment. Rather, it is seen as the desire for sharpening and steadying one's social aim or orientation to the point where one can undeviatingly walk the one true Way and turn into a civilized human being.

Walking the Way incarnates in people the vast spiritual dignity and power that resides in the Tao.

Confucius recognized four different causes for moral infractions. (1) The person was not taught well enough to be able to recognize which actions are and which are not in line with the Tao. (2) The person has not yet acquired the necessary skills to follow the Tao. (3) The person does not persist in the required effort (for lack of strength rather than by choice). (4) The person is not wholly committed to the Tao. Although the person knows enough about the Way that she *could* perform the actions that are called for, she either acts erratically or perverts the rites of *li* to serve her own personal advantage.

Yet, despite this essentially down-to-earth, secular morality, one can also find an occasional comment in the *Analects* that reveals a belief in magical powers, thanks to which some persons can implement their will directly through ritual or incantation. Magic can produce great effects effortlessly, marvelously, with an irresistible force that is itself intangible, invisible, and covert. The user of magic simply wills the end accompanied by proper ritual gesture and words. Confucius' suggestion of a magical dimension to human virtue constitutes an obstacle, of course, in the way of acceptance of his otherwise very reasonable doctrines by us sophisticates of the twenty-first century CE.

Lao Tzu. More or less contemporary with the rise of Confucianism there appeared also a rival brand of moral philosophy in fifth century BCE China. Its essential doctrines—just as those of Confucianism—are embodied in a Sacred Way, or *Tao*. Unfortunately, the traditional designation of this rival philosophy to Confucianism is 'Taoism,' even though Confucianism is no less 'Taoist' than is Taoism. It is in their conception of the essence of the Sacred Way that Confucianism and Taoism differ significantly.

The Taoist philosophical system is derived chiefly from the *Tao-te-ching*, a book that was probably written as late as mid-third century BCE and whose authorship is traditionally ascribed to the legendary founder of Taoism, Lao Tzu. He was allegedly born at the turn of the fifth century BCE, but in contrast to Confucius, about whose existence there is no doubt, there is no evidence that Lao Tzu was really a historical person. The *Tao-te-ching* describes the path taken by natural events that proceed without effort, either by spontaneous activity, such as the effortless downward flow of water, which wears away the hardest substance, or by regular alternations of phenomena, such as day invariably following night. Like flowing water, persons following the Tao must abjure all striving, and, accordingly, the ideal state of being is freedom from desire.

The main difference between the Tao of Confucianism and the Tao of Taoism is that Confucianism stresses the Tao of non-natural human society while Taoism stresses the Tao of natural phenomena. Thus the humanistic Sacred Way of Confucianism, being concerned with the political order and the practical life of the person, tries to deal with the problems inherent in social relationships. It prescribes social norms and moral precepts, for which the ways of nature are of little relevance. The natural Sacred Way of Taoism, by contrast, is a transcendental moral philosophy, whose main relevance is for the person's inner life rather than for her social relations. Taoist precepts are based on the fundamental premise that mankind is part of nature and that, therefore, human life must follow the Tao of natural phenomena. Besides abjuring all striving in following the natural Tao, people must distrust reason and attempt to attain a mental state in which they are as free from desire and sensory experiences as possible. The political doctrines developed by the Taoists reflect their quietist philosophy of withdrawal from worldly affairs. They believe that the duty of a ruler is to protect his subjects from experiencing material wants or strong passions and to impose a minimum of government. The Taoists rejected the social values embraced by the Confucians as symptoms of excessive government. Neither Confucianism nor Taoism invokes God or Eternal Reason as the source of its authority, nor does either posit the existence of any natural law or human rights. Rather, both systems endeavor to provide for mankind's harmony with its environment—the social environment in the case of Confucianism and the natural environment in the case of Taoism.

The original division of labor between Confucianism and Taoism at the time of their emergence twenty-five centuries ago is still reflected in contemporary Chinese social and political life. While Confucianism continues to guide Chinese political affairs (including the homegrown brand of Chinese Communism), Taoism is manifest chiefly in Chinese cultural life—in art and literature.

A basic tenet of the *Tao-te-ching* is that the human world is merely a part of the natural world. This tenet brought Taoism into conflict with the Confucian emphasis on the non-natural, magical aspects of human behavior and social relationships, such as ritual, virtue, and obligations entailed by familial-social relationships. The anti-Confucian Taoists taught that one should strive to restore the continuity between mankind and nature by freeing the person from the unnatural, restrictive influence of social norms, moral precepts and worldly goals. Eventually, a more or less symbiotic relation developed between Confucianism and Taoism. In this symbiosis, the Confucian bureaucracy ran the state, while the Taoist intelligentsia provided spiritual and cultural leadership.

Taoism, with its focus of attention on nature, also became the intellectual fountainhead for the development of Chinese science. But since Taoism mistrusts the powers of reason and logic and does not provide for the (Sumerian) idea of laws of nature, the evolution of Chinese science took a course very different from that of Western science. Joseph Needham (1969) epitomized this difference in the following terms: "With their appreciation of the relativism and the subtlety and immensity of the universe, [the Chinese scientists] were groping after an Einsteinian world picture without having laid the foundations for a Newtonian one."

Since Taoism regards the workings of nature to be inscrutable for the theoretical intellect, Chinese science developed along mainly empirical lines. This empirical development was slow but steady, and by Renaissance times, Chinese science and the technology it had inspired were considerably more advanced than anything that had been achieved in the West. Indeed, much of pre-Renaissance European science fed on Chinese discoveries that had percolated from East to West. Many of the key inventions that eventually produced the transformation of medieval into modern Europe, such as gunpowder, movable type, the mechanical clock, the magnetic compass, the stern post rudder, and *pasta*, were of Chinese origin. But lacking the spiritual incentive to integrate its empirical discoveries into a general theoretical framework, Chinese science remained an intellectually fragmented enterprise.

Backward Western science began its meteoric rise with Galileo's discovery that models built on mathematically expressible laws dealing with exactly measurable quantities can give a useful account of reality. Thanks to that discovery, Western science soon left Chinese science far behind. For it turned out that, contrary to the Taoist doctrine, the working of nature is not all that inscrutable for the intellect. Provided that the questions one asks of nature are not too deep, satisfactory answers can usually be found. Difficulties arise only when, as we will note in Chapters 12 and 14, the questions become too deep, and their answers are no longer fully consonant with rational thought or intuition.

Immanuel Kant. Shifting to fast forward in our survey of the development of moral philosophy, onwards from its origins twenty-five hundred years ago in the Mediterranean Basin and East Asia, to the Age of Enlightenment in the eighteenth century CE, we encounter Immanuel Kant, the towering figure of modern moral philosophy.

Kant's approach to morality is designated as *deontological*, which means that in judging the moral praise- or blameworthiness of peoples' actions, one evaluates the intrinsic principles of rightness and wrongness of the intentions that motivated them. Thus Kant differed fundamentally from Aristotle's and Bentham's *utilitarian* approaches to morality. As we noted earlier in this chapter, the utilitarian crux of moral action is the promotion of a socially felicitous goal or purpose, especially the attainment of human happiness and the good life as a harmonious fulfillment of peoples' natural inclinations. According to Aristotle, the highest Good for mankind is *eudaemonia*, or material and spiritual well being, while Bentham's paramount utilitarian end was epitomized as the goal of bringing about the greatest happiness for the greatest number of people.

From the viewpoint of the person, the utilitarian approach to moral action is straightforward, provided one has some eudaemonian Happy End in mind. One may be mistaken, of course, in expecting that one's action will actually bring about the end one desired, or, in case it does bring about the desired end, whether the end's consequences were, in fact, those one desired. The deontological approach is much less straightforward, however. How can one know whether one's intended action is in accord with the intrinsic requirements of morality? Kant proposed a solution for this quandary: One must apply his test of the *categorical imperative*, which commands

> "Act only on that maxim (that is, general rule or principle) which you can at the same time will to be a universal law."

Since the categorical imperative demands that one selects maxims on the basis of their eligibility as universal law, it presupposes that one is able to disregard one's personal inclinations and thoughts about one's own happiness in choosing a morally righteous course of action. The categorical imperative became Kant's most famous, albeit not his most important, contribution to moral philosophy. It was controversial when Kant first put it forward, and it still remains so today. One of the common objections raised by Kant's critics has been directed against his sharp distinction between *categorical* and *hypothetical* imperatives. According to Kant, the categorical imperative

You ought to do Y!

commands an action as of itself rationally necessary and endowed with an automatic reason-giving force, without regard to any other end. A hypothetical imperative, however, commands an action only as a means to some other end:

If you want X, you ought to do Y!

This objection to Kant's sharp distinction between the two kinds of imperatives does not appear unreasonable. For it seems improbable that there are any moral imperatives with an automatic reason-giving force arising *ex nihilo* from pure reason, independently of our personal inclinations and thoughts about our own happiness. For, according to Kant's contemporary, the Scottish philosopher David Hume (whom Kant credited with waking him from his 'dogmatic slumber'), reason is, and ought to be, the slave of the passions. Thus the reason-giving force of all imperatives, including that of categorical imperatives, would have to derive from the implied hypothetical proposition

If you want, (or believe, or care about) X, you should do Y!

Another troublesome problem inherent in Kant's formulation of the categorical imperative arises from its demand that the person must be able to will the maxim to be 'a universal law.' What does it mean to be able to will a maxim to be a *universal* law? Critics of Kant's categorical imperative have no trouble putting forward counterexamples that refute any candidate maxim nominated for standing as a universal law. For instance, one of the many possible counterexamples refuting the universal validity of the categorical imperative 'thou must not tell a lie' invokes a Gestapo officer who barges into a house in Nazi-occupied Amsterdam and asks the householder "Where is Anne Frank hidden?" According to the maxim, the Dutchman ought to reply truthfully: "She's hidden in the attic; Sir. Second door to the left." But the Dutchman lies and replies: "Anne Frank? Never heard of her." Is the Dutch liar acting immorally? No, he is not, because he is perfectly able to will as universal law an amendment to the maxim, to wit "thou must not tell a lie, except when you can save an innocent life."

Since Kant's time, many deontologically inclined moral philosophers have tried to provide a more secure rational basis for his categorical imperative. One of the best-known contemporary attempts was put forward by John Rawls (1971) in his book *A Theory of Justice*. To meet Kant's demand that in choosing maxims eligible for the status of universal moral law, people have to be able to disregard their personal inclinations and thoughts about their own happiness, Rawls invokes what he calls an '*original position.*' In that position people are under a 'veil of ignorance.' They do not know their own place in society—their gender, personal traits, race, and social class, or even their (utilitarian) concepts of the good life. Hence, according to Rawls, they can make their moral judgments as unbiased representatives of every member of society.

Neither Rawls' nor anyone else's modification of the categorical imperative was any more immune to philosophical criticism than had been Kant's original formulation. The most obvious defect of Rawl's 'original position' is that it is not a practical guide to moral action in any real society, even for moral people of good will. For its applicability is limited to the lucky members of a utopian, ideal democratic society, unlikely to arise any time soon in the sublunary sphere.

Despite the not wholly unwarranted criticism calling attention to its conceptual flabbiness, Kant's categorical imperative remains a plausible (albeit not infallible) guide to willing morally relevant actions in complex social situations for which no non-trivial, exceptionless rules *can* be explicitly articulated. Although not infallible, the categorical imperative may still be the best rule of thumb for judging whether a contemplated action is in accord with deontological criteria of morals in an imperfect world. Being imperfect, in such a world some willable maxims may be of more universal validity than others, just as on Orwell's *Animal Farm*, some may be more equal than others.

Coda. It is one of the curious facts of world history that the first teachings of secular moral philosophy appeared independently in Europe and in East Asia during the sixth and fifth centuries BCE. In Greece, this development was set off by Socrates, Plato, and Aristotle and in India and China by the 'Three Teachings' of Buddha, Confucius, and Lao Tzu. Among these ancient founders of moral philosophy, Buddha and Confucius were the Indian and Chinese analogs of Plato, whereas Lao Tzu was the Chinese analog of Aristotle. The dominant influence of Greek moral philosophy in the Judeo-Christian-Muslim world and that of the Three Teachings in East Asia, reaches down twenty-five centuries to our own times.

St. Augustine (354–430) in his study

Painting by Sandro Botticelli (1480)

Chapter Four

Theodicy

Christian Philosophy. Christianity spread through the Roman Empire onwards from the second century CE, offering the poor and oppressed hope for otherworldly bliss, to compensate them for all their worldly suffering. This promise of future happiness in a life *after* death provided for an optimistic and fervent approach to life *before* death with which the more pessimistic and intellectual teachings of Platonic and Aristotelian philosophy could not compete. By the fourth century, Christian beliefs had come to dominate Western world.

Having converted the masses, the time had come for the Church to win over the intelligentsia, by devising a credible system of Christian metaphysics. A new era now began in the history of moral philosophy, as Christian philosophy arose as a fusion of secular Greek philosophy with the monotheistic Israelite belief in a personal God. Greek philosophers had sought the foundations of morals in rational principles, while Jewish theologians derived their ultimate source of moral authority from God's commandments conveyed in the Torah. Upon the rise of Christian philosophy, these two disparate sources of moral standards—human reason and divine commandments—came to stand side-by-side in a single moral system, and the tension between them led to the divergent interpretations of theological doctrines that have caused sectarian strife in Christendom ever since.

Early Christian philosophers were confronted with the baffling paradox inherent in most monotheistic religions, namely that they embrace the transcendental belief in a one-and-only, all-powerful, righteous, benign God, despite the obvious empirical fact that the world He created abounds in evil. This paradox derived its modern name, *theodicy*, [which is a composite of the Greek words *theos* (God) and *diké* (justice)], from the title of a book published in the early eighteenth century by the German

59

philosopher and mathematician Gottfried Wilhelm Leibniz. The kinds of evil usually invoked under the rubric of theodicy are the physical suffering and the mental anguish of innocent people caused either by other people or by natural disasters (such as epidemic diseases, floods, and earthquakes).

Long before it received its modern name, however, the theodicy paradox had been acute in the context of the Judeo-Christian faith and the Torah's account of God's creation of the World. According to Genesis 1:26-31, God created mankind in His 'image.' So why, if He really did create mankind in His image, didn't He incorporate His own most important moral qualities of righteousness and virtue into his creatures?

Zoroaster. The theodicy paradox had not been as acute in the context of Judeo-Christianity's ancient polytheistic precursor religions, such as those of the Egyptians, Sumerians, or Greco-Romans. Although their pagan Pantheons usually included a righteous God-in-Chief, such as Re, Marduk, or Zeus/Jupiter, He was not all-powerful and had to contend with lesser, sometimes-malign fellow deities, who were regarded as the main sources of evil in the World. One ancient version of this polytheistic account of the source of evil, whose theological influence survived well into the Middle Ages, was the doctrine promulgated in the sixth century BCE by the Persian prophet Zoroaster (whom the Greeks called 'Zarathustra'). He taught that of the gods of the Pantheon only one, Ahura Mazda, was good and righteous. All the other gods, called collectively 'Angra Mainyu,' were malign. They opposed Ahura Mazda, whose power was evenly matched with theirs, so that in this everlasting divine struggle of good versus evil, it was win some and lose some for both sides. The Zoroastrian doctrine presaged also the hopeful vision of a Messianic redemption of mankind at the end of history, when good Ahura Mazda was going to score an eschatological Final Victory over the evil Angra Mainyu crowd.

Manicheanism. In the third century CE another Persian prophet, Mani, adapted the Zoroastrian resolution of the paradox of theodicy for the rising tide of monotheism that had been energized by Christianity in the first centuries CE. According to Mani's monotheistic religion of Manicheanism, which presented a farrago of the teachings of Zoroaster, Buddha, Plato, and Jesus, there rages an everlasting struggle between the divine forces of good and of evil. In this struggle, the forces of good arise in the realm of the one-and-only God and are represented by light and spirit, while the forces of evil arise in realm of the fallen angel Satan and are represented by darkness and matter. Mani regarded women as part of the forces of Satan. They seduce men, so that, if women have their way, the day of emancipation from darkness and matter will never come. After the Zoroastrians in Persia martyred Mani as a heretic in 276 CE, his religion spread rapidly throughout the Roman Empire and Southwestern Asia. By the sixth century CE, however, Manicheanism had disappeared, along with the Roman Empire.

Some early Christian theologians offered another way of resolving the theodicy paradox in the terms of Plato's mind-body dualism. They argued that the Biblical phrase 'in God's image' refers only to our soul, whose virtue we share with Him. But our body, which is a separate substance and obviously very similar to the body of many non-human creatures, we share with the animals rather than with God. Thus our animal body lacks Divine Grace and is the repository of the evil that is within us. According to that dualist view, our evil deeds arise as the result—after an internal struggle—of a victory of evil flesh over righteous soul, or of malign matter over benign spirit.

Another resolution of the paradox of theodicy was provided by the doctrine of free will. Suppose that He *did* make mankind's soul in His image and that one of God's most potent attributes is the freedom of His will. In that case He surely passed on that mark of His distinction to the humans He created. Yet, He took a considerable risk in creating humans with free will, since the gift of freedom entailed the possibility that His creatures might turn against Him, as they indeed did according to the events told in the Torah's *Genesis* 3, known as the 'The Fall of Man.' To try out their God-given free will Adam and Eve violated their creator's edict, set themselves against Him and even sought to be His peers.

Free will turned out to be an even more contentious theological issue than the origin of evil that free will had been thought capable of explaining. In fact, free will became *the* crucial moral issue upon the rise of Christianity, because of the Judeo-Christian belief that God has foreknowledge of the future. How can our will be free if He knew how we were going to decide long before we actually *did* decide freely how to act? Such divine foreknowledge did not seem to allow for the kind of free will that would provide a rational basis for the notion of moral responsibility in the first place. How can God be just in rewarding us for our good deeds and punishing us for our evil deeds, if these were all foreordained by Him?

Pharisees, Essenes, and Sadducees. At the time of Jesus' birth there flourished three Jewish sects in Palestine: the Pharisees, the Sadducees and the Essenes. They differed in their interpretation of the Torah, in the strictness of their observance of religious ritual and dietary law, in their social class, and, most importantly in the context of our discussions of the Paradox of Moral Responsibility, in their views about free will. (Stemberger, 1995)

Until the discovery of the Dead Sea Scrolls in mid-twentieth century, our knowledge about these sects was based on only two contemporary sources: the Gospels of the Christian Evangelists—especially that according to St. Paul—and the writings of the Jewish historian, Josephus Flavius. Both Paul and Josephus described themselves as Pharisees, the sect that comprised upper class Jews, including the priesthood and collaborators with the Roman Imperial administration, and whom the Gospels portray in an unfavorable light.

In his treatise, *The Antiquities of the Jews*, Josephus noted that the three sects differ in their opinions regarding the causation of human actions. The Essenes affirmed that fate determines all actions, and that nothing befalls mankind but what is determined by fate. They therefore rejected the role of free will in the causation of human actions and accepted the view that became known as 'determinism.'

The Sadducees held that fate plays no role in human affairs, there being no such thing as fate in the first place. They supposed that all our actions are within our control, so that our own righteousness is the cause of our doing what is good and that we are driven by our own folly to doing what is evil. Hence Sadducees believed in free will.

Finally, the Pharisees ascribed the cause of all human actions to fate. Yet they allowed that acting according to what is right or what is wrong is mainly within our own power, even though fate plays some causative role in every action. The Pharisees' argument regarding the compatibility of fate (and God's foreknowledge of it) with the exercise of human free will was adopted some 300 years later by St. Augustine.

St. Augustine. The task of developing the novel Christian philosophy was taken on by several Church Fathers. Among them, Augustine was the philosophically most influential, since he provided the main theological link between pagan classical antiquity and Christian Middle Ages. Augustine was born in 354 CE near Carthage in the Roman province of Africa (in what is now Tunisia) to a pagan father and a Christian mother—the future Santa Monica. At that time, ancient Greco-Roman paganism was still widely practised in the Roman Empire, even though the emperors had been Christians since Constantine the Great's conversion at the beginning of the fourth century. The Empire's last great pagan revolt and the temporary disestablishment of Christianity still occurred in Augustine's youth. His life thus spanned the years of transition of the Roman Empire from Greco-Roman paganism to the adoption of Christianity as the official state religion. He witnessed the social transformations, political upheavals, and military disasters that eventually led to the fall of the Roman Empire.

Augustine belonged to the world of late Roman antiquity, whose educational system had a decisive and lasting role in shaping his mind. That system's aim was to enable its alumni to emulate the great literary masterpieces of the past and thus tended to encourage a conservative literary antiquarianism. The culture it produced rarely rose above the sterile cult of polite letters and generally had little contact with the deeper forces at work in its contemporary society. There were many creative minds still at work, but even their best work was largely derivative. This is especially true of the philosophy of the fourth and fifth centuries.

It was in the context of this jejune culture that eighteen-year-old Augustine set out on his search for truth and wisdom, which led him far afield. Looking back on this search in his forties, Augustine declared in his autobiographical *Confessions* that it changed his interests and gave his work a new direction and purpose, namely the search for a route that would lead him back to God. According to Augustine, his way to Christianity was prepared by his reading the works of the *Neo-Platonists*, who flourished in the Empire in the third to fifth centuries CE and urged their contemporaries to return to Plato's idealist teachings. In a famous passage in his *Confessions* Augustine describes how he had discovered the distinctive Christian doctrines about God and His Word, the creation of the world, and the presence of the divine light in the books of the Neo-Platonists before reading of them in the Scriptures. What he had failed to find anticipated in the Neo-Platonist writings, however, were the beliefs in the Incarnation in Jesus Christ as the union of humanity and divinity and the Gospels' account of His life and death. Later in life, Augustine came to see a wider gulf between Greco-Roman philosophy and Christian faith. But he never ceased to regard much of philosophy, especially that of the Neo-Platonists, as containing a large measure of truth and hence as capable of serving as a preparation for Christianity.

The problem of evil, and especially the Theodicy paradox, was a life-long preoccupation of Augustine's, and the main lines of thought that he eventually developed in the effort to resolve it have been followed by most of the Christian philosophers ever since. Before his conversion to Christianity, Augustine had fallen under the spell of Manicheanism. But he had become increasingly dissatisfied with Manicheanism, not least because it implicitly denied the existence of an all-powerful God and invoked Satan as an equally powerful anti-God.

Ambrose. Augustine's studies took him from his native North Africa to Italy, first to Rome and then to Milan, where he joined Bishop Ambrose and his group of Neo-Platonist Christians. From Ambrose's circle he learned what impressed him as better philosophical approaches to the theodicy paradox than those provided by the Manichean doctrine. Thus, under the influence of his new friends in Milan, Augustine broke with Manicheanism. Moreover, he felt that he had finally encountered a more satisfactory interpretation of Christianity than he had previously found in the simple, naïve faith of his Christian mother, Monica. There was no deep gulf between the Christianity of Ambrose's circle and the resurrected Platonic philosophy, so that Augustine saw no need to sort out exactly what belonged to Christian and what to Platonic teaching. On the contrary, it struck him how much Christianity and Platonism had in common. This blend of Platonism and Christian belief won his adherence, and in 386 CE Augustine had himself formally baptized by Ambrose as a Christian.

To resolve the theodicy paradox, Augustine reexamined the concept of evil. He decided that what *appears* to be evil when seen in isolation or in too limited a context actually turns out to be a necessary element in the perception of the Good when the world is viewed as a whole. For evil provides a contrasting background that makes the Good to shine more brightly. According to Augustine, a world that contains as many different kinds of entities as are possible—good as well as bad—expresses more adequately His creativity than a world that contains only the highest type of created beings. The immense hierarchy of forms of created existence, in which each creature has its own proper place in the scheme of nature, is good and glorifies its creator. Those creatures that rank lower on the scale of being are not on that account evil. They merely represent different Goods and contribute in their own way to the perfection of the world.

Confessions and City of God. Augustine returned to North Africa from Milan and retired to a quasi-monastic life with like-minded friends, until he was ordained to assist the elderly bishop of Hippo, a city about 100 miles East of Carthage. All of Augustine's work thereafter was devoted to the service of the Church. Preaching, administration, travel, and an extensive correspondence took much of his time. Despite this multifarious activity, Augustine never ceased to be a thinker and a scholar, but his talents and achievements were directed increasingly to pastoral work and to the service of the episcopal flock. The Scriptures took a deeper hold on his mind, eclipsing the strong philosophical interests of the years immediately preceding and following his conversion.

Augustine became bishop of Hippo in 395, and shortly thereafter began writing his *Confessions*. They eventually ran to thirteen books and set the pattern for a novel literary genre of self-critical rather than self-glorifying autobiography. The first nine books of the *Confessions* describe how God opened Augustine's own mind and heart to himself. To that end, Divine Providence had arranged his intellectual conversion by the encounter with Platonist writings and the moral influence on him of fervent Christians, especially that of his devout mother. The tenth book reveals Augustine's spiritual state after his conversion and at the time that he was writing the Confessions. They are a frank self-examination, in which he squarely faces the struggle and conflict of Christian life with the confidence provided by grace and hope. Not the misery of mankind, but the mercy of God is their theme. Augustine confesses the temptations to which he was still subject from the lust of the flesh, the lust of the eyes, and the pride of life. The last three books present Augustine's meditations on the Scriptures, leading to his personal reflections on time and eternity.

Despite the demands made on him by his ecclesiastical duties, Augustine did not give up his philosophical interests. He shared with his contemporaries the opinion that it was the mission of philosophy to discover the way to wisdom and thereby show mankind the way to blessedness. Accordingly, Augustine thought of Christianity as a brand of philosophy, in that its aim to find wisdom is the same as that of the pagan philosophers. The chief difference between Christianity and pagan philosophy is that only Christianity holds that the way to blessedness was provided for mankind by Jesus Christ and that the ultimate source of salvation is revealed in the Scriptures. According to Augustine, the Scriptures superceded the teachings of philosophers as the gateway to truth. Thus religious authority rather than reason and faith rather than understanding became the essence of Augustinian Christian philosophy. Admittedly, pagan philosophers had discovered much of the truth proclaimed by the Christian Gospels. But what their abstract speculation had not, and could not have reached was the kernel of the Christian faith: the belief in the contingent historical facts that constitute the history of salvation—the Gospel narrative of the earthly life, death, and resurrection of Jesus.

According to Augustine, mankind differs from other creatures in that the motivations that drive mankind to action are very much more complex. Mankind has many desires and drives, impulses and inclinations—some of them conscious, others subliminal. And it often happens that the satisfaction of one motivation entails the foiling of another, so that the harmonious satisfaction of our desires that forms the overall objective of mankind's activity is a scarcely attainable goal. The source of this frustration of our overall objective is not merely the multiplicity of desires that go into the making of human nature. A further and more important source is the incoherence and disorder of the ensemble of mankind's desires, which have lost their original state of harmony. Augustine interpreted this troublesome aspect of the human condition as God's punishment for Adam and Eve's sin and the Fall of Man. Augustine argues, for instance, that the shame that accompanies lust is the just penalty for that disobedience, although he wonders—not unreasonably—how mankind, had it *not* sinned, would have been able to propagate itself without lust.

Next to the *Confessions*, Augustine's best-known work is his *City of God*, which is a massive defense of Christianity against its pagan critics. Here Augustine argues that all of history can be regarded as God's preparation for two cities, one heavenly—the City of God—and the other earthly—the City of the Devil—and in one or the other of which, all mankind will ultimately reside. Augustine tells how the two cities were formed by the separation of the good angels from the bad angels. He reconciles his account with the Torah's *Book of Genesis*, especially with the Fall of Man, and argues that the advent of Christ signifies God's wish to enable mankind to merit salvation, despite its sinfulness. The City of the Devil is inhabited by people who refuse to believe in Christ's mission and to repent; they will not be saved. But the City of God is inhabited by people who believe in Christ's mission and are genuinely repentant. They will establish eternal communion with God on the Day of Judgment.

On the Free Choice of the Will. One of Augustine's most enduring contributions to moral philosophy was his consideration of the problem of free will, which has come down to us via his treatise *On the Free Choice of the Will*. Its text is styled in the form of a Socratic dialogue with his disciple Evodius, who asks Augustine to explain to him why God gave us free will, when we wouldn't have been able to sin if He hadn't given it to us in the first place. Augustine asks Evodius how he can be so sure that it really was God who gave us free will. Evodius replies that there isn't anyone else who could have given us free will. After all, we owe our very existence to God, and He decreed, moreover, that for the sake of justice we deserve punishment for sinning and deserve reward for doing right. But, Evodius wonders, how it is possible that, given that God is the source of everything that is good—and justice *is* good—that justice demands that sinners be punished and the righteous be rewarded? How could God be just if He Himself is the cause of the unhappiness of the sinners and the happiness of the righteous, when both sinners and righteous are of His making?

While Augustine admits that it is true that sinners could not sin without free will, he insists that it is equally true that the righteous couldn't do right without free will either. So God didn't give us free will so that sinners can sin but so that the righteous can do right, which would be equally impossible without free will. The very fact that God punishes anyone who uses free will to sin shows that free will was given to us to enable us live righteously, for such punishment would be unjust if the *purpose* of having given us free will had been to live righteously as well as sinfully. After all, how could someone be justly punished for using free will for the very purpose for which it was given? When God punishes a sinner, isn't he saying, "Why didn't you use your free will for the purpose for which I gave it to you, namely living righteously?"

And as for the virtue that we so admire in God's justice—His punishing sins and rewarding good deeds—how could virtue even exist if human beings lacked free will? No action would be either right *or* wrong if it was not attributable to the will: punishment as well as reward would be unjust if human beings lacked free will. So God did right to give free will to mankind.

Evodius accepts the logic of Augustine's argument. Yet he still wonders why, if God gave us free will for the purpose of living righteously, He did not prevent us from perverting free will and misuse it for sinning. Why isn't it like justice, which God also gave to mankind to enable it to live well? No one can use justice to live wickedly. In the same way it ought to be the case that no one could use the free will to sin, if, indeed, it was given to us for acting righteously.

Augustine replies, with some casuistic legerdemain, that he hopes that Evodius can work this out on his own, possibly with a little help from God. Didn't Evodius just affirm hat he is sure that it was God who gave us free will? But if he now doubts that it actually was a good gift then he can't be all that sure that it was a gift of God, from whom the soul derives all its good gifts. So if we find that free will is *not* a good gift, then we must infer that God couldn't have been its donor, since it is impious to blame God for anything. But if it is quite certain that God *did* give us free will, then we must admit that it *ought* to have been given. And in exactly the way that it was given; for God gave it, and his deeds are utterly beyond reproach.

Though driven into a corner, Evodius does not give up. He assures Augustine that his faith in God is unshaken, but, all the same, he would like to understand better why free will was given to us for doing right when it can also be used for doing wrong. For if it is uncertain that free will was actually given for doing right, then it's also uncertain whether it ought to have been given in the first place. This means in turn that maybe he,

Evodius, was wrong in being so sure that free will was God's gift, if, as Augustine says, it's impious to believe that God gave us something that shouldn't have been given. So Evodius asks whether free will should be included among the good things we have, for if this can be shown, Evodius will reaffirm that God gave it to us and concede that He was right to do so.

Augustine reminds Evodius that they had already agreed that even when we find good things in the body that we can use wrongly, we do not say that they ought not to have been given to the body, for we admit that they are, in fact, good. So why should it be surprising that there are also good things in the soul that we can use wrongly, but since they are in fact good, can only have been given by Him from whom all good things come? Evodius should consider what a great Good a body is missing if it has no hands. And yet people use their hands wrongly in committing violent or shameful acts. If one sees someone who has no feet, one admits that his well being is impaired by the absence of so great a Good. And yet one would not deny that someone who uses his feet to harm someone else or to disgrace himself is using them wrongly.

Or, by way of another example, we see light and we distinguish the forms of objects by means of our eyes. They are the most beautiful things in our bodies, and we use them to preserve our safety and to secure many other good things in life. Nonetheless, many people use their eyes to do evil things, and yet one realizes what a great Good is missing in a face that has no eyes. But when they are present, who gave them, if not God, the generous giver of all things? Thus, just as one approves of those good things in the body and praise God who gave them, while disregarding those sinners who use their eyes for evil purposes, one should admit that free will, without which no one can live rightly, is a good gift. One should condemn those who misuse this good gift rather than saying that He who gave it shouldn't have given it.

Evodius is not satisfied by this argument. He wants Augustine to prove, as he has requested all along, that free will is a good thing. Upon this proof he will concede that God gave free will to us, since he, of course, admits that all good things come from God.

Augustine now sets out to prove to Evodius that free will is not only a good thing but that it ranks among the very highest of good things. It's simply perverse of Evodius to doubt the virtue of free will, when even those who lead the worst of lives admit that no one can live righteously without it. He asks which is better: something without which we can live righteously, or something without which we cannot?

Evodius admits that something without which we cannot live righteously is far superior and concedes that Augustine has finally shown to his satisfaction that free will should be included among the good things given to us by God. But now he wants Augustine to explain to him the source of the force that moves the will from good towards evil. He wants to know this because if God gave us the will in a way such that it is driven from good towards evil by a force of nature, then the will turns towards evil by necessity. So, how can there be blame for the evildoer if nature and necessity determined his will's movement?

Augustine responds with a question. Doesn't Evodius agree that the movement that occurs when a stone falls to the ground by its own weight is a movement of the stone?

Yes, Evodius agrees, but he remarks that in seeking the lowest place, the stone performs a natural movement. And if *that* is the kind of movement the will makes, then its movement is natural as well. So if the will is moved naturally, it cannot be blamed when it turns towards something evil, being compelled to do so by its own nature. However, since we do not doubt that a will's movement towards evil is blameworthy, we have to deny that it is natural, and is therefore unlike the natural movement of a stone.

Augustine concedes that the two cases are unlike but points out that the difference between them is that the stone has no power to check its downward movement while the soul cannot be moved to abandon righteousness and turn to evil unless it wills to do so. In other words, the movement of the stone is indeed natural, but that of the will is voluntary, and therefore blame- or praiseworthy. So why is there any need for Evodius to ask about the source of the force that moves the will from good to evil?

Evodius wants to know the source of the force because he can't understand how God can have foreknowledge of everything in the future—as he surely does—if the movement of any person's will either away from or towards evil is voluntary rather than necessitated by nature. How can our will be free if God foreknew that it is going to move us towards evil?

Augustine's answer, which Evodius accepts, is that God's foreknowledge of movements of the will does not create their necessity. The will He gave us could not be a will unless it remained in our power rather than in His. God's foreknowledge of how we are going to use that power does not take away its freedom.

Thus, this very early discussion of the crucial role of the concept free will in the realm of moral responsibility already ended in a paradox. And so did all subsequent efforts to find a coherent, existentially satisfactory way of dealing with free will, from the dawn of the Middle Ages in the fifth century to modern times. Resolution of the paradox turned out to be possible only by considering the problem of free will in two or more mutually exclusive, or in what we will refer to in Chapter 14 as *complementary* contexts. In Augustine's case, the complementary contexts were Christian faith and Hellenist logic.

Augustine died in 430 CE at the age of 76, as the invading Vandal hordes were closing in on his bishopric Hippo.

Peter Abelard. Throughout the Middle Ages, Christian, Islamic, and Judaic philosophy was dominated by Platonic idealism and preoccupied with religious faith and salvation. One of the few philosophically noteworthy persons during that long, intellectually dark European period was the Parisian monk and highly original thinker, Peter Abelard (1079–1142). In addition to his ever-lasting fame for having been the unfortunate lover of his student, the beautiful Héloise, Abelard is remembered also for his rediscovery some of the problems of moral philosophy left unresolved by the Early Church Fathers. He brought into clear view the distinctive feature of Christian ethics implicit in Augustine's work, in particular the split between religious and secular considerations that separates Christian from Greek ethics. Abelard held that morals are an inner quality that relates to one's motives or intentions rather than to the consequences of one's actions. This view of the nature of morals came to be stressed in the Protestant Reformation of the fifteenth century and attained its fullest development in the eighteenth century in the ethical system of Immanuel Kant. Abelard taught that one can attain virtue through reason as well as faith, and, on first sight heretical proposition in the context of medieval Christianity. In this way Abelard paved the way for St. Thomas Aquinas, the towering figure of late medieval Christian philosophy, whose elaboration of this proposition came to be incorporated into the canon of the Roman Catholic Church. Thomas provided the theological link between the Christian Middle Ages and the Renaissance, just as Augustine had provided the link between Greco-Roman paganism and medieval Christianity.

St. Thomas Aquinas. Thomas was born in the Kingdom of Naples in 1225, as a member of the family of the Counts of Aquino. Educated at the Benedictine Abbey of Monte Cassino and the University of Naples, he entered the Dominican Order of mendicant preacher-friars at the age of nineteen. He spent the rest of his life exemplifying the Order's commitment to studying and preaching. Thomas died in the Cistercian monastery of Fossanova near Rome in 1274 and was canonized in 1323.

Early in his career, Thomas came under the influence of Albertus Magnus, the great Dominican scholar who had become acquainted with the works of Aristotle. During the Middle Ages Aristotle had been largely forgotten in the Christian West, but by the thirteenth century knowledge of his works had begun to percolate back from the Muslim East to their European source. Albertus had been one of the first Christian theologians to realize the need for reconciling Aristotelian philosophy with Christianity. So Thomas made it his aim to square Aristotelian materialist science and naturalism with Augustinian Platonic idealism, after the latter had held sway over Christian theology and philosophy for eight centuries. What Thomas set out to prove was the compatibility of Aristotelian materialism with Christian idealist dogma and to construct a unified view of nature, mankind, and God.

The task Thomas had cut out for himself was not easy. Aristotle's ethics was relativistic and rational while Augustinian ethics was absolutist and fideist (that is, grounded in faith rather than reason). Evidently, at least one of these rival moral theories is totally misguided, or else there must be room in the world for two very different systems of moral concepts and principles. Thomas adopted the latter alternative and divided the ensemble of moral concepts into two realms, the 'natural' and the 'theological.' He thought that by proper training and exercise of reason one can attain the natural virtues accounted for by Aristotle, while attainment of theological virtues—faith, hope and love—requires divine grace. Thomas also distinguished two supreme Goods, or paramount goals of life: worldly happiness and eternal beatitude. The former is attained through natural virtue and the latter through the Church and its sacraments. Thomas, the Aristotelian, thus expressed a considerably more optimistic attitude toward the possibility of improving mankind's lot on earth through knowledge of nature and rational action than did Augustine, the Platonist. Thomas helped prepare the climate for the Western rebirth of natural science, whose first stirrings came in Thomas' own thirteenth century.

Thomas' influence on Christian theological thought of succeeding centuries was immense, in that his theological ideas became part of the mainline teachings of the Roman Catholic Church. They include Thomas' proposition that there are two distinct routes to knowledge of God, one of them being revelation and the other human reason. Another notion put forward by Thomas that still looms large in present-day Catholicism is the belief that each rational human soul is originated by divine creation from nothing. Thus human parents are not the total cause of their offspring; they share the work of procreation with God. This is why the Catholic Church puts so much stress on the dignity and sanctity of human reproduction, which it regards as more than a mere profane biological function.

As for the paradox of theodicy, Thomas accepted Augustine's argument that even a perfectly benign God has to allow evil to exist because the existence of evil is a necessary condition for making many good things possible. For instance, Thomas pointed out that if there were no death of their animals of prey, there would be no life for lions, and if there were no persecution from tyrants, there would be no occasion for the heroic suffering of the martyrs. Thomas, however, went beyond Augustine's argumentation by introducing an additional, essentially cognitive consideration. He pointed out that since we lack an insight into God's nature, we must struggle with the question of how to understand the terms used in the Scriptures to describe God. What do terms such as 'good,' 'wise,' and 'just' mean when they are attributed to God? Their meaning as divine attributes cannot be the *same* as that of their meanings as human attributes, because if they *were* the same, we would have the insight into God's nature that we obviously lack. Should the terms therefore be understood merely as the *opposites* of human attributes that we do understand, such as 'good' meaning 'not wicked,' 'wise' meaning 'not foolish,' and so on? Thomas rejected this solution of the theodicy paradox championed by the Jewish philosopher Moses Maimonides in the twelfth century, on the grounds that the Scriptures must mean more than mere opposites of human attributes when they apply them to God.

Thomas' own answer was that when referring to God, these terms are used only metaphorically. Since we cannot have an adequate conception of God's nature, that is, since our ideas of Him fall short of reality, we have to recognize that the qualities that 'good' and 'wise' signify exist in God at a higher level than in ourselves. It is not that God is not really, or not in the fullest sense, good, wise, just, and so on. On the contrary, He has these qualities to the fullest perfection in the most complete way possible, and it is we mortal creatures who fall short of perfection.

According to Thomas, God's perfect qualities include His perfect knowledge. He knows everything knowable. He knows the world He created, not as a spectator comes to know things he happens to encounter. Being their absolute first cause, God's knowledge of things is not even dependent upon their prior existence. On the contrary, it is the act of His knowing them that brings the things into existence in the first place. We can, so Thomas suggests, get a crude idea of the nature of God's knowledge of things before they even exist, by analogizing it with the kind of knowledge an architect has of a house before it has been built. It is because of the conception of the house in the architect's mind that the house comes into existence, whereas it is because the house already exists that the passer-by comes to know it.

Thomas succeeded to a large degree in blending Aristotelianism with Christianity, by arguing for the truth of both systems and refuting arguments of his predecessors and contemporaries that purported to show their incompatibility. Thomas held that human reasoning alone can validate the existence of God and the immortality of the soul, although for the benefit of those who cannot engage in such strenuous mental exercise, these metaphysical propositions are also divinely revealed for acceptance by faith. Divine revelation, however, extends beyond reason to validate the acceptance of such further Christian truths as the Sacred Trinity of God the Father, Christ the Son, and the Holy Ghost. Thomas thus supported the general (though not universal) Christian view that revelation supplements, rather than cancels or replaces, the theories of rational philosophy.

Summa Theologica. One of the unsolved problems of moral philosophy that Thomas rediscovered was free will, on which there had been little movement in the eight centuries that had elapsed since Augustine's death. He devoted two sections to the problem in his major treatise,

74

Summa Theologica, written between 1265 and 1273. One section was entitled 'Free Choice' and the other 'The Voluntary and the Involuntary.'
(Aquinas, 1947)

Thomas' account of free will and moral responsibility was generally
similar to that of Augustine's. Like Augustine, Thomas held that free will
not only exists but also is compatible with God's foreknowledge of our actions. But Thomas' concept of free will was more fully developed than
Augustine's, since Thomas associated the exercise of free will with rational self-determination by a process of judgmental deliberation, rather
than with a mere absence of external causal influences. To make this
point, Thomas pointed to some things that act without judgment, such as
stones, which, whenever given the opportunity, move downwards. And
although animals *do* act with judgment, they act without judgmental deliberation. A sheep seeing a wolf , for instance, judges the wolf a thing to
be shunned. But this is a *natural* but not a *free* judgment, because the
sheep judges by natural instinct rather than by rational deliberation.
Mankind's actions, by contrast, are determined by freely willed judgments, because, thanks to our capacity for rational thought, we are free to
decide whether something should be shunned or sought.

What is the rational basis for the freely willed decisions we make? According to Thomas, it is our rationally guided desires, formed by our
moral education and training. The will's freedom of choice then inheres
in the process of our deliberating the reasons for and against a particular
action. He pointed to our habits, our desires, our knowledge, and our deliberations as the faculties to which our will resorts in deciding on actions
for which we may be held responsible. Thomas did not, however, address
the further question whether these faculties are within our personal control, that is, whether we really are 'free' to choose the habits and desires
that determine our will. Perhaps we are *not* wholly 'free' after all, since,
according to Thomas, our rationally guided desires are determined by our
moral education and training. Thus, in the end, Thomas too fell short of
resolving the Paradox of Moral Responsibility.

Later theologians tended to interpret Augustine as stressing predestination and Thomas as stressing free will. Yet, it may be argued to the
contrary that Augustine's conception of free will as an inexplicable and
non-natural attribute of the soul allows the person more autonomy of his
characterological traits than does Thomas' notion of the determinative
role of education and training. Yet, for that very reason, Thomas'

account is more congenial to a scientific, especially psychological, outlook on mankind.

Candide. In the early eighteenth century, Gottfried Wilhelm Leibniz considered the problem of evil in his philosophical book, *Theodicy,* published at the very onset of that secular and humanistic modern age. Leibniz accepted Augustine's contention that there is no paradox of theodicy because of the existentially unavoidable linkage between good and evil that even the Almighty Himself could not dissolve. But, so Leibniz argued, God's essential virtue and benevolence towards mankind is manifest in His creation of the best of all *possible* worlds. It is the best, not because it contains *no* evil but because any other possible world would contain even more evil.

Leibniz's thesis was famously demolished in mid-eighteenth century by Voltaire in the most popular of all his works, his satire *Candide,* in which Voltaire also takes potshots, *en passant,* at one of his pet hates, namely religion. The young protagonist, Candide, and his mentor, Doctor Pangloss, suffer a series of incredible misfortunes and hardships, while Pangloss steadfastly insists on the Leibnizian mantra that this is 'the best of all possible worlds.' Candide, in the end disillusioned, decides that this is *not* the best of all possible worlds. He concludes that we simply have to bear our misfortunes bravely, be tolerant, do the very best with whatever bad hands we have been dealt, and simply 'cultivate our garden.' Thus Candide's resolution of the paradox of theodicy is simply that since God either does not exist, or if He *does,* He obviously lacks essential virtue and benevolence towards mankind, and everybody has to look after his or her own interest.

As we will note in Chapter 10, Voltaire's way of resolving the paradox of theodicy led the nineteenth century German philosopher, Friedrich Nietzsche, to declare that the philosophers of the eighteenth century Enlightenment had managed to kill the God we thought we all knew. Thus, according to Nietzsche, with God dead, everything has become morally permissible and mankind is about to sink into a moral abyss.

Coda. The ancient metaphysical paradox of theodicy inherent in the belief in a one-and-only, all-powerful, righteous, benign God still awaits its satisfactory resolution. The perennial failure of theologians and philosophers to account for God's seemingly flawed, quasi-schizoid character became especially troublesome in the wake of the Second World War. Admittedly, Augustine's argument may be rationally sound. Perhaps God *does have to allow* the existence of evil to provide mankind with a contrasting background that makes the Good shine more brightly and thus more easily perceptible to the dim-witted mortals. But this argument can hardly be emotionally acceptable to survivors, or to relatives of victims, of the Nazi Holocaust.

ARISTOTLE CONTEMPLATING A BUST OF HOMER

Painting by Rembrandt (1663)

Chapter Five

⟞⟞◇⟝

Personhood

Virtually every moral issue hinges on the unique metaphysical standing of persons, since personhood confers on its bearers rights and responsibilities that render interactions among them radically different from interactions between them and other living creatures that lack personhood, such as animals. Or, in terms of L. E. Lomasky's (1992) homely characterization of this difference, "one eats animals but sleeps with persons; any inversion of this procedure is apt to occasion considerable attention."

As we noted in Chapters 2 and 3, the belief in the unique moral standing of persons dates back far into human history. Yet, while the rights and duties of persons are what moral discourse is all about, it is not easy to provide an unambiguous definition of the kind of creatures to which those rights and duties entailed by personhood actually pertain. Despite its standing as a category of what Kant designated as 'pure practical reason,' personhood has remained an elusive metaphysical concept. That is not to say that we do not usually recognize a creature as a person when we see one. For just as Plato conjectured that we recognize 'justice' when we see it because there exists a perfect, unambiguous, and eternal example of justice—its 'Form'—in our mind, so can we conjecture that there exists also in our mind a perfect, unambiguous, and eternal Platonic personhood 'Form.' We will develop the concept of personhood as a Platonic 'Form' further in later chapters, after we have considered Kant's philosophy of *critical idealism* in more detail.

Identity Definition. According to the standard modern definition, such as that provided by the *Shorter Oxford English Dictionary*, "a person is an individual human being; a man, woman or child," where 'human being' denotes a member of the biological species, *Homo sapiens*. The traditional taxonomic criteria for setting specimens of *H. sapiens* apart from other creatures not belonging to their species was a subjective, fuzzy set of anatomical, physiological, and hereditary properties. But by the end of the twentieth century, in the wake of the revolution brought to the life sciences by molecular-biology, those traditional criteria had come to be replaced by a novel, more precise, and objective criterion: the nucleotide base sequence of the DNA comprising the creature's genome. We will refer to this latter-day definition of personhood as the '*identity definition*' because it can be stated in the form of an identity function.

Person ≡ Carrier of Human DNA Nucleotide Base Sequence in Genome

Although the identity definition is not problematical in natural, moral-value-free contexts, it *can* be very troublesome in non-natural/moral-value-laden contexts in which moral considerations are at issue since its scope is both too broad and too narrow. Its scope is too broad because there are some circumstances under which many people do not regard possession of a human genome by a living entity as *sufficient* to qualify it as a person entitled to the rights and duties devolving from personhood. And its scope is too narrow because there are other circumstances under which many people do *not* regard possession of a human genome by a living entity as *necessary* to qualify it as a person. In any case, the identity definition provides no rational justification for conferring special moral rights and duties on just one single biological species—namely our own—by virtue of its unique DNA nucleotide base sequence.

Psychological Definitions. Aristotle—the inventor of the concept of biological species—seems to have been aware of the philosophical shortcomings of the identity definition of personhood. For he questioned the validity of an attribution of a value-laden moral quality such as personhood to a creature on the basis of the value-free anatomical or physiological criteria by which it is assigned membership in a particular biological species. So Aristotle based his definition of personhood on the *psychological* criterion of rationality, which he considered mankind's unique possession, one that sets people apart from animals. He noted that, like other creatures, humans move from place to place and perceive phenomena via their senses, but only mankind has the capacity to reason. So Aristotle classified humans as the species of *rational* animals.

Jewish and Christian traditions perpetuated into modern times the Aristotelian criterion of rationality as a uniquely human characteristic.

This belief is epitomized in the biblical proposition of Genesis 1:26-31 that God created mankind in His image, where 'image' has to refer to a likeness of His sublime *spiritual* form. In other words, God endowed mankind, and only mankind, with a mind, that, like His own, can reason and know the difference between right and wrong.

Second-Order Volitions. In the first half of the twentieth century, upon the rise of the scientific study of animal behavior, biological psychologists came to reject the unique attribution of rationality to *H. sapiens*. They argued that many species of animals, especially those belonging to the class of mammals, manifest behaviors that meet the criterion of rationality, and yet are not generally considered to qualify for personhood. So, to save the Aristotelian criterion of rationality as the acid test of personhood, some latter-day moral philosophers searched for one or another special aspect of rationality that they considered as uniquely human.

The Princeton philosopher, Harry Frankfurt (1971), put forward one such special aspect, to which he gave the name '*second-order volitions*,' as a necessary and sufficient condition for personhood. Frankfurt asserted that human beings, as well as many species of animals, have desires, which can be described by the statement 'A wants to X.' If X is an action, such as taking a particular drug, then the statement refers to what Frankfurt calls a *first-order desire*. Such a first order desire may be weak or strong, present in or absent from A's conscious awareness, and implemented or not implemented by A, possibly because A wants to Y more than to X. That is to say, A's first-order desire may or may not be effective, and therefore, according to Frankfurt, is not 'coextensive' with A's *will*. However, if the action X is itself the act of desiring to X, then the statement turns into what Frankfurt calls a *second-order desire*, namely 'A wants to want to X.' Moreover, if, as is almost always the case in instances of second-order desires, A wants the desire to X to be his *will*, then Frankfurt refers to it as a '*second order volition*.'

Frankfurt asserts that creatures with first-order desires but lacking second order volitions, are *wantons* (meaning that they act without regard to what is right or wrong) and hence, being amoral creatures, they do not qualify for personhood. According to Frankfurt, the class of wantons includes all animals, some of which—though *contra* Aristotle but *pro* modern students of animal behavior—*may* be endowed with rationality.

Frankfurt justifies his disqualification of wantons for personhood standing by asserting that the second order volitions wantons lack are, in fact, the essence of free will.

It *is* the case that, as Frankfurt implies, the attribution of free will to an agent is a necessary condition for the agent's inclusion in the category of persons. But Frankfurt's identification of second order volitions as indicators of the presence of free will begs the critical, morally relevant question of their *autonomy*. He evidently takes it for granted that second order volitions meet the essential criterion of *autonomy* inherent in the (moral) concept of free will, rather than being subject to the all-pervasive, *heteronomous* governance of determinism that gives rise to the Paradox of Moral Responsibility in the first place.

Frankfurt's postulation of the existence of first order desires as a prelude to second order volitions is not unreasonable, but obviously irrelevant for the resolution of the Paradox. We will consider another instance of Frankfurt's shortcomings as an analyst of the free will problem in Chapter 8.

Abortion. The too-inclusive scope of the identity definition is exemplified by its begging the practical question whether such immature and anatomically incomplete carriers of a human genome as fertilized ova, embryos and fetuses, have the rights and duties devolving from personhood. Thus the identity definition would stigmatize abortion as the murder of a person and therefore deny to a prospective mother the 'freedom of choice' to terminate her pregnancy, in accord with the arguments put forward by 'right-to-life' opponents of abortion.

I first became aware of the moral irrelevance of biological criteria for justifying or refusing the ascription of personhood to an immature human being when I attended a conference misleadingly entitled '*Biology and the Future of Man.*' It was held in the *Grand Amphithéatre* of the Sorbonne in the spring of 1975 (Stent, 1976b). As I soon discovered, the real agenda of the conference's organizers had not been to prognosticate the Future of Man but to create a favorable intellectual climate for the legalization of abortion in France, which was then under consideration by the French parliament. The international bevy of conference participants included only biologists and biomedical scientists, because the organizers had evidently thought that your woolly-headed philosophers and theologians had nothing useful to contribute to the difficult moral problem under discussion.

The participants were generally agreed that the rights of persons include a right to life and that the intentional termination of a person's life is murder, which they, like *bien-pensants* all over, thought ought to be illegal. So the avowed aim of the discussions was to provide the *Assemblée Nationale* with an objective, scientific (that is, natural) criterion for defining the critical stage in prenatal human development at which the biologically immature human fetus turns into a person. Prior to that stage—so the reasoning went—there could be no moral objection to abortion.

Various speakers proposed this or that developmental stage as the critical time of onset of personhood. Each speaker supported his or her proposal with bio-scientific arguments based on descriptive, natural properties of the little creature, ranging from gastrulation of the embryo (that is, establishment of the three germinal layers designated 'ectoderm,' 'mesoderm' and 'endoderm'), through the onset of fetal heartbeat or electrical brain activity, to birth. All of these speakers provided counterexamples for the person=*H. sapiens* identity definition, since their proposals implicitly denied that the mere presence in an entity of the genome of *H. sapiens* is a sufficient condition for its personhood.

The only speaker who did not provide a counterexample for the identity definition was the eminent French cytogeneticist, Jerome Lejeune, who had discovered the chromosomal basis of Down Syndrome in 1959. Lejeune, a devout Catholic and a leader of the French anti-abortion movement at that time, argued that personhood begins with the fertilized ovum, because it is at that stage that the unique genetic identity of the person is established. Thus he ruled out abortion altogether.

None of the speakers—not even the devout Lejeune—referred to the categories of Kantian pure practical reason, such as uniqueness, sacredness, and free will, as a part of the ensemble of non-natural properties that confer personhood on a being. In fact, no one mentioned the soul (although some people did mention the *brain*) as the feature whose earliest time of development was the actual subject of the discussion. It seemed ironic that the participants of the Paris conference addressed the ethics of abortion in the Sorbonne's *Grand Amphithéatre* in wholly naturalistic terms, while facing the bigger-than-life statue of René Descartes, which graces that hall. I was half-expecting Descartes' statue, like the Commendatore's in Mozart's *Don Giovanni,* to quicken in anger and drag the discussants to Hell. For they paid no heed to Descartes' judgment (which we will consider in more detail in Chapter 9) that the moral law applies only to persons but not to automata. According to Descartes, automata lack personhood, not because only persons have this or that body part that an automaton may lack, but because persons (and only persons) have souls.

How, then, has the moral problem of legislating the latest permissible time of abortion, i.e. the advent of the moral threshold of personhood, been resolved in those jurisdictions that do allow abortion at all? At the earliest developmental stages—zygote, blastula, or gastrula—the embryo is certainly *alive* and contains a human genome that (as Lejeune emphasized) will eventually give rise to a biologically unique person. But the general perception in jurisdictions where abortion *is* permitted is that at its earliest stages of development the embryo is not yet a person. It is a mere blob of protoplasm devoid of any appearance of uniqueness. At some later stage of development, the fetus does take on some overt human features that may make it *look* like a person. But at just what stage the fetus does begin to look that way is a highly subjective call. For most, though transhistorically and transculturally not necessarily all people, that stage will be reached no later than the time of birth. This sociological claim finds support in the fact that while the latest stage of permissible abortion is the subject of vigorous contention, few people—except some hard-core anti-abortionists— consider abortion morally indistinguishable from infanticide.

The subjectivity of the criterion by which the personhood of an immature human creature is actually assessed is evident from the records of trials in which abortionists were charged with the murder of a fetus. Very often, the prosecution showed photographs of the abortus to the jury, and—not surprisingly—the chance of a verdict of 'guilty' was the greater the more advanced was its developmental stage. When asked for the grounds on which they reached their verdict, the jurors rarely mentioned any of the (objective) biological criteria put forward at the Sorbonne conference. Rather, most often they said that they found for 'guilty' when pictures shown by the prosecution evoked the (subjective) impression that the abortus had a recognizably human face.

Another counterexample for the identity definition of personhood is provided by the diminished personhood of insane people. We will discuss this counterexample in more detail in Chapter 6 in connection with the concept of moral responsibility. But in the meanwhile, we may note that insanity is a condition under which some adult specimens of *H. sapiens* are denied full moral standing as persons by an abridgment of some of their rights and duties. This denial occurs when human beings are judged to be afflicted with a defective power of reasoning due to a disease of the mind that prevents them from knowing the nature and quality of their actions, especially from knowing whether what they are doing is right or wrong. Insane people are not, however, denied the rights and protection due them by virtue of the uniqueness and sacredness of their residual personhood.

Aristotle, who morally justified the Greek practice of slavery by creating the category of 'natural slaves,' already appreciated the limits of the identity definition. As the inventor of the biological species concept, Aristotle was certainly aware of the cross-fertility of free Greeks and their unfree slaves and did not deny that slaves are ostensibly members of the human species. Yet he classified them as *'natural slaves,'* whose rational faculty is underdeveloped or absent. According to Aristotle, natural slaves are persons only in a *secondary* sense and therefore lack some or all of the rights and duties that come with *primary* personhood.

Uniqueness. The necessity of our perceiving a human being as a unique creature for bestowal of the rights and duties of personhood is yet another counterexample to the identity definition. For instance, the tendency of members of a foreign race to look all alike seems to be a precondition of racism. By thus being depersonalized, the people of another race are deprived of their souls, and racists can make themselves comfortable in the belief that these inferior creatures are little more than automata in human form. A similar process of depersonalization occurs in war, when soldiers suspend the normal dictates of their private morals regarding the sacredness of personhood. As many accounts of front-line wartime experience show, this suspension occurs more readily in brief encounters with an unknown, or even invisible enemy than *vis-à-vis* a particular member of the enemy camp (especially if he is of the same race), provided that an opportunity has been afforded to establish the uniqueness of his person. The faceless, homogeneous, and collective enemy has no soul; he is merely a dangerous beast outside the bounds of morals. Once recognized as a unique individual, however, the enemy acquires a soul, joins the family of man, and comes within the purview of morals.

Cloning. The intuitive belief that uniqueness is a necessary condition for granting personhood came to the fore in recent years by a biotechnological development that had been held to belong to the fantasies of science fiction. This is the asexual reproduction, or *cloning*, of humans, which has been achieved for some mammalian species, such as sheep and mice. The procedure consists of the transfer of diploid nuclei from the somatic tissues of a single adult donor animal—male or female—into artificially enucleated eggs harvested from a donor female of the same species. Upon reimplantation of such genetically manipulated eggs into the wombs of host females there will arise a *clone* of genetically identical offspring, all endowed with the hereditary identity of the single donor individual.

This procedure, which is bound to provide enormous benefits for animal husbandry, has aroused great concern among so-called 'bioethicists,' as well as among the general public. They fear that, before long, the cloning technology will be applied to the human species since it offers the tempting prospect of enriching our society by the artificial breeding of people with genes proven for their capacity to develop individuals with outstandingly desirable physical and mental qualities. But it seems most unlikely that the prospect of populating our planet with clones of genetically identical people is tempting at all. While it would be fun to have Kant, Beethoven, Edith Wharton, Einstein, Picasso, Clark Gable and Marilyn Monroe live on our block, the thought of having hundreds or thousands of their replicas in town is a nightmare. Why? Because the thought of beholding a horde of look-alike human stereotypes is abhorrent even to people who are quite unaware of and who lack the scientific sophistication to appreciate the long-term biological dangers inherent in such a cloning program. The reason for their horror is the intuitive belief in the uniqueness of the person. The horde of look-alike cloned humans would not seem to be real persons but creepy automata in human shape.

In addition to such cases in which a perceived lack of uniqueness may result in the denial of personhood to authentic human beings, counter examples can be cited that show that the perception of uniqueness may suffice to qualify a *non-human entity* for *inclusion* in the category of person. For instance, a child may bestow personhood on a favorite doll, by endowing this non-living artifact with rights, duties, sacredness, and free will (and treat it accordingly, including even loving it). However, the currently most vexing moral problem connected with the extension of personhood to non-human entities concerns not the treatment of dolls or other lovable inanimate objects, such as my own, precious 1963 white Cadillac convertible, or a Stradivarius violin, but the moral standing of animals.

Personhood of Animals. The least vexing aspect of the granting of personhood to animals concerns the treatment of household pets, among which domesticated cats and dogs provide the most common examples. Cats and dogs are in a particularly favorable position for elevation to personhood, not least because they were bred from their wild ancestor species for the very purpose of providing companionship for their human masters. The masters generally acknowledge their pets' individuality, perceive them as unique specimens of their kind, and attribute to them a mind with non-natural Kantian categories of pure practical reason, such as free will and being an end in itself. The masters extend the protection of the moral law to their pets, give them personal names and treat them with the same consideration as that granted to the human members of the household. Moreover, they also tend to ascribe moral responsibility to their pets as well. Thus the master may scold, or even punish the animal for soiling the carpet with excrement or killing a song-bird in the garden, while also praising, or even rewarding their pets for killing household vermin, such as rats or mice.

Most animal species are not likely candidates for elevation to personhood, however. They belong to invertebrate phyla, such as the annelids, mollusks, and insects, about which it is hard to believe that they have a soul that provides them with consciousness and rational thought. And even among the vertebrate species there is only the class of mammals that includes some creatures whose behavior is sufficiently complex that attributing to them a conscious and rational mind might cross the threshold of credibility. Yet even among those mammalian candidate species few specimens attain personhood status, because of their lack of opportunity to be recognized as unique individuals by a human being and be granted moral standing by virtue of the authority vested in We the *Homo sapiens* people to confer that honor.

In the context of the Western religious and moral traditions, philosophical discussions regarding personhood were only rarely concerned with animals prior to the end of the eighteenth century, except by way of a counterexample illustrating the difference between mindless brutes and thinking human beings. No doubt, the identity definition, which excludes animals from personhood, is a legacy of those times. Descartes, like his philosophical predecessors and contemporaries, still considered animals as unthinking automata, whose behavior is wholly accounted for by bodily functions. The possibility that animals might have minds was not taken seriously beyond the context of the fairy tale until the latter part of the nineteenth century, when the recognition of the evolutionary continuity between animals and humans lent it some credence, at least among biologists. And by the middle of the twentieth century the topic of animal mind came to be more widely discussed, upon the rise of *ethology*, the discipline that is dedicated to the evolutionarily oriented study of animal behavior.

So, maybe some animal species *do* have minds capable generating consciousness, rational thoughts, intentions, and feelings. It would not necessarily follow from that hypothetical premise, however, that we have to believe that the minds of these species also include the non-natural properties, such as uniqueness, sacredness, and free will that are ascribed to the human soul. That is, even if animals *do* have minds, they might still fail to qualify for personhood and lack the moral standing claimed on their behalf by the advocates of 'Animal Rights.' (Radner and Radner, 1989)

Vegetarianism. There is one context in which the personhood of animals was at stake long before the end of the eighteenth century, namely vegetarianism. In fact, the view that we should avoid eating animal meat has moral roots reaching back three millennia to Hindu beliefs about the sacredness of *all* life and the reincarnation of deceased persons in animal form. Vegetarianism also had some philosophical support in classical Greece and Rome. For instance, in the sixth century BCE Pythagoras, abstained from eating animals because of his belief that humans and animals do share a common soul. And in the first century CE the Hellenist philosopher and historian, Plutarch, provided a detailed argument for vegetarianism in his essay *On Eating Flesh*, on the grounds of justice and humane treatment for animals. The Judeo-, Christian or Muslim Scriptures provided little support for vegetarianism, however. So it remained a rare custom in the Western and Near-Eastern worlds until interest in vegetarianism was revived in the nineteenth century, inspired not only by idealistic moral concerns about the humane treatment of animals but also by pragmatic dietary considerations.

Notable British proponents of vegetarianism included the poet Percy Shelley, the writer George Bernard Shaw, and especially Henry Salt, who coined the term 'Animal Rights' by way of the title of an influential book he published in 1892. The German philosopher Arthur Schopenhauer, too, thought that, for moral reasons, we ought to become vegetarians. To his regret Schopenhauer noted, however, that we are not free to give up meat because mankind cannot survive without feeding on it.

Since the advent of postmodernity in the 1970s, the popularity of vegetarianism has risen greatly in the (mainly Protestant) countries of the Western world, swayed by ecological as well as moral arguments. The ecological argument against eating meat is two-pronged. One prong is directed against hunting (or fishing) animals living in the wild, which used to provide the only source of meat for human consumption until the agricultural-urban revolution of the late Stone Age. Lately, hunting and fishing became vilified, however, because they are said to impoverish or even destroy, the natural environment and lead to an evolutionarily harmful reduction in the diversity of biological species. The other ecological argument is based on the contention that raising animals as a source of food is very inefficient. Typically, grain is grown on fertile agricultural land and fed to animals confined indoors or, in the case of cattle, in crowded feed lots. Much of the nutritional value of the grain is lost in the process, and this form of animal husbandry is also energy-intensive. So the concerns for world-hunger, for the land, and for energy conservation are claimed to provide an ecological as well as moral basis for a vegetarian diet, or at least one in which meat consumption is minimized.

Arguments for a reassessing the moral standing of animals have supported vegetarianism as well. People who believe that animals have rights, i.e. are entitled to have their interests given equal consideration with the similar interests of human persons, naturally infer that there is no moral justification for killing animals and dining on them for our own ends. Moreover, from the viewpoint of Aristotelian moral utilitarianism, (according to which pleasure and the satisfaction of desires as the sole element of the Good) it has been argued that it is immoral to raise animals as a source of food. For by doing so we inflict more suffering on animals than people gain pleasure by eating them.

Animal Experimentation. The personhood of animals is at stake as well in the controversy regarding the permissibility of using them for scientific experiments. The parties to this dispute generally try to disqualify their opponents by claiming that they are morally unworthy discussion partners. On the one hand, the opponents of animal experiments usually attribute selfish motives to their adversaries, even claiming that biomedical scientists do their experiments mainly to satisfy a sadistic yen for torturing animals. Accordingly, they allege that one cannot expect that just those researchers who are most qualified to evaluate the scientific or medical need for animal experimentation would actually meet their moral responsibility vis à vis the creatures they victimize. On the other hand, the biomedical scientists under attack maintain that they not only try to treat animals humanely in their experiments, but also that the principal goal of their research efforts is precisely to avert pain and suffering of animals as well as of humans. According to them, the Animal Rights movement comprises mainly sentimental fools and hypocrites, who, though they have managed to gain a disproportionately powerful political influence, cannot be engaged in any rational discourse.

As a formerly practicing neurobiologist, I recognize the unavoidable necessity of the conduct of animal experiments, without which it is hard to imagine progress in biomedical research. Yet, I was dismayed to note that representatives of the Animal Rights movement skilled in ethical disputation easily defeated the arguments put forward in defense of animal experiments by my colleagues. For instance, many biomedical scientists profess that they have a moral duty to protect life in general and animals in particular. So they concede that they are faced with a moral problem in the killing of animals to provide people with food and clothing, destroying them as pests and vermin, and condemning them to extinction in their natural state by ever-expanding our living space. Yet, they do claim that putting humans and animals on a moral par is a chimera that puts into question the human primacy embedded in the Western moral tradition, and thus of human existence on the whole. For in the same passage of Genesis 1:26, which reports that God made mankind in His image, it is said also that he let mankind "have dominion over the fish in the sea, and over the fowl of the air, and over the cattle, and over all the earth, and over every creeping thing that creeps upon the earth." Thus, within the context of Biblical canon, animals are not ends in themselves, and their exploitation use for human ends presents no moral problem.

The adherents of the Animal Rights movements stoutly reject the bio-medical scientists' claim that putting humans and animals on a par is a chimera. They point out that in the United States it was not all that long ago that putting women and black Africans on a par with white males was also considered a chimera. Admittedly, this historical comparison does not provide a logically compelling argument, but, all the same, the claim that the granting of Animal Rights would represent a goal representing moral progress over Biblical canon cannot be dismissed all that easily. After all, there have long existed Far-Eastern cultures whose moral traditions are based on the atheistic ethics of Buddhism, according to which animals and humans are considered on a par to a much greater extent than they are in the West. Since Buddhists do not believe in God in the first place, they can hardly hold that He created mankind, but not the animals, in His own image. All the same, putting mankind and animals on a moral par is a belief whose general acceptance would bring about a radical transformation of the Occidental life style that even the adherents of the Animal Rights doctrine would be unlikely to welcome.

A comparison of Sweden and the United States is instructive in this connection. On the one hand, the regulations governing animal experimentation are much more stringent in Sweden than in the United States. As far as I know, neurophysiological experiments with higher mammals, not to speak of primates, are almost impossible to carry out in Sweden. But the regulations governing human experimentation are much more lax in Sweden than in the United States. Thus the Swedish legislature is apparently much closer to the chimera of the moral parity of humans and animals than is the American.

Actual and Potential Persons. There is an assumption that has underlain our discussion of personhood thus far, which is implicit in the identity definition as well as in Aristotle's and Frankfurt's psychological definitions. This is the assumption that persons and only persons are morally considerable beings, which establishes a threshold that generates a moral discontinuity. To fall on one side of the threshold is to be a creature qualified for the full panoply of rights and duties that characterize persons; while to fall on the other side is to be, strictly speaking, a thing without any moral standing at all. But as all the practical cases requiring

91

judgments regarding personhood we have discussed—abortion, slavery, insanity, uniqueness, and animals—showed, if rigidly applied, these all-or-none thresholds lead to counterintuitive moral judgments in some, by no means far-fetched instances.

For that reason, some philosophers have sought to smooth the discontinuity by distinguishing between *actual* and *potential* persons. Actual persons bear full moral responsibility for their willed actions, while the moral status of potential persons is intermediate between that of actual persons and non-persons (or mere things). Unfortunately, there inhere at least two difficulties in this approach. One is that while it is not too difficult to distinguish between actual persons and non-persons (or things), it is far from obvious how one is supposed to tell that something is a bona-fide potential person. To what criteria can one resort for deciding whether one is dealing with an actual person, or with a potential person, or with a non-person thing? One problem posed by this approach is that it may be difficult to specify the kinds of beings that qualify as potential persons. If newborn babies are clear instances of potential persons, what about fetuses, embryos, or fertilized ova? The other problem is that if potentiality is a matter of more or less, how is one to devise a system of moral criteria that covers a broad range of approximations of the status of actual personhood?

To highlight this difficulty with the (on the whole, not unreasonable) category of potential persons, Lomasky presented the following analogy. The individual who is actually the president of the United States possesses constitutionally (and otherwise) defined rights and duties. For instance, he or she has the right to veto congressional legislation and is also entitled to Secret Service protection. Let us suppose that a candidate for the presidency is a *potential president*. This individual does not have the right to veto legislation but does have a right to Secret Service protection. It is not, however, the logic of rights that generates these results. Reasoning analogously, from the proposition that actual persons enjoy a right not to be killed, nothing follows concerning whether potential persons do possess a similar right not to be killed. Thus an entire additional and independent set of ethics might be needed to spell out the claims of potential persons.

Coda. Creatures—human or animal—are *actual* persons, provided they have been granted full moral standing, that is, have moral duties as well as moral rights; and have a rational mind to which we attribute uniqueness, being an end in itself, and free will. This statement is not meant to be normative, but merely intended to call attention to the sub-jective operational criteria by which the judgment of personhood is actu-ally made, even by those people who may profess other criteria on reli-gious, biological, or humanistic grounds.

DAVID HUME (1711–1776)

Portrait by Allan Ramsay (1766)

Chapter Six

━━▷◆◁━━

Responsibility

Causal and Moral Responsibility. In everyday speech, the word 're-sponsibility' may refer to at least two different concepts. One of them is *causal responsibility*, which denotes the relation that obtains between two events, of which one causes, or helps to cause, the other. It is exemplified by the statement that hitting an iceberg was responsible for the sinking of the *Titanic*. Causal responsibility is a *descriptive* concept, in that it refers to what the speaker believes to be an empirical fact. Causal responsibility is always implied when the event identified as the cause is *not* the action of a person. A personal action may, of course, be identified as an instance of causal responsibility as well, as exemplified by the statement that the helmsman's sudden turn of the wheel was responsible for the *Titanic*'s veering leeward.

The other concept is *moral responsibility*, which denotes the relation that obtains between an action performed by a person and the duties and obligations of that person. According to the British philosopher of law, H.L.A. Hart (1951, 1968), moral responsibility is an *ascriptive* concept, which attributes duties and obligations to a person that devolve from moral, legal, or ritual imperatives. The concept of moral responsibility forms the basis of our judgmental interpretation of a person's action.

Two different kinds of moral responsibility, *prospective* and *retrospective*, can be distinguished. Prospective moral responsibility is exemplified by the proposition that the *Titanic*'s captain was responsible for the safety of his ship's passengers. This statement implies that it was the captain's duty and obligation to ensure the passengers' safety. In this example the re-sponsibility was prospective (because that for which the person was re-sponsible lay in the future). Thus to bear prospective moral responsibility for something means to have a duty or obligation to see to it that this thing will occur or obtain.

The other kind, retrospective moral responsibility, is exemplified by the statement that the *Titanic's* captain was responsible for the passengers' deaths. The intended meaning of this proposition is not that it was the captain's duty to ensure the passengers' death. On the contrary, since the deaths referred to lie in the past rather than in the future, what is meant is that the captain acted in a blameworthy manner in a past action by failing to perform his duty. Retrospective moral responsibility can also imply praise- rather than blameworthiness, as exemplified by the statement that the *Titanic's* first mate was responsible for saving many lives by his diligent command of the lifeboats. Our further discussion of responsibility will be restricted to the retrospective moral kind, since it is for their past actions that people are judged morally and legally. Thus unless otherwise specified, in these pages the locution 'moral responsibility' will refer to '*retrospective* moral responsibility.'

The intuitive concept of moral responsibility, which provides the rational foundation for regarding persons as moral creatures in the first place, is embodied in both religious and secular laws. The concept would be incoherent unless persons' actions were attributable to their very own, freely willed choices. Free will, moreover, is more than a mere theoretical speculation. It is a direct personal, or *subjective*, experience, since sane persons have no doubt that they *are* in control of their own volitions.

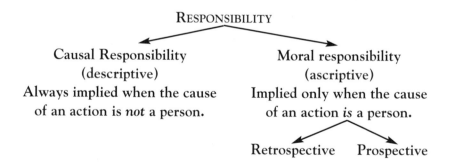

RESPONSIBILITY

Causal Responsibility
(descriptive)
Always implied when the cause
of an action is *not* a person.

Moral responsibility
(ascriptive)
Implied only when the cause
of an action *is* a person.

Retrospective   Prospective

Criteria for Moral Responsibility. To simplify our discussion, we will take it for granted that persons are morally responsible only for their *actions*, even though this stipulation is not universally accepted. For instance, it is widely held among Christian moralists and theologians that people can be held blame- or praiseworthy also for their thoughts, emotions, desires, and other mental states that did not necessarily lead to any actions. Thus, President Jimmy Carter once confessed publicly that, in accord with the Christian gospels (Matthew 5:27-28), he was blameworthy for 'lusting' after women other than his wife, even though, unlike some of his predecessors and successors in the White House, he undertook no actions to satisfy his sinful lust.

That is not to say, of course, that the mental states of people are not highly relevant for the judgment whether some particular action of theirs was praise- or blameworthy in the first place. As Peter Abelard had pointed out in the eleventh century, morality is not an *outer* quality that we infer from the consequences of their actions. Rather, morality is an *inner* quality that we ascribe to peoples' motives. In other words, people are not praise- or blameworthy for the effects that their actions actually produced. What they *are* responsible for are the motives that led them to perform their actions in the first place, depending on whether these motives do or do not conform to the imperatives of ethics.

As is the case for the meaning of many terms of moral discourse, so is the meaning of 'moral responsibility' rooted in our preformed, mostly intuitive and tacitly held (Platonic) Forms that we bring to any discussion about *deserved* praise or blame. Four criteria are usually considered necessary and sufficient for holding a person *morally* responsible for an action:

(1) The person was *causally* responsible for the action.

(2) The action was related to the person's duties and obligations devolving from moral, legal, or ritual imperatives.

(3) The person was aware that in acting as she did, she was doing moral right or wrong and was not mistaken in that awareness.

(4) The person willed to undertake the action *autonomously*, i.e. it was open to her to choose *not* to undertake it.

Determinism. As we briefly discussed in Chapter 1, the fourth of these criteria, namely being able to will something autonomously, conflicts with another of our transcendental intuitions, namely *determinism*. According to determinism, there exists a seamless web of causal connections that governs whatever happens in the world. Hence, any event would be an effect of (or necessitated by) a chain of prior events that were themselves necessitated by yet earlier events. This belief in determinism is not a mere superstition, in that it provides the rational foundation for our intuitive concept of an orderly world and thus for our scientific understanding and highly successful manipulation of nature.

Determinism thus implies that all the world's future events, including any person's willing to perform an action, are fully decided in advance. In other words, freedom of the will would be an illusion if persons were not able to will their actions differently from how they actually *do* will them. So it would make no sense to hold them morally responsible for having willed to act in one way rather than in another if that decision was not autonomously their own but forced on them by the unbreakable causal chain of the world's past events.

Paradox of Moral Responsibility. Thus criterion (4) for holding a person morally responsible for an action, namely that she autonomously willed to undertake it, confronts us with the *Paradox of Moral Responsibility*. The Paradox can be stated in terms of two premises, an argument, and a conclusion.

Premise 1: Some of the world's events are governed by *determinism* and the remaining events occur as a result of random chance.

Premise 2: Persons are morally responsible only for those of their actions that they will autonomously.

Argument: To the extent that the will of persons to perform an action *is* governed by determinism, it is predetermined. Thus persons could not have willed differently from how they *did* will, and their will was not free. To the extent that their will to perform an action is *not* governed by determinism, they *could* have willed differently from how they *did* will. But since, according to premise 1, events that are not governed by determinism occur as the result of random chance, the will of persons is no more under their direct control in the absence of determinism than in its presence.

Conclusion: It follows from premises 1 and 2, therefore, that persons are never morally responsible for their actions. Although this conclusion seems to flow logically from two reasonable premises, it is self-contradictory, and hence paradoxical in the light of our moral intuition.

The Paradox of Moral Responsibility dates back to the very beginnings of philosophy in ancient Greece, but it became especially vexing in recent times because, being the beneficiaries of a science-oriented culture, we modern people are rationally committed to the determinism doctrine.

Lately, moreover, we have also turned into politically correct, cosmic egalitarians, to whom the belief in free will ought to appear as the height of species-chauvinist conceit. How can we believe that our human will is the only causal force in the world that can escape determination by the unbreakable chains of natural causes and effects that govern all the others of the world's events? Yet, at the same time, we find it equally impossible to believe that our own actions actually do form part of those unbreakable cause-effect chains, that is, that we are not real persons but mere automata.

The Paradox of Moral Responsibility would *not* be resolved even if, contrary to our intuition, determinism does *not* obtain universally. In fact, as we will note in Chapter 14, determinism does not obtain in the world's atomic and subatomic (or *microcosmic*) realm, where there do occur some events that are *not* fully determined in advance. Hence if human volitions were among those events, people *could* sometimes have willed differently from how they *did* will. However, as set forth in the Argument of the Paradox of Moral Responsibility, such random events would be no more under the autonomous control of persons than fully predetermined events. Philosophers who accept this as a genuine, irresolvable paradox, are known as '*Incompatibilists*,' in contrast to the '*Compatibilists*' who hold that the Paradox of Moral Responsibility is false, or *can* be resolved. We will consider some Compatibilist arguments in Chapter 7.

Exculpations. So far we did not take into account that there exist also *exculpations* from blameworthiness for actions for which persons are morally responsible and that are clearly violations of the imperatives of ethics, but on which, nevertheless, no blameworthiness is conferred.

Moral philosophers recognize two distinct kinds of exculpation from blameworthiness, *justifications* and *excuses*.

(1) A *justification* is an argument for exculpation that can be invoked under a condition that renders an action permissible, or even praiseworthy, even though it would have been impermissible and blameworthy, in the absence of that condition. For instance, a driver would be *justified* in exceeding a posted speed limit on his way to the hospital with a critically injured person on board. Thus a normally impermissible action is permissible provided that it is justifiable.

(2) An *excuse* is an argument that can be invoked under a condition that leaves an action still impermissible, yet not blameworthy, or may

even be praiseworthy, because it was inspired by noble motives. For instance, Jean Valjean, the protagonist of Victor Hugo's novel, *Les Misérables*, may be excused for stealing a loaf of bread to feed his starving child. (The French court that condemned Valjean to the galleys for this theft did not see it that way, of course.)

An alternative theory of excuses was put forward by David Hume (1740). According to Hume, persons may be excused from wrongdoing if their actions were not the result of *a morally reprehensible character trait*. By 'character trait' Hume meant an enduring personality attribute (which may be either a social asset or a social liability) that is itself within our voluntary control or expresses itself in behavior that is within our voluntary control. Thus courage and generosity are character traits, whereas intelligence and a sense of humor are not. On this view of excuses, Jean Valjean has an excuse for his theft of the loaf of bread because his action was attributable to the noble character trait of compassion rather than to the ignoble trait of thievishness.

Hume's theory of excuses does not take into account the possibility that the origin of a person's reprehensible motivational state (that forecloses excuses) may not have been under her voluntary control. How can one hold a person blameworthy (or praiseworthy) for her ignoble (or noble) character traits when her biological heredity and her personal history are likely to have played a major role in their development? Hume rejected such retrospective deterministic reasoning about the origins of character traits because it would entail a causal regress all the way back to Adam and Eve. So he resolved the Paradox of Moral Responsibility by simply denying any role to free will in decisions about moral-value-laden actions. As Hume saw it, persons with reprehensible character traits perform blameworthy actions, and those with laudable character traits perform praiseworthy actions. For Hume, the moral value of an action—blameworthy or praiseworthy—depends only on the moral character of agents, regardless of how they acquired it and came to be that way.

The importance of clarifying the grounds for excusing persons from blameworthiness for impermissible actions for which they are causally responsible extends beyond the satisfaction of our intellectual quest for insights into moral philosophy. Such clarification is essential for the administration of criminal justice in the law courts, which are the workshops of applied moral philosophy, where moral responsibility is the paramount problem to be addressed.

Coercion. Actions that persons were *coerced* to undertake by dire threat applied to them by other persons belong to a special category of excusable, albeit impermissible, and ordinarily blameworthy deeds. As we noted in Chapter 3, Aristotle had emphasized that an agent may be excused from blameworthiness for an, on first sight impermissible deed if the agent undertook it only to avoid an even greater evil, or to achieve some higher purpose. By way of an example, Aristotle mentioned compliance with an order to undertake an evil action by a tyrant who has the agent's parents or children in his power, under the dire threat that in case of refusal, the agent's beloved would be put to death. Aristotle pointed out, however, that justifying an excuse from blameworthiness of a person who is faced with such a moral dilemma is not all that clear-cut, since, after all, the agent *was* offered a choice at the time he acted. Hence an excuse from blameworthiness attributable to a morally righteous goal of an action can be vindicated only by taking into account the entire context of the occasion in which the action occurred. Strictly speaking, all human actions (other than reflexes and movements implemented by the autonomic nervous system) are voluntary (and designated as such by neurophysiologists) in the concrete. An action, therefore, can be regarded as 'coerced' only in the abstract, namely by supposing that the person would never have chosen to carry it out in the absence of the dire threat.

Brainwashing. The need for taking into account the entire context in which a morally relevant action took place in judging its blameworthiness is shown by the condition of brainwashing. Let us consider an authoritarian state. For many years, the rulers of that state have so successfully controlled what its citizens read, what views they encounter, and how in their youth their minds and dispositions were skillfully molded by their teachers so that almost all of them desire what their rulers desire them to desire. Hence these citizens do not know that there *are* alternatives to the life style to which they are accustomed, or that their freedom to choose has in any way been circumscribed. Thus they are not aware of any coercion or constraints on the satisfaction of their desires. Yet, we would scarcely concede that the citizen of that state enjoyed much freedom, even though there is no overt coercion in the usual sense. In fact, coercion by the rulers had become unnecessary. So it is at least arguable that, despite the absence of overt coercion, a citizen of that state is not blameworthy for some actions that would entail their blameworthiness in a less authoritarian society.

Insanity. The foregoing discussions have taken it tacitly for granted that the persons to whom moral responsibility can be ascribed are of sound mind. But what about insane people who are not of sound mind, that is, are afflicted with a mental disorder? Are they to be held responsible—morally and/or legally—for their freely willed offenses, just as is any sane person? The attempts to resolve the problem whether insanity is an exculpating condition have provided some of the most cogent debates on the justification of excuses for *blameworthy* actions. How should insanity be defined, and why does it—if it does—excuse a person? On some accounts, insanity exculpates just because it is a special case of other generic excuses, such as ignorance and compulsion. On other accounts, insanity has to be understood as a unique kind of excuse that must not be conflated with ignorance or compulsion.

It is widely accepted in most modern liberal and compassionate societies that a person afflicted with a mental disorder may be excused for an offense for which a sane person is judged blameworthy. Such a demand for a general, non-specific excuse relief of mentally disordered persons from moral responsibility is obviously too broad, however. For instance, while an exhibitionist might be excused for exposing his private parts in public, he ought to be held morally responsible for a theft. Conversely, while a kleptomaniac may be exculpated for a theft, he ought to be held morally responsible for a rape. The principle governing exculpation in such cases is that there must exist some close connection between the nature of the person's mental disorder and the offense for which exculpation is sought.

But even though the existence of a close connection between an offense and a mental disorder may be a necessary condition, it is not a sufficient condition for exculpation. For instance, suppose that a person is caught stealing some merchandise from a department store and it is then discovered that he is afflicted with kleptomania. Should this provide an automatic excuse for his theft? One commonly held opinion is that, in view of his particular mental disorder, the thief should be excused. For, so it is argued, his disordered mind did not allow him to do otherwise, and he is therefore not responsible for his action. The validity of this reason for exculpation cannot be taken for granted, however, since a kleptomaniac thief is not *automatically compelled* by his disorder to steal as he would be compelled by the patellar reflex to kick out his lower leg by a well-placed tap on his kneecap. Rather, kleptomania is a disorder that makes it merely more difficult, but not impossible, for an afflicted person to resist an impulse to steal. So why, if there was still the possibility of his resisting the impulse, should the kleptomaniac thief be excused from failing to resist it?

The issues surrounding exculpation of the insane have been fiercely debated in the courts, foremost among them being the definition of insanity itself. Under American criminal law the first and most common insanity test is the M'Naghten rule, which excuses defendants whose mental disorder caused them to be ignorant of the nature, quality, and blameworthiness of the action for which they stand accused. This criterion of legal insanity was formulated in 1843 by English judges in response to the public outcry that resulted when Daniel M'Naghten was acquitted on grounds of insanity of murdering the private secretary of Sir Robert Peel (the organizer of the first modern police force, the London 'Bobbies'). M'Naghten had mistaken the secretary for Peel and killed the secretary while suffering from paranoid delusions about Peel's evil intentions towards him.

The judges sought to provide a morally sound, legally workable criterion for determining whether the murderer was entitled to acquittal on the grounds of insanity. The criterion they promulgated declares that to establish a defense on the ground of insanity it must be clearly proved that, at the time of committing the action, the accused was suffering from a disease of the mind that produced so great a defect of reason that he did not know the nature and quality of his action.

Or, more simply stated, the crux of the M'Naghten rule is whether the accused knew the difference between right and wrong at the time he committed his blameworthy deed. A different kind of insanity defense is sometimes produced on behalf of accused persons who do know the difference between right and wrong and who are fully aware of the criminal nature of their actions. That defense—which is often advanced on behalf of wealthy shoplifters—alleges that the defendant's offence was caused by an irresistible and possibly subliminal psychopathological compulsion.

There exists a substantial minority opinion, however, which rejects the doctrine that persons afflicted with a mental disorder should be excused from responsibility for *blameworthy* actions for which a normal person could be held responsible. For instance, the British sociologist, Barbara Wootton (1963), maintained that—the M'Naghten rule notwithstanding—no rationally coherent criterion of criminal insanity can be formulated in the first place. Starting from a determinist position, she asserted that all efforts to formulate an adequate criterion of mental disorder, and in the final analysis, of responsibility itself, founder on the Argument of the Paradox of Moral Responsibility. Since, according to that Argument, the will of every person—sane or insane—is ultimately beyond that person's autonomous control, there is no point in assessing moral responsibility in the context of the criminal law. According to Wootton, the law should be concerned solely with treating offenders so that they will not repeat their offenses. It is clear that Wootton's determinist approach to the criminal law would sweep away not only the M'-Naghten rule but any kind of excuse on the grounds of insanity for what, on first sight, would appear to be blameworthy actions.

Like Wootton, the Hungarian-American psychiatrist Thomas Szasz (1973) argued for the abandonment of any kind of insanity plea, but for reasons that are diametrically opposed from Wootton's. Szasz does not deny the existence of an autonomous free will and enthusiastically endorses the concept of responsibility. But he rejects the notion of mental illness as a noxious metaphor, claiming that mental illness is not a genuine disease and that psychiatry is not a bona fide medical specialty. According to Szasz, insane persons are not really ill and psychiatrists are not really doctors. To treat insane people as if they were sick is to confuse medicine with morals. He argued that if and insofar as it is deemed that so-called 'mental patients' endanger society, society can, and ought, to protect itself from the 'mentally ill' in the same way it does from the 'mentally healthy'—that is by means of the criminal law.

A Way without Crossroads. The foregoing discussion was meant to show that the concept of responsibility is a central, foundational, and yet troublesome problem of morals. As we noted, upon analysis of its premises—especially that of 'choice'—within the context of (Western) moral philosophy 'moral responsibility' turns out to be a philosophically ambiguous, indeed paradoxical concept. It is noteworthy, therefore, that Confucius, in his account of the ethics of the humanistic *Tao*, does not mention the concepts 'choice' and 'responsibility.' Terms roughly equivalent to them occasionally turn up the *Analects*, but Confucius does not develop or elaborate them in a way commensurate with their overarching importance for the Western philosophical understanding of morals. Dedicated to defining and illuminating what we would call moral issues, how could Confucius fail to consider the complex of moral notions centering on 'choice' and 'responsibility?'

No doubt, people in sixth century BCE China *did* make (what we would consider) morally relevant choices and some people *did* act more (what we would consider) responsibly than others. Yet Confucius and his Chinese contemporaries did not even have a language with which to express the concepts of 'moral choice' and 'moral responsibility' that were of such great concern to their contemporaries in Greece and Southwestern Asia. As we noted in Chapter 3, what the Ancient Chinese did talk about was the *Tao*, the right or normative Way or Path of Life to an ideal human existence. In this figurative context, the concept of moral choice could have been easily captured by the metaphor of taking one of several forks at a crossroads along the Way. Yet Confucius never uses this metaphor. Why not? Because for him following the correct fork at a crossroads is not a matter of choice but of having learned which fork is the right one. There is no scope for free autonomous decisions. Or, put in more general terms, Confucius did not view the moral life as a series of freely willed choices between alternative actions but as a series of classifications of actions as objectively right or wrong, according to the learned scheme of virtue, or *jen*.

Confucius tells the story of a man called 'Upright' Kung whose father stole a sheep. Kung testifies against his father. The Duke, who reports this case to Confucius, praises what he considers to be Kung's uprightness. But Confucius disagrees with the Duke. He tells the Duke that in Confucius' own homeland of Lau they teach that a son who protects rather than incriminates his father is the one who is considered upright (or, in the context of our discussion, 'praiseworthy').

This story serves as a model for demonstrating the dilemma of having to choose between two conflicting moral obligations. A Westerner would almost always emphasize that when two weighty obligations conflict, it is up to us to choose which of them to honor, because the seed of tragedy, of punishment, of guilt and remorse lies in the necessity to make a personal choice for which one bears moral responsibility. But however obvious the problem of internal moral conflict exemplified by the 'Upright' Kung's story may be for a Westerner, Confucius' fails to see or to mention it. This failure is of a piece with the absence from the *Analects* of any discussion of moral responsibility and its associated problems. These problems do not exist for Confucius because he does not believe that moral decisions involve any choice in the first place.

Classical Western morality embedded in the Greco-Judeo-Christian tradition regards punishment as a retributive response to past moral wrongdoing. Its function is to erase the guilt incurred by morally responsible persons. Their repentance is not simply a device that is appropriate or not depending on its psychological consequences on the malefactors. Rather, repentance is meant to remove the moral disequilibrium present in the world due to the existence of an unpunished, blameworthy action. This was not Confucius' view of the function of punishment, because he lacked the concept of morally responsible agents. He shared the view generally prevalent in Ancient China (and among the strain of Western moral philosophers inspired by Aristotle), that punishment serves as a utilitarian deterrent for the commission of future crimes, rather than as a just retribution to erase guilt for past crimes.

The central moral issue for Confucius is, therefore, not the responsibility of a person for actions she has by her own free will chosen to perform, but the factual question of whether a person has been properly taught the Way and whether she has the desire to learn it diligently. According to the Confucian view, the proper response to a failure to conform to the prescribed ritual order of the *li* is not guilt for having made a blameworthy autonomous choice, but self-education to remedy a deficiency in one's moral development.

Coda. The concept of *moral responsibility* provides the rational foundation for regarding human beings as moral creatures in the first place. It refers to the human intuition that persons can be judged as *praiseworthy* or *blameworthy* for the volitions that motivated their actions, with the judgment being based on established ethical criteria, such as those found in the Torah's Ten Commandments. The following three conditions are generally considered necessary and sufficient for holding a person morally responsible for an action:

1. Her action was related to her duties and obligations.
2. She freely willed to undertake the action (i.e. that it was open to her to choose *not* to undertake it).

3. She was aware that in acting as she did, she was doing moral right or wrong.

The condition that persons are held morally responsible for an action only if they freely willed it leads to the *Paradox of Moral Responsibility*, according to the Conclusion of which persons can *never* be held morally responsible for their actions. For some of the world's events are governed by *determinism* and the remainder occur as a result of *random chance*. To the extent that the will of a person *is* governed by determinism, it is not free and the person could not have willed differently from how she *did* will. And to the extent that the will of a person is the result of random chance, it is no more under her direct control than it would have been under the governance of determinism. Although this Conclusion seems to flow logically from two reasonable premises, it is self-contradictory and hence paradoxical in the light of our moral intuition.

There exist two kinds of *exculpations* from blameworthiness for actions for which persons are morally responsible and that are clearly violations of the imperatives of ethics, but on which no blameworthiness is conferred. One kind, *justification*, is an argument for exculpation that can be invoked under a condition that renders an action permissible, or even praiseworthy, even though it would have been impermissible and blameworthy, in the absence of that condition. The other kind, *excuse*, is an argument that can be invoked under a condition that leaves an action still impermissible, yet not blameworthy, or may even be praiseworthy, because it was inspired by noble motives.

PIERRE SIMON, MARQUIS DE LAPLACE (1749–1827)

Commemorative stamp issued by the French Postal Service in 1955

Chapter Seven

⟫•⟪

Determinism

Natural Laws. By the eighteenth century BCE the Sumerians had developed the idea that Marduk—patron god of Babylon—had ordained explicit natural laws whose obeisance by nature generated cosmic order out of cosmic chaos. The Sumerians had thereby laid the rational foundation for the project that eventually came to be known as 'science,' dedicated to the discovery of those divinely ordained natural laws. The concept of natural laws entails the doctrine of *determinism,* according to which all events in the world are necessitated by a chain of past events that were themselves necessitated by yet earlier events. Hence by conceiving the notion of a lawful cosmic order the Sumerians had laid also the rational foundations for the Paradox of Moral Responsibility. Their proto-scientific notions had made it seem impossible that there *could be* any scope for free will in a world in which natural law renders future events as fixed and unavoidable as past events.

Although this conceptual tension between doctrines of determinism and of moral responsibility was of some concern to the philosophers of classical antiquity, it became a crucial theological issue upon the rise of Christianity. The Christian Fathers wondered how God's certain foreknowledge of the future could possibly allow for the kind of freedom that would provide a rational basis for the notion of moral responsibility in the first place. How could God act justly in rewarding some people for their righteous deeds and punish others for their evil deeds if all actions were foreordained? Didn't God know all along how everybody was going to behave?

As we noted in Chapter 5, Augustine resolved this dilemma by maintaining that God's foreknowledge of the autonomous decisions that our free will is going to make does not entail their necessity. The will God gave us could not *be* a will unless it remained within our power to choose freely. According to Augustine there is no paradox: God's divine power to know in advance how *we* are going to use the will He gave us does not preclude its freedom to make autonomous decisions.

Pierre Simon de Laplace. In late eighteenth century, the French mathematician and astronomer, Pierre Simon de Laplace, provided the doctrine of determinism with very strong support. Laplace had managed to account for the eccentricity of the Earth's orbit around the sun, for the irregularities of the orbits of Jupiter and Saturn, and for the mysterious pattern of terrestrial tides in terms of interplanetary interactions according to Isaac Newton's law of gravitation. Thus Laplace explained these phenomena—previously considered aberrant, irregular natural happenings—in terms of a regular, determinate law of physics. This inspired him to claim that whatever happened in the world's past was—or whatever is yet to happen in its future will be—totally determined by the laws of physics and the world's initial conditions. This all-encompassing Laplacian determinist proposition left little scope for any exercise of an autonomous human free will.

The tension between the doctrines of free will and of determinism is felt especially acutely by modern people who live in a secular, enlightened, and science-oriented world. They are rationally committed to determinism and reject the possibility that miracles and prayer can influence future events by transcending natural law. Moreover, in recent years that tension became especially acute for those politically correct, cosmic egalitarians, to whom the doctrine of free will appears as the height of anthropocentric chauvinist conceit. Why should our human will be the only agency in the world that is not subject to the determinist cause and effect chains that governs all other phenomena? Yet, at the same time, how can sane persons deny their direct, subjective experience of freely willing their own actions and view themselves as mere Zombies, who form part of the world's predetermined, mindless chain of happenings?

Behaviorists, Immaterialists, Libertarians and Compatibilists. The Paradox of Moral Responsibility still remains one of the most vexing problems of moral philosophy. It has persisted from Augustine's days down to our own postmodern era, except that in the meanwhile Augustine's doctrine of God's omniscience and omnipotence as the antithesis of free will was replaced by its secular equivalent, namely the scientific doctrine of determinism. Much philosophical effort has been expended on trying to resolve that paradox, to rescue the transcendental concept of moral responsibility, which provides one of the metaphysical foundations of human social relations. Philosophers who have joined in this attempted rescue mission can be assigned to at least four different sets, according to their metaphysical starting positions. They are the *Behaviorists*, the *Immaterialists*, the *Libertarians* and the *Compatibilists*. As we shall see, most of these would-be-rescuers failed because they looked on the Paradox from the viewpoint of the monist solution to the mind-body problem, within the context of which moral responsibility turned out to be a rationally incoherent notion.

Behaviorists, such as the American psychologist B. F. Skinner (1971), asserted that free will—even if it *did* exist—has nothing to do with moral responsibility in any case. They argued that the only reason for holding people morally responsible in this determinist world is to create a rhetorical smoke screen behind which the antisocial behavior of social misfits can be modified psychotherapeutically. According to Behaviorists, the term 'responsibility' merely denotes the susceptibility of persons to abandoning their asocial behavior in *response* to the psychological pressure applied to them by the moral judgments of their blameworthiness by other persons or by the state. And if a verdict of blameworthiness will not change a person's social behavior in wholesome ways, then there is no point in making a fuss about her moral responsibility.

Very little needs to be said about the Behaviorist approach to moral responsibility, except to mention that, being obviously incompatible with any intuition about morality and justice, behaviorism cannot provide a philosophically satisfactory resolution of the Paradox of Moral Responsibility.

Immaterialists, such as Colonial America's best-known moral philosopher, the eighteenth century Puritan theologian, Jonathan Edwards (1957), derived their appellation from having stood on its head Aristotle's *materialist* doctrine that the human mind is an attribute of the human material body substance. For Edwards and his followers were beholden to Plato's *idealist* doctrine that the human body, just as all other perceptible objects of the world, are attributes of our *immaterial* mind substance and that it is these mental ideas that constitute the world's sole permanent reality.

In accord with his religious proclivity for John Calvin's doctrine of the predestination of human fate, Edwards was a staunch determinist. He believed that since the principle of causality, according to which everything

111

that happens is determined by a cause, applies to the human will as it does to everything else God has created, people have no freedom to will their actions. God alone is free, in the sense that He *can* control His volition, as we cannot control ours. But Edwards rejected Premise 2 of the Paradox, which states that that no person is responsible for her actions *unless* she is free to will them. The reason for his rejection was that he did not consider the will to be an autonomous, self-determining force. Rather, Edwards considered the will as a passive relay station that is moved heteronomously to implement actions determined by external circumstances. In carrying out this relay function, our will is moved, not by physical causes, but by our wishes, our passions, and our affects that are presented to the will, with the strongest of them determining how the will is going to move. Thus the importance of the will lies not in its making *free* choices but in being the target of the determinist action of our soul (or *ego*, as Sigmund Freud would later refer to the ensemble of such motivational mental states). In other words, according to the Immaterialist doctrine, determinism still leaves the actions of persons under their control and makes them subject to moral responsibility, even in the absence of any autonomous free will.

Although Immaterialists believe in an all-pervasive determinism just as much as do Behaviorists, they differ from Behaviorists in accepting the philosophical centrality of moral responsibility. But Immaterialists dismiss the Paradox because they reject the very idea of free will, arguing that, understood as self-determination in a determinist world, the concept of free will implies an infinite regress of acts of personal self-causation. According to Edwards, free will can imply no more than a person's random preference for one action over another. For, according to Premise 1 of the Paradox, all mental events that are *not* governed by determinism (as volitions, to be worthy of the predicate *'free,'* must not be) occur as a result of random chance. So even if free will did exist, its random, uncaused volitions could not account for moral responsibility and the cultivation of a virtuous character.

Edwards insisted that the ordinary meaning of being 'free' to do something is *compatible* with determinism. He asserted that there is no Paradox of Moral Responsibility because moral responsibility devolves from doing what one wants to do most, and if what one wants to do most is morally wrong, one is blameworthy. Sinners merit retributive punishment—either in the here-and-now or in the hereafter—because they chose to do wrong when doing wrong was what pleased their soul most.

Critics of the Immaterialists' argument had no trouble demonstrating the incoherence of Edward's argumentation, by showing that determinism is *incompatible* with statements of the form 'Person P could have willed X rather than Y.' For the normal use of expressions such locutions as 'was free to,' 'could have,' and 'was able to' implies more than a lack of *external* constraints on action. Freedom of the will does not mean 'freedom of action' but 'freedom of the *decision* to act.' Hence absent under determinism of any freedom of the will to decide what it would please its owner's soul most, it could never have been the case that a person could have willed otherwise than she did.

Libertarians, in contrast to Behaviorists and Immaterialists, believe that free will *does* exist. They accept Premise 2 of the Paradox of Moral Responsibility, which asserts that persons are morally responsible only for those of their actions that they willed autonomously. And Libertarians accept the first part of Premise 1, which asserts that there are *some* actions that are not fully determined by antecedent circumstances. But Libertarians reject the second part of Premise 1, which implies that to the extent that human actions are among those that are *not* fully determined in advance, they would have to occur by pure chance. Hence Libertarians do not accept the proposition that the person's will is no more in autonomous control of her actions that were *not* fully determined in advance than in actions that were fully determined.

To make room for free will and for the concept of moral responsibility, Libertarians distinguish between *three* types of actions, the first two of which confer exemption from responsibility.

(A) Actions that are fully determined by antecedent *external* circumstances.

(B) Actions that were caused pure chance, beyond the person's control.

According to Libertarian thought, however, the third type of actions does entail responsibility.

(C) Actions that are (at least in part) determined autonomously by antecedent *internal* circumstances. These internal circumstances correspond to a person's rational states of mind, which determine the decisions of her will and to whose freedom from *external, heteronomous* influences we ascribe her responsibility.

Conclusion: Therefore there is no paradox.

O'Connor (1970) criticized this Libertarian resolution of the Paradox, asserting that "the Libertarian's attempt to make free will dependent on reason has failed. He has fallen from one kind of determinism into another, exchanging the whips of causal regularity for the scorpions of logical necessity." But O'Connor's criticism misses the point, since the reason for the failure of the Libertarians' argument is not their replacement of the whips of causal regularity by invocation of the scorpions of logical necessity. Rather, the reason for the argument's failure is that it begs the question, by positing the existence of type C actions, which is explicitly denied in Premise 1 of the paradox. If there *did* exist type C actions, the Libertarian's attempt to make free will dependent on reason would not have failed, since there is no inconsistency in invoking scorpions of logical necessity in the determination of free will based on the person's autonomously arisen rational states of mind.

Compatibilists hold that moral responsibility and determinism are mutually compatible rather than mutually exclusive. In the seventeenth century, Thomas Hobbes (1651), the founder of English moral philosophy, provided an early statement of the Compatibilist position. Contrary to Edwards, Hobbes argued that to be 'free' means no more than an absence of external constraints that prevent one from doing what one has the will (that is, the desire or inclination) to do. He does *not* mean (an impossible) freedom of the will from causal necessitation by natural laws. One is 'free' insofar as one is able to follow one's own desires and inclinations and to implement one's will. The fact that our desires and inclinations are states and events of which each has its own causal history and explanation, does not make them any less our own, and hence they do entail our moral responsibility. Thus, the morally relevant antitheses are not volitionally 'free' as opposed to volitionally 'determined' actions but 'free' as opposed to externally 'coerced' actions.

In the eighteenth century, David Hume (1740) further developed Hobbes' distinction favored by Compatibilists between coerced action and volitional determination. Hume argued that to equate coerced action and volitional determination is to conflate *prescriptive* and *descriptive* causation. For example, the laws of the land are prescriptive causes of social behavior because they coerce certain uniform standards of conduct by imposing penalties for deviations from them. But the laws of celestial mechanics do not coerce the planets to move in their orbits; they simply *describe* the way planetary motion is determined. Nor do the laws of chemistry coerce acids to react with alkalis. They merely *describe* the way the acid-alkali reaction pattern is determined.

While Hume's proposition that there is an important difference between prescriptive and descriptive causation is no doubt valid, that difference is epistemological rather than conceptual. The difference is epistemological (that is, related to how we come to know a cause) rather than conceptual (that is, related to the concept of causation *per se*) for the following reasons.

As for *prescriptive* causation, I infer *deductively* that a red traffic light coerced a driver of an automobile to stop his car until the light turned green, even though no other cars were in sight. For I know that the State vehicle code prescribes stopping at red lights and provides for fines in case of non-compliance. As for *descriptive* causation, however, I infer *inductively* that a cover of ice on the road caused a driver to slow his car down to a crawl. For I know from past experience that drivers tend to reduce their speed because they fear the natural danger presented by a slippery road.

There is no basic conceptual difference, however, between prescriptive and descriptive causation regarding our notion of causality. In either case we posit that there is a link—always *overt* in the case prescriptive causation and often *covert* in the case of descriptive causation—that causes a person to perform an action. Admittedly, philosophers have found it very hard to define or explicate the nature of such a causal link. This does not alter the fact, however, that causation is generally recognized as a Platonic Form, or, as we will consider in some detail in Chapter 10, as a category of Kantian pure theoretical reason.

In any case, Hume's distinction between prescriptive and descriptive causation does not advance the Compatibilist cause. It seems to have little relevance for the Paradox of Moral Responsibility, inasmuch as the abrogation of our freedom of action by *overt* coercion (such as that exerted by the laws of the land) is trivially obvious and not the subject of philosophical controversy. What *is* controversial is how the belief in free will and moral responsibility can be reconciled with the ever-present *covert* determination (such as that exerted by the all-pervasive natural laws). After all, one of the main reasons for the well-nigh-universal belief in free will is our subjective experience of choosing freely in many situations.

This experience does not arise in the presence of prescriptive, and especially not in the presence of coercive causes, of which we *must* be consciously aware for them to be effective in the first place.

For instance, the captured partisan guerilla fighter must be aware of being tortured by the soldiers of the occupying army to be coerced to reveal the hiding place of his comrades, and he is unlikely to think that he is excercising his free will. By contrast, as I am writing these lines, I do have the experience of acting freely. I am blissfully unaware not only of the prescriptive rules of English grammar that restrict my freedom of choice of the next word, but even more importantly, of the multitudinous physiological events in my brain—past or present—that determine which symbols I strike on my computer keyboard. It is only under these seemingly unconstrained conditions that I might wonder whether I am *really* choosing freely.

A fundamentally different, and in my view much more satisfactory Compatibilist resolution of the *Paradox of Moral Responsibility* was put forward at the turn of the twentieth century by the British philosopher, F.H. Bradley (1927). He too rejected the Paradox's Premise 1 that between them, determinism and random chance share the governance of all the world's happenings. Bradley insisted that in considering the implications of determinism, it is necessary to distinguish, not between determination and coercion, as did Hume, but between a person's internally self-determined action and an action that is heteronomously determined by circumstances external to the person. Why did Bradley insist on making this distinction? Because, in line with the dualist solution of the mind-body problem (which we will examine in more detail in Chapter 9), Bradley maintained that circumstances external to the person exert their determinate effects directly on the body, which implements the action commanded by the mind. The internally self-generated mental commands for action, however, are determined by the mind's free will, which is not wholly subject to the otherwise all-pervasive determinism. Therefore there is no paradox.

In Chapter 10 we will develop Bradley's Compatibilist resolution of the Paradox further and take into account that free will is a *non-natural attribute* that moral reason obliges us to *ascribe* to the mind of persons. Therefore, unlike the determinist causation in terms of which we try to account for the natural phenomena, whose occurrence we perceive and *describe* in both mind and body, free will belongs to the transcendental world of *a priori* ideas.

In anticipatory support of this argument, it ought to be borne in mind that the concept of 'responsibility' is *ascriptive* as well, just as is its rationally essential precondition, namely free will. Thus, in speaking of her responsibility we *ascribe* to the person some duties and obligations arising from moral, legal or ritual imperatives, rather than *describing* some empirical fact.

Determinism and Predictability. Laplace's determinism had inspired also a secondary doctrine that was commonly supposed to be entailed by it. According to this doctrine determinism should enable us—at least in principle—to predict all of the World's future events on the basis of our knowledge of the laws of Nature and of the World's present conditions. So when at the beginning of the twentieth century some physical systems were discovered whose future events turned out *not* to be predictable, it was inferred that they are not subject to determinism and designated *indeterminate* rather than *unpredictable*, as they ought to have been. This unfortunate conflation of the concepts of determinism and predictability led to the conclusions that determinism is *not* a universal feature of the world's events, that there is no *Paradox of Moral Responsibility*, and that therefore there would be room for moral responsibility based on free will after all. Finally, by the middle of the twentieth century these developments gave currency to the liberating postmodern thought that the world is not 'Laplacian' after all. (Volkenstein, 1980)

To appreciate that the *Paradox of Moral Responsibility* cannot be resolved all that easily, one needs to disentangle the two conflated concepts. Under the doctrine of determinism, any event is the effect of a prior series of causal events necessitated by even earlier causal events, so that the initial and final states of any determinate system are linked via a causal chain. Determinism implies, therefore, that all future events are as fixed and unalterable as past events. Predictability, however, is an attribute of only a *subset* of all determinate systems. For that subset future events can be forecast by application of natural laws to observations of past events, while for the remainder of determinate systems future events are *unpredictable*. The proof that a system whose events are unpredictable may nevertheless be determinate is that their *retrodiction* (that is, provision of a rational account of the causes of a present event as an effect of past events) *is* possible. This insight came upon the study of some physical phenomena, such as the weather, whose events cannot be precisely

117

foretold, even though they are still linked by rigid causal connections with their antecedent events. (Stent, 1983)

As we shall now see, it transpired that determinism does not *entail* predictability, even though the very idea of a rational predictability of the world's future events has the doctrine of determinism as its metaphysical foundation.

Chaos. In the 1960s, the French mathematician Benoit Mandelbrot (1963) drew attention to the highly irregular nature of the statistical data gathered by quantitative observations of some natural and social phenomena, such as the weather and the stock market, which he called '*second stage indeterminism*.' These phenomena differ fundamentally from what he called '*first stage indeterminism*,' of which the outcomes of the *croupier's* repeated spinnings of a roulette wheel are an example. To circumvent the confusion arising from the conflation of 'determinism' and 'predictability' in the context of discussions of the Paradox of Moral Responsibility, I shall refer to two categories of phenomena identified by Mandelbrot as manifesting 'first stage' and 'second stage' *unpredictability*.

First and second stage unpredictability phenomena are alike in that both are determinate phenomena, whose final state could be predicted *in principle* to some degree of accuracy, provided all the relevant parameters characterizing the initial state are known to a corresponding degree of accuracy. The phenomena are unpredictable *in practice* because, due to fluctuations in the values of the parameters, such knowledge about their initial state is almost never available.

For a first stage unpredictability phenomenon, however, it is at least possible to make an accurate prediction of the *average values* of the parameters descriptive of the final state in a series of its repeated occurrences. This is the case because the fluctuations tend to offset one another in the long run, an effect known to statisticians as the "ergodic principle." A roulette wheel in which the fraction of the total number spinnings of the wheel in which the ball comes to rest on a red number is predictable exemplifies a first-stage unpredictability phenomenon.

Such predictions are not possible, however, for the average diameter and wind velocity over the next century of hurricanes on the American East Coast, which exemplify second stage unpredictability phenomena. By the 1970s, the realm of second stage unpredictability had come to be called 'Chaos' and had developed into a specialized subdiscipline of the study of complex natural and social phenomena. The reason for the chaotic behavior of second-stage unpredictability phenomena turned out to be that their cause-effect relations are governed by complex *non-linear dynamics*, in contrast to the *linear dynamics* that govern 'well-behaved,' predictable, as well as first-stage unpredictable phenomena.

Linear dynamics are described by mathematical functions whose variables (such as *x*, *y*, *z*, *t*, and *u*) appear only to the first power, are multiplied only by constants (such as *A*, *B*, *C*, and *D*), and may be combined only by addition and/or subtraction, e.g.

$$x = Ay + Bz - Ct$$

Non-linear dynamics, by contrast, are described by mathematical functions, some of whose variables appear to powers higher than the first, and may be combined not only by addition and subtraction but also by multiplication and/or division.), e.g.

$$x = Ay^2 \times Bz^3/(Ct^4 + Du^5)$$

Under linear dynamics, the variation in the magnitude *x* of an effect is generally proportional to the variation in the magnitude of its causal variables. Under non-linear dynamics, however, there may occur enormous variations in the magnitude *x* of an effect produced by small variations in the magnitude of its causal variables, with tiny variations in the causal variables sometimes resulting in huge variations in the magnitude of the effect.

Thus the roulette wheel is a first stage unpredictability phenomenon because it is governed by linear dynamics. The final resting position of the ball depends on the angle and timing of croupier's toss of the ball into the spinning wheel and on the initial rotational force applied by him to the wheel. Moreover, the variations in the final resting position are directly proportional to the variations in the croupier's manipulations.

By contrast, a hurricane, being governed by complex non-linear dynamics, is a chaotic phenomenon. Here the variations in the diameter of the funnel-shaped rotating cloud (which may reach a mile) and in its velocity (which may reach 300 miles per hour) are vastly greater than the corresponding variations of the atmospheric events that set off tornadoes hundreds of miles removed from their future epicenters. In fact, it came to be realized eventually that most natural phenomena are fundamentally attributable to chaotic systems, although some phenomena are more chaotic than are others. As it turned out, the successful theories resulting from past scientific efforts had addressed mainly the relatively rare quasi-non-chaotic phenomena, such as the rotation of the planets around the sun.

Prediction vs. Retrodiction in History. Since human affairs belong to the world's most chaotic phenomena, the second-stage unpredictability of human history was appreciated long before Mandelbrot drew attention to its prevalence in the phenomena addressed by the natural and social sciences. Historians approach their subject from the premise of determinism, just as do physicists. They believe, just as do physicists, that the events they study do not happen haphazardly but are effects of (or necessitated by) a series of prior events that were themselves necessitated by even earlier events. And just as do physicists, so do historians try to explain how an event of interest came about by seeking to uncover the causal chain linking it and the earlier events that necessitated it. Retrodiction of present or past events (rather than prediction of future events) is therefore the main research goal of historians.

Historians differ from physicists, however, in that in their retrodictions historians cannot call on generally valid laws of history (since there are none) and in that, partly for this very reason, their power of reliable *prediction* of future events is much more limited than that of physicists. This difference is attributable not to the intellectual shortcomings of historians as compared to physicists, but to the much greater complexity and highly non-linear dynamics of historical phenomena as compared to physical phenomena.

For instance, historians would generally agree that some retrodictive account can be provided, at least in principle, of the causal chain that linked the sequence of events portrayed in Tolstoy's great novel, *War and Peace*. For a scholar who believed that there *is* nothing to explain retrodictively about these events and that they just happened by haphazard chance would be a mere chronicler of them rather than an historian.

But the opinions of historians differ greatly on the extent to which the state of Russia at the end of the Napoleonic invasion in 1813 was *predictable* on the basis of the state of Russia and France at its beginning in 1812. Tolstoy himself was beholden to the historical determinism propounded by the nineteenth century German philosopher G. H. F. Hegel, who regarded history not only as a determinate but also as an essentially *linear* process. According to Hegel's linear, determinist view of history, the magnitude of an event, such as the extent of Napoleon's devastation of Russia, is roughly proportional to the magnitude of its cause, such as the aggressive forces unleashed by the French Revolution. It would follow, therefore, that if there had not been any General Napoleon Bonaparte, the French would still have invaded Russia under the direction of some other commander, say General Gaston Dupont, who would have been defeated by Tsar Alexander, just as was Napoleon. Thus according to Hegel, prediction of the course of history is at least *thinkable*.

By contrast, the 'Great Man' view of history—no Napoleon Bonaparte, no invasion of Russia in 1812—was championed by the nineteenth century Scottish historian Thomas Carlyle. He regarded history as determinate process as well, but one characterized by non-*linear* *dynamics*. Under Carlyle's view of the course of history, very small causes, (such as the birth of a baby to the Bonaparte family in Ajaccio in 1769), can have huge effects (such as changing the entire course of European affairs). From Carlyle's 'Great Man' standpoint of non-linear historical dynamics, prediction of historical events is virtually impossible.

Thus the existence of chaotic phenomena in the world studied by the natural and social sciences does not put in doubt the existence of determinism and is not in conflict with Premise 1 of the Paradox of Moral Responsibility. Consequently the invocation of chaos (in its modern technical meaning) is of no help for the resolution of the Paradox.

The True Indeterminism of Quantum Physics. Though determinate causal relations do govern second stage unpredictable, chaotic phenomena such as tornadoes, there exists another class of phenomena that *does* put doubt on the universality of the rule of determinism. These phenomena belong to the realm of nature to which we will refer as the '*microcosm*' in Chapter 12. The objects of the microcosm comprise atoms and subatomic particles, such as electrons (the elementary particles of electric charge) and photons (the elementary particles of light). It is the subject of quantum physics, which was inaugurated by Max Planck at the turn of the twentieth century.

As we will note in Chapter 14, the microcosm of atomic and subatomic physics is an Alice-in-Wonderland world. First, this world is not determinate, and yet many of its phenomena are sufficiently well behaved to manifest first-stage (rather than chaotic second stage) unpredictability. Its moving objects do not follow definite trajectories. Instead, their motion can only be represented by probability functions, which merely lead to correct predictions for the *likelihood* of the outcome of experiments that are designed to measure their spatial distribution. Second, the objects of this world are not conserved; they are created and annihilated, disappearing down a rabbit hole. They disappear singly, in the case of absorbed photons, or doubly in the case of annihilated negative and positive electron pairs. Third, the category of identity is abolished in this world. In a system that contains several objects of the same kind, it is impossible in principle to mark them individually for later identification. These three counterintuitive properties of subatomic objects are essential parts of the formal structure of atomic physics.

We will return to these bizarre aspects of the microcosm of quantum physics in Chapter 14. For the time being we merely note that even if the *truly* indeterminate phenomena of the atomic and subatomic microcosm *were* to play a role in human decision making and people could sometimes have willed differently from how they *did* will, this possibility would not provide any support for a compatibilist resolution of the Paradox of Moral Responsibility. For according to the Paradox's Argument presented in Chapter 6, random events that are not fully determined in advance can be no more under a person's autonomous control than can fully predetermined events.

Coda. Determinism, the doctrine according to which every event is an effect of a prior series of events, implies that all future events are as fixed and as unalterable as past events. One of the doctrine's most vigorous champions was the eighteenth century French Mathematician, Pierre Simon de Laplace. Determinism seems incompatible with the concept of moral responsibility, however, and thus confronts us with the Paradox of Moral Responsibility. The would-be resolvers of the Paradox have included *Behaviorists, Immaterialists; Libertarians* and *Compatibilists*, but none of their proposed resolutions have withstood incisive philosophical criticism. Some developments in twentieth-century physics, however, have aroused doubt regarding the all-pervasiveness of determinism in the world and inspired the idea that there is scope for free will after all. Yet, these developments also fail to provide a logically coherent resolution of the Paradox.

ÆTHERNA IPSE SVÆ MENTIS SIMVLACHRA LVTHERV
EXPRIMIT AT VVLTVS CERA LVCÆ OCCIDVOS
·M·D·XX·

MARTIN LUTHER (1483–1546)

Etching by Lukas Cranach the Elder (1520)

Chapter Eight

=⟫⬩⟨=

Freedom

Meaning of Freedom. It is freedom of the will rather than freedom of action that lies at the root of our attribution of moral responsibility to the person, and hence also of the troublesome Paradox of Moral Responsibility. For the action of a person is judged as being praiseworthy or blameworthy, not so much for the *results* that it actually produced as for the will that led the person to undertake the action in the first place. But we have yet to clarify the meaning of 'freedom,' as that term applies to willing and acting, except that it is opposite of 'determinism.'

'Freedom' can take on several basically different meanings, some of which apply to natural, value-free situations. Physicists, for instance, speak of 'degrees of freedom,' by which they mean the number of theoretically possible independent modes of change a physical object can take on, such as a change in the direction of motion of a gas molecule, upward or downward, backward or forward, and rightward or leftward. This meaning of 'freedom' is *not* the opposite of 'determinism,' inasmuch as which of several theoretically possible modes of change a physical object actually does undergo *is* subject to the causal chain of determinism.

Other meanings of 'freedom' do apply to non-natural, value-laden situations. Thus when philosophers speak of 'freedom of the will,' they mean an unfettered human choice of volitions and refer to the concept that *ascribes* to persons the capacity to choose *autonomously* among alternative actions. This ascription of autonomy to the will does not imply, however, that volition is totally immune to causal influences by the person's physiology, heredity, and past experience, or by other persons, or by the natural world. What freedom of the will does imply is that, such *heteronomous*, determinist influences on a person's will not withstanding, there remains a substantial residue of independence of them, by virtue of which the rational faculty of persons remains the final arbiter of what the person actually wills. The outcome of this autonomous arbitration process is not capricious or random, but causally determined by the person's soul, or, in the parlance of modern psychology, by the person's *self*. This meaning of freedom *is* an opposite of determinism.

Constraints. Although the concept of 'freedom of the will' has to be distinguished from the concept of 'freedom of action,' the two concepts are closely related. Thus while freedom of the will refers to the presence of an autonomous *volition to undertake* an action, the concept of 'freedom of action' entails also the person's *capacity for actually undertaking it*.

What are the necessary conditions for persons to be 'free' to arrive at some particular volitional state of mind? What is needed for persons to be able to choose their own goals? What actions are available to implement them? One obvious necessary condition is the absence of *social constraints* imposed on the agent by the will of another person, or of the state, or of any other authority. In addition to the volitional liberty provided by the absence of such *social* constraints there is another kind of necessary condition for freedom, namely the absence of *natural constraints* that may also limit a person's freedom to choose among alternatives. For instance, a San Franciscan is not free to choose between bicycling and flying to New York if she has to attend a conference on the East Coast on the following day. Yet another, albeit more controversial claim has been made on behalf of a necessary condition for freedom, namely that one cannot be said to be *truly* free to choose some preferred alternative unless one has the power and means to implement it. For instance, some philosophers contend that poverty-stricken or poorly educated people are less free than rich and well-educated people are because fewer alternatives are open for choice to the former than to the latter.

Does it follow from this argument that the extent of freedom in a society is directly related to the number of available alternatives, in that the more alternatives are open for choice to its members, the freer they are? The answer is "yes and no." Yes, because a larger measure of individual freedom is likely to obtain in a society in which a wider variety of beliefs are expressed and where there is a considerable diversity of tastes, pursuits, customs and codes of conduct, as well as ways and styles of living. No, because however numerous may be the alternatives among which persons may choose, they will not consider themselves to be free if the *one* alternative they would prefer most is the one that is forbidden. For instance, in a society that forbids the preaching of Roman Catholic doctrine and the practice of Roman Catholic forms of worship, Roman Catholics would not concede that they enjoy religious freedom just because they are still free to be Anglicans, Methodists, or Buddhists. Thus a meaningful assessment of the extent of freedom in a particular society has to take into account the interests of its individual members and of their ways of living.

Thus far, our considerations about freedom in non-natural, value-laden situations have focused on the absence of constraint imposed on personal actions by the state or some other authority, which can be categorized as 'freedom *from*.' But we need to take into account also the *kind* of freedom on behalf of which freedom is being claimed, or what amounts to a claim of 'freedom *of*.' This latter kind of freedom is actually the subject of most political and sociological discussions about freedom. For the 'freedoms of' are almost always concerned with demands for the removal of obstacles to the exercise and satisfaction of specific interests and forms of activity that are generally accepted as endowed with special moral and social significance. They include freedom of thought, speech, association, assembly, and religion, as well as the choice of one's employer or occupation, namely the specific spheres of human activity within which the right for individual choice and initiative really matter.

Another kind of 'freedom from,' which President Franklin D. Roosevelt often mentioned in speeches advocating his 'New Deal,' is basically different from the freedoms we have been discussing thus far. It refers neither to the absence of constraint nor to any specific interest on behalf of which freedom is claimed, being exemplified by the terms 'freedom from want' and 'freedom from fear.' These Rooseveltian locutions were meant to characterize an ideal society whose political and economic structures shelter its members from hunger and physical threats. This kind of freedom must not be confused with the kind of freedom that has always been considered as central and fundamental for the tradition of liberal thought. For the freedoms from want and from fear can be provided by a well-run, humanitarian prison that drastically restricts the range of personal freedom of its inmates within important spheres of human activity.

Principle of Alternate Possibilities. How is one to decide whether a person willed an action freely and thus bears moral responsibility for what happened? According to Van Inwagen (1975), almost all philosophers agree that for holding a person morally responsible for an action and its results, it is necessary to believe that the person could have refrained from undertaking it. This necessary condition, which is known as 'Could-Have-Done-Otherwise,' seems like an intuitively plausible criterion for freedom of action and attribution of moral responsibility. It is tantamount to one of the four criteria we considered in Chapter 6 as necessary and sufficient for the attribution of moral responsibility for an action, namely

(4) The person willed to undertake the action autonomously, i.e. it was open to her to choose *not* to undertake it.

Despite its plausibility and general acceptance perceived by van Inwagen among his colleagues, the criterion of 'Could-Have-Done-Otherwise' has been the subject of much discussion in the contemporary philosophical literature. (Dennet, 1984; Fischer 1982; Van Inwagen 1973; 1983)

Martin Luther. One likely reason for so much discussion is that the denial of freedom implicit in that criterion's inverse, namely '*Couldn't* Have Done Otherwise,' may not necessarily grant automatic relief from moral responsibility for a person's action. Dennett (1984) sought to provide an example of this ambiguity inherent in the criterion's inverse by examining Martin Luther's famous statement "Here I stand! I can do no other." Luther is supposed to have made it at his trial in 1521 before the Imperial German Diet at Worms, after responding "negative" to the Prince Electors' question whether he was willing to recant his heretical, rabble-rousing sermons. The source of this statement is an inscription on the pedestal of Luther's memorial statue in Worms, erected in 1868. According to the leading historian of the German Reformation, Leopold von Ranke, Luther did not say anything at his trial about being unable to do otherwise. He merely asked God to help him. (Buechmann, 1884)

But supposing that Luther *had* actually said it, Dennett would be almost certainly correct in supposing that Luther was not asking the Electors to absolve him of moral responsibility because he could not have done otherwise. What Luther *would* surely have meant is, as Dennett pointed out, that being the kind of person he *is*, his soul allows him to will only one action, namely refusing to recant.

As for the Prince Electors, many of them acknowledged the influences that gave Luther cause for promulgating his heresies, such as the corrupt practices of the Roman clergy. The Prince Electors might even have gone along with Luther in granting that, having his kind of soul, he could have willed only as he did. But they held him morally responsible for his actions all the same.

One of the most notorious critics of the Could-Have-Done-Otherwise criterion of moral responsibility, was Harry Frankfurt (1969), [whose personhood criterion of "second order volitions" we criticized in Chapter 5.] He called the Could-Have-Done-Otherwise criterion the '*Principle of Alternate Possibilities*,' which he formulated as follows:

"A person is morally responsible for what she
has done only if she could have done otherwise."

Frankfurt asserted that, its intuitive plausibility notwithstanding, "the Principle of Alternate Possibilities is false. A person may well be responsible for what he has done even though he could not have done otherwise. The Principle's plausibility is an illusion, which can be made to vanish by bringing the relevant moral phenomena into sharper focus."

Frankfurt's Counterexample. To bring the relevant moral phenomena into sharper focus, Frankfurt devised a counterexample, by means of which he meant to show that, contrary to the Principle, in some situations we *do* hold a person morally responsible even when that person could *not* have done otherwise. Frankfurt presented several variants of a scenario in which a Mr. Jones had decided to kill a Mr. Smith. All the variants shared the bizarre feature that before actually killing Mr. Smith, a Mr. Black happened to demand of Mr. Jones to undertake that very action. To enforce his demand, Mr. Black threatened Mr. Jones that if he did not kill Mr. Smith, Mr. Jones would suffer a penalty so harsh that no reasonable person would have been willing to risk it. Mr. Jones goes ahead and kills Mr. Smith, as he had intended to do all along. So Frankfurt asks: "Was Mr. Jones morally responsible for Mr. Smith's death?

Most peoples' moral intuition, evidently including also Frankfurt's own, would find that in view of Mr. Jones' prior decision to kill Mr. Smith, Mr. Jones *was* morally responsible for Mr. Smith's death. But, according to Frankfurt, it is also the case that in view of Mr. Black's dire threat, Mr. Jones could not have done otherwise than killing Mr. Smith. Hence, it would follow from the Principle of Alternative Possibilities that, contrary to moral intuition, Mr. Jones *was not* morally responsible for Smith's death. So Frankfurt asserted that the Principle of Alternate Possibilities is false, because he believed that his counterexample shows that an absence of moral responsibility is *not entailed by* (i.e., does not flow automatically from) Mr. Jones' inability to do otherwise than killing Mr. Smith.

Blameworthiness. Frankfurt's argument in support of his proposition that the Principle of Alternate Possibilities is false is itself defective in at least two of its crucial aspects. First, Frankfurt's argument conflates the concept of moral responsibility for actions that relate to the duties and obligations of a person with the concept of the blameworthiness of the person's volitions that energized these actions. While it *is* the case that there is a close connection between intuitions about moral responsibility and about blameworthiness, they are distinctly different concepts. Frankfurt's failure to take this difference into account undermines one of his main arguments.

As we first noted in Chapter 1, the very notion of moral responsibility refers to the intuition that persons can be held blameworthy or praiseworthy for some of their actions. And in Chapter 6 we listed four criteria that are generally considered necessary and sufficient for holding a person *morally* responsible for an impermissible action. So, in case the four criteria are met, the person is held morally responsible.

However, as we noted in Chapter 6 as well, it does not follow necessarily from a finding of moral responsibility of a person for a normally impermissible action that the person is therefore *blameworthy*. For there may exist two kinds of extenuating circumstances under which an *exculpation* of the morally responsible agent from blameworthiness may be granted. Under one kind, the granted exculpation is designated '*justification*,' which renders an action permissible, or even praiseworthy, even though it would have been impermissible and blameworthy, in the absence of these circumstances. Under the other kind, the granted exculpation is designated '*excuse*,' which leaves the action still impermissible, yet not blameworthy, or possibly even praiseworthy, because it was inspired by noble motives.

A special class of excusable (albeit impermissible and ordinarily blameworthy) actions is represented by cases in which an agent was *coerced* by dire threat to undertake them. As we noted in Chapter 3, Aristotle had emphasized in his *Nichomachean Ethics* that an agent may be excused from blameworthiness for an, on first sight impermissible action, provided that the agent undertook it only to avoid an even greater evil, or to achieve some higher purpose. By way of an example, Aristotle cited undertaking an evil action in compliance with an order by a tyrant who has the agent's parents or children in his power, under the dire threat that in case of refusal, the agent's beloved would be put to death.

As Aristotle pointed out, however, vindicating an excuse from blameworthiness of a person who is faced with such a moral dilemma is not all that clear-cut, since, after all, the agent *was* offered a choice at the time he acted. Hence to vindicate an excuse from blameworthiness for an impermissible action on the grounds that the agent did it for a morally righteous reason it is necessary to take into account the entire context of the occasion in which the action occurred. Strictly speaking, all human actions (other than reflexes and movements implemented by the autonomic nervous system) are voluntary (and designated as such by neurophysiologists). An action, therefore, can be regarded as 'coerced' only by supposing that the person would never have chosen to carry it out in the absence of the dire threat.

Coercion plays a central role in the argumentation of Frankfurt's counterexample. Frankfurt takes it for granted that the coercion exerted by Mr. Black's dire threat to make Mr. Jones kill Mr. Smith is tantamount to Mr. Jones being *unable* to do otherwise. Hence Frankfurt concludes that the Principle of Alternative Possibilities is false, because Mr. Jones, despite being unable to do otherwise, is morally responsible and (since Frankfurt does not distinguish between responsibility and blameworthiness) blameworthy as well for Mr. Jones' death. But when Frankfurt says that, in view of Mr. Black's threat, Mr. Jones *couldn't* do otherwise, he actually means that Mr. Jones *wouldn't* do otherwise. Mr. Jones *could* have done otherwise, had he been willing to suffer the consequences of his refusal to do what Mr. Black demanded of him (which, as Frankfurt stipulates), no reasonable person would have been willing to risk.

Thus Frankfurt's scenario is not a counterexample for the Principle of Alternative Possibilities at all. What the scenario *does* address is the problem of *exculpating* agents from blameworthiness for actions of theirs that are clearly violations of the imperatives of ethics and for which they are clearly morally responsible. Under ordinary conditions, the agents would be held blameworthy for these actions, but under some special conditions, such as coercion, they may be granted relief from blameworthiness. The actual question posed by Frankfurt's counterexample is whether, given Mr. Jones' prior decision to kill Mr. Smith and Mr. Black's dire coercive threat, Mr. Jones was or was not *blameworthy* for killing Mr. Smith. But, as we saw in Chapter 6, to answer that question the entire context in which Frankfurt's scenario is set has to be taken into account, which Frankfurt fails to do. For instance, Frankfurt does not stipulate Mr. Jones' motives for his original decision to kill Mr. Smith. If, like William Tell, Mr. Jones had decided to kill Mr. Smith to free his people from a fiendish foreign governor, or if, like King David, to make Mrs. Smith his wife, he would be praiseworthy or blameworthy, respectively, regardless of any threats made by Mr. Black.

Limitations of Counterexamples. There inheres another crucial defect in Frankfurt's argument in support of his claim that the Principle of Alternate Possibilities is false—quite apart from the bizarre scenario of his counterexample and his conflation of the concepts of moral responsibility and exculpation from blameworthiness. This other defect is rooted in Frankfurt's evident lack of appreciation that the logical force of counterexamples for the disproof of propositions is strong in some disciplines and weak in others. In philosophical argumentation counterexamples can serve two distinct functions, both mentioned explicitly, albeit conflated by Frankfurt.

One function is to *clarify* some concept, or to *show its inadequacy*. For instance, the concept of democracy can be brought into sharper focus by considering the counterexample of the totalitarian state. Or, as we found in Chapter 5, by considering counterexamples from everyday life, the 'identity definition' of personhood is both too inclusive as well as too restrictive for capturing the concept of 'person' in morally relevant contexts. The clarifying function is applicable in principle to all disciplines, although perhaps not in practice. For instance, it may not be possible to provide a useful clarifying counterexample for the complex concept of the 'soul,' described in Chapter 1 as the seat of consciousness, thought, volition, emotions, and feelings.

The other function of counterexamples is to *disconfirm* some proposition, as exemplified by Frankfurt's claim that his counterexample "disconfirms the Principle of Alternate Possibilities." Counterexamples *do* have a compelling logical force in disconfirming allegations of particular facts, such as disconfirming the statement "No computer program has ever beaten a chess master," by pointing to the game in which the IBM program 'Deep Blue' beat the world champion chess master Garry Kasparov.

The logical force of counterexamples is compelling also in disconfirming a general proposition or a 'law,' in 'hard' disciplines, such as mathematics or physics. For example, Fermat's 'last theorem' of number theory, which states that there are no positive, whole numbers a, b, and c that satisfy the equation $a^n + b^n = c^n$ when $n > 2$, remained unproven for more than three centuries, until it was finally proven in 1992. All the while, some mathematicians had suspected that the theorem hadn't been proven because, maybe, it wasn't true in the first place. And so they sought to disconfirm the theorem by searching for a counterexample, namely a triplet of whole numbers a, b, and c that *does* satisfy the equation for $n > 2$. If they had succeeded in finding just one such triplet, then Fermat's last theorem would have been decisively disconfirmed. They didn't find one, because the theorem turned out to be true.

The logical force of counterexamples is much less compelling, however, in disconfirming general propositions in 'soft' disciplines, such as biology and social sciences (including moral philosophy). One reason for calling these disciplines 'soft' in the first place is that they know no (non-trivial) exception-less laws, except the one law that affirms the absence of universally valid laws. These 'soft' disciplines know only generalizations whose validity is based on the preponderance of plausible evidence and of which it can be said that, as in jurisprudence, hard cases make bad law.

For instance, one of the most generally valid biological propositions is Darwin's principle of the role of natural selection in the evolution of the species. This principle is not disconfirmed by the many counterexamples to which students of evolution can point in which evolutionary change is attributable to processes other than natural selection, such as random genetic drift. Similarly, one of the most generally valid sociological propositions is the incest taboo, which forbids marriage between close relatives, especially between brothers and sisters. The counterexamples provided by the custom of brother-sister marriages in the royal houses and noble families of Ancient Egypt do not disconfirm the principle of incest taboo as a generalization of social practices.

Nevertheless, despite the far-fetched character of his counterexample, Frankfurt stoutheartedly asserts that "the [Principle of Alternate Possibilities] argument's plausibility is an illusion, which can be made to vanish by bringing the relevant moral phenomena into sharper focus." So it comes as a surprise that after these strong words, Frankfurt implies at the conclusion of his essay that the Principle of Alternate Possibilities may not be all *that* mistaken. For, he suggests that it should be replaced by the following proposition:

> "A person is not responsible for what she has done if she
> did it only because she could not have done otherwise."

Admittedly, Frankfurt's proposed change in wording of the 'could-have-done-otherwise' criterion does provide a more easily defensible support of the Principle of Alternate Possibilities than the original version, especially in the complex variants of Frankfurt's bizarre scenario. But Frankfurt's suggested revised wording is no more immune to Frankfurt-style, far-fetched counterexamples than the original version.

Consider, for instance, an (admittedly unlikely) SS guard in a concentration camp who has some residual feelings of compassion for his prisoners. He obeys his commander's order to inflict some particularly horrible atrocity on them that he would not have done unless his own execution would have been the penalty for refusing to obey the order. So according to Frankfurt's revised principle, the SS Guard is not morally responsible for committing the atrocity because he did it *only* because he could not have done otherwise.

At the 1946–47 Allied War Crimes Trials held at the former SS Divisional Headquarters at the Dachau concentration camp (which I attended when I was a member of the U.S. Military Government for Occupied Germany), not a few indicted SS guards did indeed make such a claim in their own defense. They alleged that they did those horrible things to their prisoners only because they could not have done otherwise. But the tribunal held the accused morally responsible all the same. Taking into account the entire context of the case, the judges found that the accused could have done otherwise than volunteering for service in the elite SS in the first place, knowing full well that SS guards were expected to treat their prisoners brutally.

Coda. The notion of freedom, which is an essential ingredient of the judgment of personal moral responsibility, is another elusive metaphysical concept of central importance for moral philosophy. To what criteria can one resort in everyday life for justifying the ascription of freedom to a moral agent in holding that person praiseworthy or blameworthy for having willed and performed an action? Frankfurt and other critics of the Principle of Alternate Possibilities notwithstanding, the Principle appears to be the only serviceable—but by no means infallible—criterion actually used in every-day-life for that purpose. The Principle does not, of course, apply to cultures whose moral traditions are based on the 'Three Teachings' of Buddha, Confucius, and Lao Tzu, who, as we noted in Chapter 3, are strangers to the concepts of free will, choice, and moral responsibility in the first place.

RENÉ DESCARTES (1596–1650)

Painting by Frans Hals (1649)

Chapter Nine

——◆——

Mind-Body Problem

The enduring, ancient philosophical chestnut known as the '*Mind-Body Problem*' dates back to the emergence of moral philosophy in fourth century BCE Greece as a secular rather than religion-based subject of intellectual inquiry. The problem had arisen in connection with the effort to resolve the Paradox of Moral Responsibility and to find a place for human beings as creatures endowed with an autonomous free will in a world whose events are governed by determinism.

Physicalist-Mentalist Dualism. To resolve the Paradox of Moral Responsibility, some Greek philosophers had proposed that there is a basic difference between mind and body. They conjectured that it is only the person's body that is subject to the heteronomous forces of determinism, while the person's mind is free to will autonomously the actions for which that person is morally responsible. In support of this conjecture, they noted that the *physicalist* statements that we make about peoples' bodies are different in kind from the *mentalist* statements we make about peoples' thoughts and feelings. As we noted in Chapter 1, the thesis that mental phenomena, especially willing, are basically different from bodily functions, in that they *are not* subject to determinism, came to be known as *dualism*. And the antithesis of dualism, namely the counter-thesis that mental phenomena, including willing, are nothing other than bodily functions, and hence *are* subject to determinism, came to be known as *monism*.

Substances-Attributes Dualism. Modern believers in monism usually make light of the alleged difference between physicalist and mentalist statements, which they simply attribute to our still very incomplete understanding of the mechanisms by which the brain implements such mental processes as thoughts and feelings. But the Greeks, who took this difference seriously, accounted for it—and hence for the difference between dualism and monism—by invoking a conceptual distinction between *substances* and *attributes*. A substance, such as a stone, can exist in the world on its own, whereas an attribute, such as weight, *cannot* and must ultimately refer to something that *is* a substance. According to that distinction, the human body is obviously a substance, and its functions, including those of its attributes, ought to be subject to determinism. And what about mind? If, according to monism, mind were an attribute of the body substance, mentalist functions would be no less subject to determinism than all the other functions of the body. In that case, the only available resolution of the Paradox would be to declare moral responsibility an incoherent concept, based on mankind's subjective illusion of a non-existent freedom of the will.

Suppose, however, that in accord with the doctrine of dualism, mind *were* an independent substance rather than a mere attribute of the body substance—an autonomous mental substance, so to speak. In that case mind might have some special properties that would provide it with freedom from the forces of determinism to which ordinary substances, such as those of which the rest of the human body is composed, are subject. Then freedom of the will *could* exist and the Paradox of Moral Responsibility would be resolved.

Platonic Dualism. The ancient Egyptians, who believed that the immortal soul, or *ba*, survives independently after it leaves the mortal body, or *ka*, upon a person's death were steadfast (albeit, unwitting and premature) dualists. Had they been aware of the distinction between substances and attributes they would have certainly taken it for granted that the immortal soul is an independent substance rather than an attribute of the body.

Plato, who was under the sway of Egyptian metaphysical traditions, was a dualist. He argued on behalf of dualism that persons are to be identified with their reason and capacity for thought, which reside in the soul rather than in the body. (Plato tended to refer to the mind as 'soul' because that term connotes more closely than 'mind' the venue of the transcendental concept of moral responsibility that dualists actually have in mind.) Since the soul, with its rational intellect and innate knowledge of Platonic Forms, belongs to the set of imperceptible, unchanging (that is, permanent) substances, the person's soul is immortal, whereas the person's body, belonging to the set of perceptible, changing substances, is mortal.

138

THE MIND-BODY PROBLEM
Are mental states fundamentally different from body states?

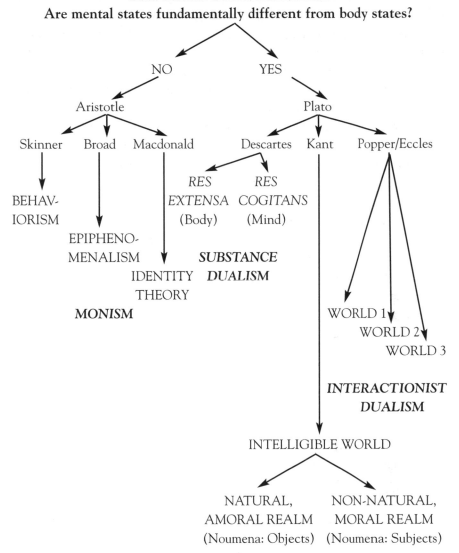

Citing examples of psychological conflict, Plato argued that we do, in fact, identify ourselves with the rational thoughts arising in our souls rather than with our non-rational impulses and appetites arising in our bodies. This identification would not be rational if the soul were a mere attribute of the body. According to Plato, acceptance of this dualist view of ourselves as possessors of a substantial and immortal soul leads to the moral conclusion that in living a virtuous life we prepare ourselves for the eternal afterlife that begins once our immortal soul is finally released from our mortal body.

Plato favored dualism because he was beholden to the *idealist* doctrine that the world's reality consists of the transcendental forms that exist only in our consciousness and reason. He emphasized that this difference between physicalist and mentalist statements is especially acute in the context of ethics, where human will looms large in moral judgements. Thus Platonic dualism might resolve the Paradox of Moral Responsibility.

Aristotelian Monism. Aristotle rejected Plato's dualist concept of mind being a distinct substance, and accepted the monist concept of the mind being a mere *attribute* of the body. He favored monism because he was beholden to the *materialist* doctrine that physical matter is the world's only reality, with all existence and all phenomena being accountable as manifestations or attributes of matter. He also believed that there is no essential difference between the physicalist statements we make about peoples' bodies and the mentalist statements we make about their thoughts and feelings, since, as he saw them, both kinds of statements obviously refer to states of physical matter.

Aristotle thought, moreover, that the body organ to whose state mentalist statements actually refer is the *heart,* of which he considered mind to be an attribute. That there is a close connection between heart and mind—with the mind substance investing the heart under dualism or the mind being an attribute of the heart substance under monism—is likewise an idea that the Greeks had imported from Egypt.

It would be another 500 years until the Alexandrine physician Galen provided monism with strong empirical support. He showed in mid-second century CE (by vivisection of condemned prisoners) that the brain (albeit not the heart), is the seat of consciousness and sensation. Galen's demonstration provided the empirical basis for the modern materialist-monist credo that mentalist statements simply refer to *brain* states. Yet the ancient Egyptian soul-is-in-the-heart concept survives in modern language and ritual. The heart is still referred to as the organ of love; "will you be my Valentine?" cards exchanged by would-be lovers are still heart-shaped; and in pledging allegiance to the national flag, the right hand is still placed over the heart.

Arguments regarding the mind-body problem have persisted into modern times, because, Galen notwithstanding, mental phenomena might still be *more than*, or *fundamentally different from*, brain states. Moreover, there always remained the metaphysical paradoxes entailed by monism for the morally indispensable belief in free will.

Augustinian Dualism. At the dawn of the Middle Ages, in the fourth century CE, Platonic dualism was carried over into Christianity by Augustine, who adopted it as the solution of the mind-body problem. Augustine regarded the soul not, as a monist would, as an attribute of the body, but as a substance endowed by God with reason to rule the body. Augustine did not consider this mind-body interaction as reciprocal, but thought that while the soul can act on the body, the body cannot act on the soul. Augustine epitomized his dualist view by characterizing the person as an immortal and immaterial rational soul, which invests a subservient mortal body during her secular lifetime and discards that body after death, at the onset of eternal after-life.

Cartesian Substance Dualism. The most notorious dualist solution of the mind-body problem was put forward in mid-seventeenth century by René Descartes, the French mathematician-philosopher, who is generally considered the father of modern philosophy and is best-known for formulating the only undoubtedly true existential proposition, namely 'I think; therefore I exist.' He was born near Tours in the Valley of the Loire in 1596, educated at a Jesuit College, and graduated from the law faculty at Poitiers. After traveling all over Europe for twelve years—for a while as a mercenary soldier—he eventually settled in Holland, living quietly and writing his philosophical works such as *Discourse on the Method* and *Meditations on First Philosophy*. In 1649, Descartes left Holland for Stockholm upon Queen Kristina's invitation to tutor her in philosophy. But the Swedish climate, as well as the rigors of life at Kristina's court, did not agree with him, and within a few months of his move to the Venice of the North, he died there of pneumonia.

Discourse on the Method, a condensed exposition of his system of philosophical investigation, is remarkable for its highly personal, autobiographical tone, as well as for having been written in French (rather than in Latin, as was then customary among European savants). Two features of the Cartesian system stand out. ('*Cartesian*' is the adjective that specifies that something belongs to Descartes). One feature is its intent as an *analytical* method, which seeks solutions to complex problems by resolving them into their simpler constituent elements. Descartes' model for this method was the resolution of complex mathematical curves by use of *analytical geometry*, a branch of mathematics that he developed and which commemorates his contribution by referring to the axes of its graphical representation as 'Cartesian coordinates.'

The other remarkable feature of the Cartesian method is that it was intended not only for mathematical or scientific studies, but also for any rational inquiry whatever. Descartes had a vision of the unity of all knowledge—philosophical as well as scientific—which he likened to a tree of knowledge, whose roots are metaphysics, whose trunk is physics, and whose branches are the other sciences, including medicine and ethics. This simile was meant to suggest the continuity of metaphysics and science, and much of Descartes' writings imply just this visionary ideal of philosophy and the natural science, unified in a grand single system of scholarship.

As did Plato, so did Descartes regard human beings as a composite of two distinct substances, or *res*. One of them is the material body, the extended substance, or *res extensa*, of which Descartes thought as the kind of mechanical automaton in human or animal form that enjoyed great popularity in seventeenth century France. But, so Descartes pointed out, humans are also moral creatures, who possess spiritual qualities that automata obviously lack. These spiritual qualities are attributes of the composite's other substance, namely the non-material soul, the thinking substance, or *res cogitans*, which, lacking extent in physical space, is not itself part of the body. Therefore, a human being is more than an automaton with the body shape of a great ape. According to Descartes, it is from their non-material *res cogitans* that persons derive both their free will and the responsibility for their actions, without which there would no such thing as morals. Because of its invocation of two substances, *res extensa* and *res cogitans*, Cartesian dualism came to be called '*substance dualism.*'

Unlike Plato's dualist doctrine, however, Cartesian substance dualism did not assume that the body-automaton owes its very life in the here-and-now to the soul, and that the direct cause of a person's death is the departure of her soul from her body. Instead, Descartes'—for its time revolutionary—conception of death was that live bodies differ from dead bodies as stopped clocks differ from running clocks. The body does not die because the soul leaves it, but because the automaton suffered a mechanical breakdown. And the soul leaves the body only because it cannot inhabit a lifeless body. The exit of the soul from the body is therefore a consequence rather than a cause of death.

Today, this distinction between the alternative causes of death may seem like trivial metaphysical hairsplitting. Yet, Descartes' concept of the human body as an automaton that owes its life to the proper operation of its working parts and its death to a mechanical breakdown of the automaton stimulated the progress in medicine and the life sciences that would be made in the following three centuries. For this concept entailed the fruitful notion that to understand the function of the body, one must study its components and find out how they make the automaton work. It was to provide the conceptual basis for the rise of physiology. And out of physiology developed the modern disciplines of biochemistry and genetics, with their immense practical benefits for human welfare.

Cartesian Physiology. In his treatise, *Passions of the Soul*, Descartes provided some details of his ideas about the nature of the body-soul composite. He emphasized that the mind's role in the composite is not that of a helmsman, whose only contact with his vessel is via the steering apparatus. Rather, the mind is connected to all parts of the body, so that it *directly* feels the body's pains and other sensations. Descartes conjectured that this connection is mediated by the *pineal gland,* located in the human brain just above the third ventricle. He selected the pineal gland for this central role because it lies as a single organ on the midplane of the brain, and he believed (incorrectly) that the natural distribution of the pineal gland is limited to the human species. In fact, the pineal gland is present in the brains of all vertebrate animals (and is now known to subserve the regulation of diurnal physiological rhythms set by the daily light-darkness cycle).

According to Descartes, the soul communicates with the pineal gland and thus intervenes in, as well as being affected by, the interaction between sensory input channels and motor output channels. That interaction Descartes supposed to be mediated by nerves (whose function he thought was of a hydraulic rather than, as we now know, an electrical nature). Descartes incorporated into this view a pioneering theory of visual perception that he had previously developed but which was published

LXXVIII.
Comment
vne idée
peut eftre
côpofée de
plufieurs;&
d'où vient
qu'alors il
ne paroift
qu'vn feul
objet. Et de plus, pour entendre icy par occafion, comment, lors que les deux yeux de cette machine, & les organes de plufieurs autres de fes fens font tournez vers vn mefme objet, il ne s'en forme pas pour cela plufieurs idées dans fon cerveau, mais vne feule, il faut penfer que c'eft toujours des mefmes points de cette fuperficie de la glande H que fortent les Efprits, qui tendant vers divers tuyaux peuvent tourner divers membres vers les mefmes objets: Comme icy que c'eft du feul point b que fortent les Efprits, qui tendant vers les tuyaux 4, 4, & 8, tournent en mefme temps les deux yeux & le bras droit vers l'objet B.

Descartes' theory of visual perception, published posthumously in his *Traité de l'Homme*. The pear-shaped cerebral structure labeled "H" is the pineal gland, thought by Descartes to be the gateway to the soul, where the percept is formed. Thus, according to this view, it is to the pineal gland that information from the sensory input projects, and it is from the pineal gland that the commands to the effector part issue.

[From the Kofoid collection of the Biology Library of the University of California, Berkeley. Courtesy of the University of California.]

only posthumously in his *Traité de l'Homme*. There he clearly outlined the overall process of visual perception. He described how light rays emanating from a visual object in space, such as an arrow, pass through the lenses and form an inverted, complete image of the arrow on the retinas at the back of both eyes. The retinas transduce the light stimulus into a (hydraulic) representation of the arrow, which is transmitted to the brain via the paired optic nerves across the optic chiasm. Once past the optic chiasm, the representations of the bilateral images converge on the pineal gland, where the soul converts them into a unitary, single percept of the arrow.

These insights into the physiology of visual perception represent a triumph of the Cartesian method, although the mechanism of visual perception turned out to be enormously more complex than Descartes could have imagined. Moreover, although the pineal gland does turn out to process visual sensory input, it does not participate in transforming it into a conscious percept.

Descartes believed that physiological studies leave the final step of forming a conscious percept from the retinal image of the arrow untouched. This is why he assigned that final step to the soul, whose nature he thought to be inaccessible to scientific analysis.

The concept of visual perception developed by Descartes turned out to be way ahead of its time, ridiculed and not pursued further for the next two centuries. But when it was finally resurrected in the nineteenth century, it provided the formation for modern vision research.

Great advances *have* been made in the analysis of the function of the human visual system since Descartes' time. Yet, there is still no better explanation available for that final step than postulating a tiny inner person—a homunculus—who watches the projection of the arrow's image onto a little screen in the subject's theater of the soul.

The analysis of the production and reception of human language appears to be heading for the same conceptual impasse, as does the analysis of vision. Thus, Noam Chomsky, the most influential investigator of linguistics of the latter half of the twentieth century, encountered a similar difficulty in explaining the final step of forming a conscious percept of the spoken word. Chomsky, who views himself as carrying on the line of linguistic analysis begun by Descartes, was unable to account for how a speaker produces speech acts and how a listener extracts meaning from them. Great advances *have* been made in linguistics since Descartes' time. Yet there is still no better explanation available for the final step of decoding the spoken words carried to the listener's brain by his auditory system than postulating a tiny inner person who looks up their meaning in a little dictionary in the subject's library of the soul.

Brain Science. Descartes' was aware that there are many functions that the body, working as a purely mechanical system, performs without participation of the soul. These mechanical, mindless functions involve direct interactions between sensory input channels and motor output channels. Examples of such *reflexive* reactions are provided by our throwing out our hands on stumbling to save ourselves from falling or by responding to some distressing news by behavior expressive of emotions, such as crying. In such cases, our body is functioning as a reactive Cartesian automaton, with the sensory stimuli producing bodily change through the subconscious mechanisms of the brain and nervous system.

It was Descartes view, moreover, that the behavior of all animals is reactive in this mindless, automatic sense while humans may have at least some awareness of these automatic processes—for instance in the form of experienced emotions. This is not the case for animals, which he thought have no consciousness at all. Actually, he was not wholly consistent in his denial of the presence of consciousness in animals, but on the whole, he does seem to have held the strong thesis that has usually been ascribed to him. His main reason for restricting possession of a conscious mind solely to human beings and denying it to animals hinged on the argument that only humans have the ability to reason. He took it as a particularly cogent support for this argument that only human beings have language, which (so Descartes supposed) no automaton or animal could possess. Nor did he believe that an automaton or animal could have free will, for which he thought conscious rational deliberation is required.

In the context of contemporary brain research, mind is considered as a wholly natural thing, whose understanding is a principal objective of the discipline of *neurobiology*. The findings of neurobiological studies leave no doubt that the overall function of the human brain, just as the overall function of all other organs of the human body, is governed by the principles of physics and chemistry. Accordingly, it ought to be feasible to ascertain whether mental states, including morally relevant volition, can be accounted for in terms of physicochemical brain states, such as electrical activity patterns in the network of cerebral nerve cells. If they can be, mental states would be subject to the natural laws of causal determination, just as are all others of our bodily functions, such as respiration or digestion.

During the recently ended 'Decade of the Brain' proclaimed by the elder President George Bush in 1990, some important methodological progress was actually made in the study of mental states that did bring significant advances in our understanding the biological bases of thoughts and feelings. Probably the most promising among these novel methods is 'brain imaging,' which permits the observation of states of the very parts of the living human brain that are involved in the generation of mental phenomena. Thus many of the most mysterious functions of the human brain, such as language, emotions, and cognition that cannot be studied in experimental animals, recently became accessible to neurobiological investigations on human subjects. (Damasio, 1999)

Yet, it seems unlikely that the results of these promising neurobiological advances will succeed in actually disposing of the free will problem. That problem has endured for millennia, not because of our hitherto insufficient neurobiological understanding of the human brain, but because the answer to the question whether our will is free is a paradoxical 'yes' *and* 'no.'

Monists usually make light of the alleged difference between physicalist and mentalist statements, which they ascribe to our still very incomplete neurobiological understanding of the mechanisms by which the body implements its mind attribute. And as we reached the end of the Decade of the Brain, many monists believe that the time is near (albeit not quite here yet) when mental phenomena will be explained in terms of physicalist statements about brain states and dualism can be buried at last.

Mental Phenomena and Brain States. Probably the deepest of the mentalist phenomena that remained unsolved at the end of the Decade of the Brain was *consciousness*. (Stent, 2001). The absence of a useful theoretical handle on consciousness is the reason why we still lack any satisfactory explanation of the final steps that convert the image projected by an arrow onto the retina into a visual percept. In fact, until recently, the riddle posed by consciousness appeared so deep that it was widely seen as a philosophical rather than neurobiological problem.

One of the main reasons that is usually advanced for excluding consciousness from the realm of soluble biological problems is the intrinsic subjectivity of the experiences it provides. This subjectivity of conscious

147

experiences is reflected in their qualitative aspects (or 'qualia'), such as the redness of the setting sun or the salty taste of seawater, which cannot exist in the absence of a conscious living observer. Soluble biological problems, by contrast, are posed by phenomena such as metabolism and heredity that can exist in the absence of a conscious living observer.

Other arguments that have been advanced by psychologists and philosophers for the rejection of the possibility of developing physicalist explanations of mental phenomena include two further claims. One of them asserts that the *intentionality* of some mental states makes them 'emergent' properties of brain states, and hence not wholly reducible to them. [In this context, the term 'intentionality' refers to the directedness of conscious mental states—especially those that lead to speech acts— that they are *about* something]. Another asserts that such mental states as feelings, beliefs, and desires are imaginary, *ad hoc* concepts that do not correspond to anything in the real world, no more than did the mean- while abandoned, old-time concepts of 'vital force' of naive biology or of 'phlogiston' of naive thermodynamics. These claims by psychologists re- garding the in-principle impossibility of reducing psychological theories about mental states to neurobiological theories about brain states have been effectively refuted. In any case, the fact that some mental states, in- cluding consciousness, intentionality, as well as feelings, beliefs, and de- sires, may differ essentially from other bodily functions does not exclude them from the realm of biological phenomena. They are obviously the product of processes that occur in our brain, whose understanding is equally obviously a biological problem, albeit an especially difficult, fas- cinating and troublesome one.

The view of the biological nature of mental phenomena does not com- mit one to the belief, however, that their *complete* explanation in terms of biological theories is actually possible in practice. The reason for this caveat is that the brain belongs to a class of phenomena whose high de- gree of complexity limits the extent to which theories developed to ex- plain them can be successfully reduced by theories developed to explain less complex phenomena. That is why the project of a complete biologi- cal explanation of mental phenomena is probably utopian in practice, even though it *ought* to be possible in principle. (Stent, 1975, 1986)

Modern Monism. Although the latter-day developments in brain re- search have not yet led to a detailed account of the mechanisms of very many important mental phenomena (including volition), many neurobiologists confidently expect that all those recent technical breakthroughs will soon reveal the physical bases of mental states. For they, as well as many contemporary philosophers—such as Gilbert Ryle, (1984), who had lampooned dualism as invoking a 'ghost in the machine'—believe that all being and phenomena can be explained as manifestations or results of matter. As materialists they follow the Aristotelian monist tradition and consider the mind-body enigma as a pseudo problem, while relegating dualism to the historical garbage heap of abandoned theories. In their view, Aristotelian monism is the only game in town. The mind *is* the brain. (Churchland, 1986)

So how *is* mind instantiated as an attribute of the brain? The following two proposals, which were widely discussed by philosophers during the twentieth century, exemplify the conceptual poverty of the efforts to answer that question.

1) *Epiphenomenalism*, envisages that there exist both mentalist states as well as conceptually separate physicalist brain states. (Broad, 1925) Thus, on first sight, epiphenomenalism appears to be a kind of *existential* dualism. However, epiphenomenalism is actually a kind of *functional* monism, in that it regards mental states as causally ineffective and gratuitous byproducts, or *epiphenomena*, of physicalist brain states. In other words, Epiphenomenalists deny that mental states have any influence on behavior, which is governed entirely by mindless neurologico-physicalist brain processes. Like Skinner's behaviorism, which (as we noted in Chapter 7) denies the existence of mental states altogether) epiphenomenalism seems incompatible with any philosophically reasonable intuition about morals and justice. Moreover, in view of its allegation of causal inefficacy of subjective mental experiences, such as pleasure and pain, it reduces persons to Zombies.

2) The *Identity Theory* is a modification of epiphenomenalism. Like epiphenomenalism (but unlike behaviorism), it admits the existence of mental states as attributes of brain states in living creatures that have a conscious mind. It therefore qualifies as a monist theory. But unlike epiphenomenalism, the Identity Theory *does* consider mental states as causally effective and hence capable of influencing behavior. It asserts that mental processes are identical with certain physical brain processes, albeit of a special kind that presents different aspects to objective extro-

149

spection from the outside and to subjective introspection from the inside. The Identity Theory attributes the causal efficacy of mental states to some kind of 'identity' between certain mental states and certain brain states. (Macdonald, 1989)

Just as the two popular names 'Evening Star' and 'Morning Star' denote different aspects of the same planet Venus, so do 'mental states' and 'brain states' denote different aspects of the same organ of our body. We just happen to know about the mental state aspects of our brains first hand from its inside while our theories about physicalist states of the brain aspect simply describe the same thing from the outside, based on second hand information provided by neurobiological brain studies.

Thus the identity theory is more obviously a monist theory than is Epiphenomenalism, since it holds that mental states *are* brain states, albeit of the special kind that presents different aspects from inside and outside. The identity theory is of no help for the resolution of the Paradox of Moral Responsibility, of course, since, if mental processes were identical with brain processes, they would be subject to the forces of determinism and hence incompatible with free will.

Most contemporary neuroscientists and philosophers of mind are beholden to the doctrine of materialism. Since materialists believe that all being and phenomena can be explained as manifestations or results of matter, they simply follow the Aristotelian monist tradition. Seemingly unaware of the fundamental inability of monism to provide a satisfactory rational basis for morals, they are convinced that there is no need to bring any metaphysical considerations to the mind-body problem, and they declare stoutly that the mind *is* the brain.

Interactionism. The contemporary obituary notices of dualism seem premature, since they merely reflect the failure of modern devotees of monism to fathom the deep moral roots of the mind-body problem. However incisive and illuminating may have been the neurobiological progress made in recent years, monism remains the existentially unsatisfactory solution of the mind-body problem that it has always been. While monism may be an adequate, or maybe even the only way to deal with mind as a *natural* phenomenon, it cannot give a satisfactory account of mind as a *moral* phenomenon.

One of the few noteworthy latter-day proposals for a dualist solution of the mind body problem was put forward under name *'interactionism'* by two eminent twentieth-century scholars, the philosopher Karl Popper, and the neurophysiologist John Eccles. In their 600-page collaborative essay, *The Self and its Brain*, Popper and Eccles (1977) accepted the Platonic concept of the person as a morally responsible, autonomous person with free will. Their aim was to reconcile the notion of the autonomy of the person with modern neurophysiological insights into brain function. Interactionism is a brand of substance dualism, in that it envisages that mental processes exist as distinct entities rather than as mere attributes of brain processes.

According to Popper and Eccles' interactionism, we live in three metaphysically distinctive worlds. One of them is World 1, comprising the universe of physical objects that are the source of sensory impressions. Another is World 2, comprising the universe of mental states that include psychological dispositions and conscious as well as unconscious states of mind. And yet another is World 3, which comprises the contents of thought, and, in particular, the intellectual products of the human mind. The nub of Popper's and Eccles' theory is that the mental processes that represent Worlds 2 and 3 interact with the brain processes that are responsible for handling the sensory input from World 1 and producing the motor output to World 1. This interaction is reciprocal. On the one hand, the mental processes of Worlds 2 and 3 are causally effective in governing behavior by interacting with the brain processes responsible for the physical implementation in World 1 of the decisions made by mental processes. On the other hand, the brain processes responsible for sensory input from World 1 are causally effective in influencing the mental processes that represent Worlds 2 and 3. Interactionism provides for the autonomy essential for the exercise of free will by allowing the possibility of an intervention by the self [or 'soul,' as it used to be called] in the interaction between mental processes and brain processes. Popper and Eccles tried to clarify this idea with a metaphor, namely that "the self plays on the brain as a pianist plays on a piano."

In a review of *The Self and its Brain*, Donald MacKay (1978) found that "what makes [Popper and Eccles'] joint effort so remarkable is that it seeks to reverse an all-but universal trend in contemporary thinking about the relation of mind to brain. For a couple of decades at least, the great majority of brain scientists have proceeded on the working assumption that the central nervous system is a physically determinate system in the same sense as the heart or lungs or any part of the body. Yet here, in 1977, is a book in which two acknowledged leaders in scientific thought condemn this whole trend as misguided and obstructive of progress."

According to MacKay, monism and all of its latter-day versions, such as behaviorism, parallelism [he meant 'identity theorism'], and epiphenomenalism, are fatally deficient because they cannot give "the fullest recognition of the moral and spiritual dimensions to our human nature." Dualism, by contrast, "offers the only way to do justice to the data of experience." Yet, MacKay concluded his review by saying that he does not believe that Popper and Eccles have established their case for an 'interactionist' version of dualism. In particular, they failed to put forward any neurophysiologically credible mechanism to account for the supposed interaction between mental and brain processes, or for the intervention in that interaction by the soul in the service of free will. All the same, MacKay wishes *The Self and Its Brain* "whatever the fate of its more adventurous speculations, a long life as a spur to the theorist of cognitive functions."

MacKay's good wishes did not materialize. Insofar as *The Self and Its Brain* is still known at all, it is remembered as a philosophical *folie-à-deux* of a pair of *éminences grises*.

Persistence of Dualism. Despite its general overt rejection by neurobiologists, psychologists and philosophers, dualism remains alive and well in modern secular societies, albeit surviving mainly underground as a tacitly held belief. How has dualism managed to persist through all those years, as other myths and unscientific misconceptions have fallen by the wayside in the course of ever-growing, no-nonsense scientific sophistication? One plausible answer is that dualism is more compatible than monism with the ancient theory of human nature according to which mankind is partly animal and partly divine, that mankind lives both in as well as out of nature. The Israelite version of this theory has been passed on to us via the Torah and its story about Adam and Eve's ejection from the Garden of Eden once they stopped being amoral animals and turned into moral persons who, like God, know evil. As archaeological records eventually revealed, this theory of the bipartite human nature dates back at least to predynastic Egypt, long before the Torah was written.

152

Coda. On the basis of Plato's perception that statements about peoples' bodies are obviously different in kind from statements about their thoughts and feelings, he put forward the dualist doctrine of mind and body being separate substances. Thus the Paradox of Moral Responsibility would be resolved if, unlike the body substance, the mind substance and its organ of free will were immune to influence by the heteronomous forces of determinism. Two thousand years later—in the seventeenth century CE—René Descartes developed Platonic mind-body substance dualism further. By the eighteenth century, however, the success of Newtonian physics had made Descartes' concept of a non-material substance hard to accept. As we will note in the next chapter, Immanuel Kant then replaced Cartesian substance dualism with his *epistemic dualism*, the gist of which is that we live in the two metaphysically distinct worlds, both of which are constructs of the human mind.

Critik

der

reinen Vernunft

von

Immanuel Kant

Professor in Königsberg.

Riga,

verlegts Johann Friedrich Hartknoch

1781.

TITLE PAGE OF KANT'S CRITIQUE OF PURE REASON

First Edition (1781)

Chapter Ten

◆

Critical Idealism

In mid-eighteenth century, Immanuel Kant presented a dualist solution to the mind-body problem that was significantly different from any that had been previously put forward. Kant's solution, to which we will refer as *'epistemic dualism'* (Stent, 1998a), was based on his epistemological theory of *critical idealism,* which disentangled the seemingly intractable antinomy of free will and determinism.

Kant is generally considered as one of the most important European philosophers of modern times, though unfortunately not as one of the clearest expositors of philosophical ideas. He was born in 1724 in the East Prussian city of Königsberg, where he spent his entire life and died in 1804. He studied philosophy (which in those days included also the natural sciences) at the University of Königsberg from 1740 to 1746, and then worked for a time as a private tutor. In 1755, Kant began lecturing at the University in a wide variety of academic disciplines, including mathematics, physics, anthropology, pedagogy, and physical geography, as well as the more restricted subject to which we refer nowadays to as 'philosophy.' He was appointed Professor of Philosophy in 1770 and published his masterpiece, *Critique of Pure Reason*, in 1781.

In addition to the opacity of Kant's writing style there is another obstacle in the way to understanding his works. He uses many terms in special technical senses that do not match their common, everyday meanings. For instance, with the phrase 'critique of' in the title of his *Critique of Pure Reason*, Kant meant 'careful examination' or 'reasoned clarification,' rather than cantankerous criticism or faultfinding. Similarly, whereas in ordinary speech the adjective 'pure' refers to something that is unsullied, or to someone who is uncorrupted, in the context of Kantian philosophy the phrase 'pure reason' refers to rational thought based on principles that are intuitive, or innate, rather than being derived from experience. Thus for Kant, the 'pure' in 'pure reason' was a quasi-synonym for his equally unconventional use of the word 'transcendental.' Nowadays this latter term is generally taken to mean 'supernatural' but Kant meant it to designate innate ideas that we *apply to* our experience *a priori*, rather than *derive from* our experience *a posteriori*.

Kant's novel approach to the Paradox of Moral Responsibility forms only one part of his all-encompassing epistemological doctrine of '*critical idealism*.' That doctrine qualifies as a brand of idealism, since it shares with other brands of idealism, such as Plato's, the rejection of the materialist creed. According to the materialist creed championed by Aristotle, physical matter is the only essential reality, with all things, processes, and phenomena being attributable to physical matter. Unlike other brands of idealism, however, Kant's critical idealism also rejects the traditional idealist creed that the only things that really exist are minds and their contents. Instead, Kant's critical idealism invokes a source external to our minds of the phenomena we perceive, and it provides a coherent, closely reasoned account of how we come to *construct* the reality in which we spend our lives.

One of Kant's goals that led him to the development of his critical idealism was to show that there does exist such a thing as pure (or transcendental) knowledge that transcends experience. Prior to Kant, in the late seventeenth and early eighteenth centuries, British empiricist philosophers, such as John Locke and David Hume, had denied the existence of transcendental knowledge and claimed that experience is the only source of authentic knowledge.

A priori-Synthetic Propositions. Philosophers had long recognized that there exist two different kinds of propositions (that is, statements that are capable of being either true or false), namely *analytic* propositions and *synthetic* propositions. An analytic proposition is a statement whose truth is entailed *a priori* by the meaning of the words of which it is composed, such as

> 'No bachelor is married,'

and whose negation,

> 'Some bachelors are married,'

is self-contradictory.

A synthetic proposition, by contrast, is a statement whose truth is inferred *a posteriori* from experience, such as

> 'No bachelor is happy,'

and whose negation,

'Some bachelors are happy,'

is *not* self-contradictory.

Yet, so Kant noted, there exists a third kind of propositions whose truth appears to be both *a priori* as well as *synthetic*, which Kant designated by the oxymoron '*a priori-synthetic*' propositions. An example of such an *a priori*-synthetic proposition is

'Every event has a cause.'

This proposition, which provides the rational foundation for our belief in determinism, is one of the two mutually contradictory propositions that generate the *Paradox of Moral Responsibility*. Its truth is neither entailed analytically by the meaning of the words of which it is composed nor is it inferable *a posteriori* from experience. So, Kant wondered how there could there be such things as true *a priori*-synthetic propositions.

Four Antinomies. Kant noted also a second troublesome problem posed by some propositions that he designated as '*antinomies*' and that are paradoxical contradictions between two apparently equally valid propositions. He considered the following four antinomies, or pairs of propositions, of which each pair comprises a seemingly true *thesis* and its seemingly equally true contradiction, or *antithesis*.

	Thesis	Antithesis
First Antinomy	The world is finite. It has a beginning in time and limits in space.	The world is infinite. It has no beginning in time and no limits in space.
Second Antinomy	Every composite thing in the world is made up of simple parts.	No composite thing in the world is made up of simple parts.
Third Antinomy	Freedom exists. Not everything in the world takes place solely in accordance with the causal laws of nature.	There is no freedom. Everything in the world takes place solely in accordance with the causal laws of nature.
Fourth Antinomy	One absolutely necessary being exists in the world.	No absolutely necessary being exists in the world.

A Copernican Revolution in Philosophy. Kant believed that, lest they be resolved, the conceptual problems posed by *a priori*-synthetic propositions and by the four antinomies would lead to a hopeless philosophical skepticism, which he termed 'euthanasia of pure reason.' He thought that he could resolve both problems by means of the doctrines of what he himself referred to as his 'Copernican Revolution in Philosophy.' [Copernicus had resolved the formerly intractable physical quandary of planetary motion by putting forward the revolutionary and counterintuitive theory that the Earth moves around the Sun.] And so Kant set out to resolve the intractable metaphysical quandaries by putting forward the revolutionary and counterintuitive theory that for the world's things to be knowable for us they must conform to our subjective ways of knowing.

In support of that theory Kant claimed that our perception of space and time are examples of such subjective ways of knowing, thanks to which our mind abstracts meaning from the phenomena that we observe. This Kantian critical-idealistic view of our *subjective* perception of space and time is radically different from the materialistic view backed half a century earlier by Isaac Newton and Gottfried Wilhelm Leibniz. Newton considered space and time as self-subsisting, *objective realities*, while Leibniz regarded them as *objectively existing relations between* self-subsisting objects.

In his *Critique of Pure Reason*, Kant developed the epistemological dogma that the world's things become known to us by reaching our mind, not as they may be *in themselves* but as abstract forms. In other words, according to Kant's Copernican Revolution, we can know things only as they *appear* to us, but not as they are actually *in themselves*.

Critical Idealism. The basic idea that underlies Kant's theory of critical idealism is Plato's insight that our direct contact with the world is limited to a *sensible world* of appearances, or phenomena, which we perceive via our senses, such as sight, smell, hearing, and touch. To orient ourselves in that sensible world of phenomena, that is, to extract meaning from it, we take it for granted that the sources of the phenomena we perceive are not phantoms but real things-in-themselves, or *noumena* of an *intelligible world*. [The Greek word *noumenon* means 'that which is conceived.' It is the opposite of *phainomenon*, which means 'that which appears.']

However, according to Kant, it is not given to us to perceive that intelligible world of noumena directly via our senses, so that the *noumena* we take for granted are not actually *knowable as they really are*. But they are at least *thinkable* and thus can serve as the elements of an indirectly inferred intelligible (that is, understandable) world of our own making.

To construct that intelligible world and its noumena, we interpret the phenomena we perceive in terms of *a priori* categories that inhere in our rational faculty, such as time, space, good/evil, and free will. In this interpretive procedure we also resort tacitly to *categorical propositions*, which inhere in our rational faculty as well and whose validity we similarly accept *a priori* rather than inferring them a *posteriori* from experience. An example of such an *a priori* categorical proposition is 'some A are B; therefore all A are B' (to which philosophers refer as *induction*). Another example is the proposition 'the occurrence of a set of conditions A is both necessary and sufficient for the occurrence of B' (to which philosophers refer as causation by A of B).

Kant considered these categories and categorical propositions to be universally applicable to all phenomena. Their rational use allows our mind to construct an intelligible world from our sensory perceptions of the phenomena of the sensible world. Indeed, it is only in the process of constructing the intelligible world that sensory perceptions of phenomena *become* experience, that is, become meaningful, once the mind has interpreted them in the terms of its innate categorical endowment. Hence the Kantian categories and categorical propositions have *transcendental* status, since we resort to them for *creating* experience rather than *deriving them from* experience.

Kant designated that part of our rational faculty whence the categories spring as *pure* reason—'pure' because it is not corrupted by our unreliable, incomplete and possibly misleading sensory impressions of the sensible world of appearances, as described in Plato's *Parable of the Cave*. Kant knew, of course, that many of our reactions to sensory stimuli provided by the sensible world, such as the reflexive withdrawal of the hand from a hot stove, do not involve any rational interpretation of their noumenal source in the intelligible world. Since such automatic reactions to sensory stimuli are determined subliminally by the causal forces of natural laws, they are obviously not instances of the exercise of pure reason.

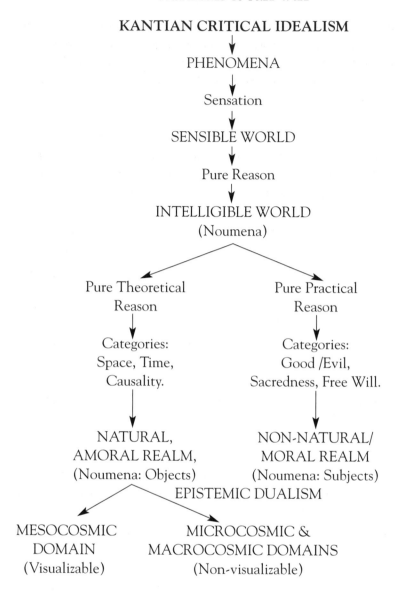

KANTIAN CRITICAL IDEALISM

↓

PHENOMENA

↓

Sensation

↓

SENSIBLE WORLD

↓

Pure Reason

↓

INTELLIGIBLE WORLD
(Noumena)

Pure Theoretical Reason	Pure Practical Reason
↓	↓
Categories: Space, Time, Causality.	Categories: Good /Evil, Sacredness, Free Will.
↓	↓
NATURAL, AMORAL REALM, (Noumena: Objects)	NON-NATURAL/ MORAL REALM (Noumena: Subjects)

EPISTEMIC DUALISM

MESOCOSMIC DOMAIN (Visualizable)	MICROCOSMIC & MACROCOSMIC DOMAINS (Non-visualizable)

Epistemic Dualism. By the latter part of the eighteenth century, the explanatory success of Isaac Newton's physics in the natural world had discredited the Cartesian theory of substance dualism. So, based on his epistemology of critical idealism, Immanuel Kant developed a novel brand of dualism, to which we will refer as '*epistemic dualism*' (Stent, 1998, 2002). Unlike Aristotelian monism or Platonic dualism, Kantian epistemic dualism is not a descriptive theory that is meant to represent the physical world. It is not concerned with the empirical question whether mental states are or are not fundamentally different from body states. Rather, Kant's epistemic dualism, which is philosophically more palatable than Descartes' substance dualism, is a metaphysical theory meant to connect two of the fundamental aspects of existence, namely being and knowing.

Epistemic dualism flows readily from Kant's theory of critical idealism, in that it envisages our existence in two metaphysically distinct realms of the intelligible world. Both realms are of our own making, their noumena being products of our interpretation by use of our pure reason of the phenomena we perceive in the sensible world.

One realm, the natural/amoral realm, we construct by use of that part of our pure reason that Kant designated as '*pure theoretical reason*.' (As used here by Kant, the adjective 'theoretical' denotes the concern of pure reason with the difference between truth and falsehood.) For constructing the natural/amoral realm, pure theoretical reason resorts to value-free, natural categories, such as space, time, causality, and object. The noumena of natural/amoral realm are material objects, such as stars, stones, and animals. Their existence in the world is governed by the natural laws of causal determination. They include also human beings, insofar as *Homo sapiens* are one of the many species in the class of mammals of the vertebrate phylum of the animal kingdom.

The other realm, the non-natural/moral realm, we construct by use of that part of pure reason that Kant designated 'pure practical reason.' (As used here by Kant, the adjective 'practical' denotes a concern of pure reason with moral decisions.) Pure practical reason resorts to non-natural categories, such as good and evil, sacredness, free will, and personhood. The noumena of the non-natural/moral realm are human subjects, or persons, in so far as we consider them as being governed by the moral laws of freedom within them.

In his *Critique of Practical Reason* Kant (1949) epitomized the psychological consequences of his epistemic dualism in a famous epigram. "Two things fill the mind with ever-increasing wonder and awe, the more often and the more intensely the mind of thought is drawn to them: The starry heavens above and the moral law within me."

Resolution of the Paradox of Moral Responsibility. Kant's epistemic dualism thus resolves the Paradox of Moral Responsibility. For it recognizes that our perception of the causes of a person's action are fundamentally different when we encounter that person in the context of the natural/amoral realm or in the context of the non-natural/moral realm of the intelligible world. In the context of the natural/amoral realm—especially in a biological or psychological setting—we regard the person as an unfree object whose actions form part of the events heteronomously determined by the laws of nature. But in the context of the non-natural/moral realm—especially in a jurisprudential setting—we regard the person as a free subject whose actions are autonomously willed by her mind.

As Kant argued in his Critique of Pure Reason, the existence of free will is an *a priori* synthetic proposition, whose truth cannot be demonstrated by empirical observations. Moreover, there is an obvious antinomial contradiction inherent in our categorical attribution of free will to the person and our categorical belief that everything that happens in the world is determined by causal necessity. Kant sought to resolve this antinomy of free will and causal necessity by means of two arguments.

First, Kant insisted that the belief in free will is a precondition of morals and has its roots in the non-natural/moral categories of pure practical reason. Hence free will does not need to be established as a fact of nature. From the practical point of view it suffices that we adhere to the belief that freedom of the will *does* exist, since a person who believes in her freedom is by this fact alone effectively free.

Second, Kant saw no difficulty in believing in free will, inasmuch as there are no primary sensory data provided by the sensible world that contradict the categorical belief that people have the power to will their actions autonomously. Regarding persons as phenomena of the sensible world, I may use my *pure theoretical reason* to deem them noumenal objects in the amoral/natural realm. Using my *pure practical reason*, however, I may also deem them noumenal subjects in the non-natural/moral realm. Thus depending on the context, I can consider the actions of another person either as determined heteronomously by causal necessity or as willed autonomously by her free will.

Some philosophers have rejected the proposition that attribution of an autonomous free will to an entity necessarily excludes it from the natural/amoral realm. Dennett (1984), for instance, argued that animals with an autonomous free will, such as smart dogs, do belong nevertheless to the natural/amoral realm. However, as we noted in Chapter 5, the owners of smart dogs tend to confer personhood, and hence membership in the non-natural/moral realm, to their pets, precisely in appreciation of the animals' intelligence. Dennett also pointed to some *inanimate* artifacts, such as smart machines that possess some of the aspects of free will that we attribute to persons, would have to be conferred membership in the non-natural/moral realm. The chess playing 'Deep Blue' program would provide an example of such a smart artifact. It has reliable expectations about what will happen next, can make what appear to be autonomous rational choices on the basis of its expectations, and has projects, interests, and values it creates in the course of its own self-definition.

Dennett's counterexamples highlight the obstacles along the way of reaching definitive, logically consistent and universally valid conclusions regarding the paradoxical aspects of the free will problem. However rational and autonomous the choices of smart dogs and smart machines may appear, few people would infer that any moral responsibility devolves from their actions, except perhaps on the part of their human owners.

Why should this be so? It is so because, as Kant evidently realized when he developed his non-naturalistic ethics, the paradoxical character of morality is one of the innate human qualities. Far from being regrettable, however, this paradoxical character bids fair reflecting a felicitous adaptation of our cognitive faculties to the human condition. For if the two domains constructed by pure theoretical reason and pure practical reason were *not* inconsistent, we might, indeed, will actions that would serve our ends better. But in that case we would not will these actions as a matter of moral duty but for pragmatic (that is, utilitarian) reasons. And thus mankind would be emotionally poorer, for if pure reason were not inconsistent, we should lose the opportunity to show good will, the only thing in the sublunary sphere—or even beyond of it—that can be taken without qualification as an instance of the Good.

Resolution of the Quandary of A Priori Synthetic Propositions. The possibility of the existence of true *a priori*-synthetic knowledge of things of potential experience provides the very foundation of Kant's critical idealism. Unlike the truth of an analytic proposition, the truth of the *a priori* component of an *a priori*-synthetic proposition, such as 'every event has a cause,' is *not* entailed logically by the meaning of the words of which it is composed. Accordingly, the negation of an *a priori*-synthetic proposition, such as the statement 'some events have no cause,' is *not* self-contradictory.

Kant contends that the truth of the *a priori* component of the proposition 'every event has a cause' devolves from the presumption inherent in our pure theoretical reason that to become objects of knowledge for us in the first place, phenomena have to conform to the categorical concept of causality. And the truth of the synthetic component of that proposition devolves from our failure to observe any phenomena about which we can confidently assert that they represent instances of its negation, that is of instances of events that have no cause. Kant thus resolved the problem of the truth of *a priori*-synthetic propositions by attributing their justification to the *a priori* categories of pure reason that provide the metaphysical basis for his doctrine of critical idealism.

Resolution of the Antinomies. Kant was less successful in disposing of the paradoxes entailed by the mutually contradictory theses and antitheses of the four antinomies. The antinomies exist because our reason allows us to construct valid proofs for either of the two conflicting, all-encompassing propositions, justifying Kant's ultimate sardonic judgment about the quality of human reason, namely that

> *Out of timber so crooked as that from which mankind is made,*
> *Nothing wholly straight can be built.* (Kant, 1784)

As for the first antinomy regarding the finiteness or infinity of the world in time and space, Kant argued that all things of which we have experience are always associated with other things that had previous existence in time and that exist beyond them in space. So when we put these experiences provided by the phenomena of the sensible world together into an intelligible world of noumena, it is no more conceivable that this intelligible world is finite in both time and space than that it is infinite.

As for the second Kantian antinomy regarding the quandary whether composite substances are or are not made up from simple parts, Kant pointed out that in dealing with this question our pure theoretical reason tries to grasp the constitution of matter by extending our reasoning from our experience with composite substances to the ultimate material elements of which they are composed. We know from our experience that we can usually break any sample of matter into smaller parts and then

164

break these smaller parts into yet smaller parts. Eventually, the parts may become too small to be directly perceptible to our senses, but our pure theoretical reason tells us that they cannot be simple, indivisible elements. For when we reflect on their nature we find that we cannot help conceiving them as occupying space and therefore (in principle) breakable into further parts. Thus such parts are not the simple material elements of reality of which we are in search. And if in the process of breaking up things we do reach parts that are no longer breakable into smaller parts, they cannot be occupying space and therefore are no longer matter. That is to say, the answer to the question what matter consists of would be the paradoxical proposition "matter consists of nothing at all."

Kant resolved the quandary of his first and second antinomies by concluding that their theses *and* their antitheses are both *false*. For two propositions that may seem incompatible at first sight are not truly antinomial if one or both of them is false. Kant's way of resolving the first and second antinomies did not fare well upon the development of twentieth-century physics, according to which the *theses* of the first and second antinomies both happen to be *true*. As for the first antinomy, the world *did* have a beginning with the Big Bang about 10-15 billion years ago and can look forward to an (at least *conceivable*) end upon the gravitational collapse of the Big Crunch. The world also turns out to have a finite size, presently estimated to correspond to a radius of about 10 billion light years. And as for the second antinomy, the world *does* contain some unbreakable, simple parts, such as electrons.

Had he been still alive in mid-twentieth century, Kant ought not to have been surprised to learn of this shipwreck of his proposed resolution of the first and second antinomies. For he himself had concluded that our reason inevitably falls into contradiction with itself whenever it ventures beyond our direct experience and tries to think of the world as a whole (as his reason did in conceiving the first and second antinomies). Kant erred in his judgement that both theses and antitheses of the first and second antinomies are false. But he was right in foreseeing the intrinsic limitations on our understanding of the world as a whole that came to light long after his death and which we will consider in Chapters 12 and 14.

The long and short of the third and fourth antinomies regarding the presence or absence of freedom in the world and the requirement or dispensability of the existence of an absolutely necessary being (a.k.a. "God") in the world is that there can be no overarching rational resolutions of them. We simply have to come to terms as best as we can with our paradoxical mental endowment provided for us by critical idealism. Thus thesis and antithesis of the third antinomy epitomize the contradiction between freedom of will and determinism. The thesis is a rationally necessary condition for the concept of moral responsibility of pure practical reason, while the antithesis is an equally rationally necessary condition for the concept of natural law of pure theoretical reason. And thesis and antithesis of the fourth antinomy epitomize the contradiction inherent in the concept of God, which is a category belonging to pure practical *as well as* pure theoretical reason. While the existence of God is a rationally necessary condition for the foundations of morals, He is (or possibly only *may be*) also conceptually indispensable for the operation of natural law.

It had not escaped Kant's notice that whereas his first and second antinomies deal only with the world's natural/amoral realm of pure theoretical reason, his third and fourth antinomies deal also with the world's non-natural/moral realm of pure practical reason. Thus in the case of the third antinomy, its thesis that freedom exists pertains to the non-natural/moral realm, while its antithesis that freedom does not exist pertains to the natural/amoral realm. And in the case of the fourth antinomy, the thesis that God (the one absolutely necessary being) exists deals with the non-natural/moral realm, while its antithesis that God does not exist deals with the natural/amoral realm.

Existence of God. Three formal arguments were cited by Kant that were often advanced on behalf of fourth antinomy's thesis, 'God exists.' The first argument asserted that the very concept of God implies that God could not *not* exist. Thus the existence of God would be an analytic truth. The second asserted that the existence of the world entails that God exists, because only He could have been the First Cause that brought it into existence. And the third asserts that the structure and function of the world is such that it could not have arisen naturally but must have been designed by Him.

Kant demolished all three arguments on rational grounds, which proves neither that the thesis is false nor that its antithesis, "No God exists," is true. All that can be said on behalf of the antithesis is the reply that Laplace made to Napoleon when Napoleon asked Laplace whether he believes in the existence of God: "*Sire, je n'ai pas besoin de cette hypothèse.*"

166

This is not the answer that Kant would have given to Napoleon. Kant did reject the standard proofs of God's existence by resort to arguments based on pure *theoretical* reason. But Kant not only believed in the existence of God but also held that His existence can be justified by pure *practical* reason as a rationally necessary condition for the foundations of morals. Kant's proof of the existence of God was based not on a descriptive proposition about some objective facts in the world but on the subjectively experienced moral situation.

He reasoned that, absent God, people might still applaud and admire the magnificent precepts of morals. The precepts alone, however, could not serve as sufficiently strong mainsprings for driving moral intentions and actions in accord with the categories of pure practical reason that are present *a priori* in every person.

Immortality of the Soul. The central transcendental problem connected with a person's death, namely the immortality of the soul, became more, rather than less troublesome over the years. In medieval and Renaissance Europe, the immortality of the soul was held to be self-evident, in view of the generally accepted Egypto-Christian belief of a life after death and of a reward or punishment in heaven or hell for one's acts in the here-and-now. According to that belief, death is more a beginning than an end of existence; it marks a kind of graduation from a transient, secular probationary period, to the onset of the eternal, transcendental existence during which persons receive their just deserts.

With the decline of religiosity in the eighteenth century, set off by the Enlightenment, the belief in life in the hereafter could on longer be taken for granted. Yet, it proved very difficult to dismiss the idea of the immortality of the soul as just so much nonsense. Descartes, and after him Leibniz, continued to believe in the soul's immortality, but they grounded that belief neither in the revelations of the Christian religion nor in personal mystical experiences. Descartes and Leibniz held that, what Kant would soon designate as 'pure practical reason,' obliges us to believe that the soul is immortal.

The rationalist arguments of Descartes and Leibniz did not persuade the monist French philosophers of the Enlightenment, however. They simply denied the immortality of the soul and developed a materialist outlook on death. According to them, there is no such thing as the soul in the first place. All there is, is the mind, which is merely an attribute of the mortal body. Hence the question of the soul's immortality after death of the body is moot. It is merely a pseudo-question, since humans are no more than Cartesian automata after all, whose function simply ceases upon death. Death, therefore, being the final breakdown of the automaton, obviously entails the total annihilation of the person, as its body disintegrates and returns to the dust whence it came.

Where does the idea of the soul and its immortality come from in the first place? According to the Enlightenment philosophers, the immortality of the soul is simply a fairy tale made up by the lying priests. Their goal was to keep the downtrodden poor content with their miserable fate in the here-and-now and to persuade the rich to endow monasteries where lazy, good-for-nothing monks would pray for their souls in the hereafter. This lie must be exposed to provide for a better living of mankind. It is the amelioration of the human condition in the here-and-now rather than in after-life that ought to be the paramount goal of our earthly strife. Indeed, as pointed out by one of the Enlightenment philosophers, the Marquis de Condorcet, a person's service on behalf of the betterment of mankind in the here-and-now not only provides a real purpose for life but even offers an opportunity for achieving for genuine immortality.

Here too it was Kant who fathomed the real depth also of the existential problem of the immortality of the soul, just as he had in the case of the epistemological problem of how we come to know what we know. He conceded that the immortality of the soul is not an empirical proposition, since, even it were true, its truth would not be demonstrable. But Kant pointed out that if there were no immortality of the soul, there would be no counterargument against the claim that it makes no difference how we conduct ourselves in the-here-and-now, since death annihilates saints and sinners equally. Here Kant did not mean that the belief in immortality and its attendant eternal reward or punishment is needed as a (utilitarian) inducement for good conduct. Instead, what he had in mind was the proposition that unless there were a God and a life in the hereafter, there would be no Supreme Wisdom according to which the moral worth of our actions could be judged. And there would be no way for us to know eventually whether we acted well or badly during our earthly sojourn. Absent God and an immortal soul, life would of necessity be amoral.

Hence to be a moral creature it is necessary to be committed to the belief in the immortality of the soul, or, in Kant's terms, "in an infinitely

168

prolonged existence and identity of one and the same rational being." Just as are the problems of free will and of God's existence, so is the immortality of the soul one of the central concerns of metaphysics, which cannot be disposed of by simply declaring them to be nonsense or a pack of priestly lies.

Death of God. Kant's moral argument in support of the immortality of the soul and God's existence made relatively little impact in the French- and English-speaking countries, where the materialist view of death as total annihilation still retains many professed adherents to this day. In this respect, Kant's moral argument in support of God's existence and of an immortal soul suffered a similar fate as his theory of knowledge, which also lost out to empiricism as the main philosophical inspiration of nine-teenth-century science. However, Kant's ideas on death were taken up, elaborated, and modified by a succession of nineteenth century German philosophers. But none of these post-Kantian thinkers was able to strengthen the argument in favor of an immortal soul sufficiently to ward off the ever-growing dominance of their materialist opponents.

Finally, towards the end of the nineteenth century, Friedrich Nietzsche saw the full implications of that development. Whereas, according to Niet-zsche, Kant was correct in asserting that without believing in God people cannot lead a moral life, the French philosophers of the Enlightenment, such as D'Alembert, Diderot, and Voltaire had nonetheless managed to kill Him. Thus, according to Nietzsche, everything had become permissible and mankind was about to sink into a moral abyss. To survive mankind must now transcend its animal nature and become truly human, that is, to become Supermen, so that their actions will be beyond good and evil.

Though Nietzsche's Supermen have yet to make their appearance, we did manage to survive into the twenty-first century CE, albeit just by the skin of our teeth, mainly because God, though seemingly moribund, was not dead after all. He was still alive and well because the Enlightenment philosophers and their influential disciples, foremost among them Karl Marx, were atheists in name only. They merely provided a new vocabu-lary for justifying the established moral values of old-time Judeo-Chris-tianity without really abandoning the tacit belief in the transcendental source of their authority. Yet, by Nietzsche's time, the eighteenth-century project of seeking a wholly materialistic, scientific basis for moral con-duct reached the end of its road.

169

Nietzsche's exposure of the moral bankruptcy of materialism paved the way for a different view of mankind, which by the middle of the twentieth century had become a serious rival to the Enlightenment, namely the counterenlightenment. Its focus is on mankind's existence, a concept that was put forward at about the time of Nietzsche's birth by Søren Kierkegaard. Here the word 'existence' does not refer so much to persons' presence in the world as to their interrelations and to their peculiar nature. Kierkegaard appreciated that Descartes' mind-body dualism is more than an academic philosophical truth. It is the key to the human psyche. Not only philosophers, but also all persons know that they embody the union of irreconcilable opposites, of an animal body and of self-conscious soul. While believing that they possess divine freedom and immortality, persons are nevertheless aware of the limitations and inevitable death of their animal body. The illicit coming into that knowledge is, according to Kierkegaard, the real meaning of the Biblical myth of the Fall and the First Couple's ejection from the Garden of Eden. Because of that knowledge, which animals lack, humans are the only creatures that can be said to 'exist.'

One of the most important insights into that existence was provided by Kant's invocation of the concept of the two realms of the intelligible world of critical idealism and its epistemic dualism; namely the non-natural/moral realm with its free subjects and the natural/amoral realm with its unfree objects. Insofar as I exercise my faculty of pure practical reason, I belong to the non-natural/moral realm of the intelligible world. All my actions would be driven by my autonomous free will, and I could have willed otherwise. Insofar as I exercise my sensuous faculties, however, I belong to the natural/amoral realm of the intelligible world. All my actions would be driven by natural necessity, and it would make no sense to think that I could have willed otherwise.

Reconciliation of Ancient East Asian Philosophy with Critical Idealism. How can it be the case that, in accord with the canon of Kantian critical idealism, the *a priori* categories of pure practical and pure theoretical reason are shared by all human beings? Do not the seemingly incompatible differences between the metaphysical beliefs in which Western and East Asian philosophies are rooted prove otherwise? No; not necessarily, according to some students of the comparative aspects of these two philosophical systems. In their opinion, Buddha set off a

Copernican Revolution in East Asian Philosophy long before Kant made his Copernican Revolution in Western Philosophy, or even long before Copernicus himself made his eponymous, prototypical revolution in Astronomy.

The stimulus for Kant's development of his revolutionary philosophy of critical idealism had been the philosophical impasse created by the two rival Greek epistemological systems of materialism and idealism, which advocated diametrically opposed views about the nature of reality. And similarly, the stimulus for Buddha's development of his revolutionary philosophy of *Madhyamika* had been the philosophical impasse created by two rival Indian epistemological systems. One of them, the *Atma-Vada*, is the Indian analog of Aristotelian materialism. It holds that physical matter is the world's only essential reality, and that all being, processes, and phenomena can be accounted for as manifestations of matter. The other, the *Anatma-Vada*, is the Indian analog of Platonic idealism. It holds that the world's essential reality is transcendental, existing only as an idea of the human mind—in its consciousness and reason—and that there are no material substances with permanent, stable identities.

Buddha's *Madhyamika* and Kant's critical idealism agree in their conception of the main mission of philosophy, namely to provide a critique of human consciousness and reason, rather than to provide an account of the nature of reality. Thus, both Buddha's and Kant's systems may be considered as philosophies of philosophy—as reflective awareness of the working of philosophy. (Murti, T.R.V. 1960)

The Greek philosophers (and many of their modern ideological successors) believed that the origin of the incompatibility of our two alternative concepts of reality—materialism and idealism—is attributable to a conceptual error in one, or both, metaphysical systems. But as Kant showed in his *Critique of Pure Reason*, it is not a conceptual error but the intrinsically paradoxical nature of human reason itself that forestalls our development of a wholly consistent intelligible world.

Similarly, Buddha called attention to the paradoxical nature of human reason, by presenting a set of metaphysical problems, the *Avyakrta*, which he declared to be insoluble. That set included four unanswerable questions, which bear a striking resemblance to the four antinomies formulated by Kant more than two millennia later.

171

Buddha's *Avyakrta*

1. Does the world have both a beginning and an end in time, or only one or the other, or neither?
2. Is the world finite in space, or is it infinite?
3. Are body and soul one and the same thing, or are they different things?
4. Is there a Perfect Being who can know things as they really are and is immortal?

How did Buddha account for our inability to answering such seemingly reasonable questions about time and space, body and soul, and a Perfect Being? By attributing it to the incoherence of human reason, as manifest in its innate adherence to the two antithetical metaphysics of *Atma-Vada* and *Anatma-Vada* (i.e., of idealism and materialism).

But how can one account for the absence from the Far-Eastern Three Teachings of such key Western moral concepts as 'choice' and 'responsibility'? It does not follow, of course, from the lack of a developed language of choice and responsibility in a culture that its people fail to make morally relevant choices or are not judged praiseworthy or blameworthy for their actions. Surely, it did not escape Confucius' notice that in Ancient China some people behaved more righteously than did others. It also seems indubitable that—the concept of the Tao notwithstanding—Chinese people made morally relevant choices and were certainly punished for their blameworthy acts. The Confucian justification of punishment, however, is the utilitarian-behaviorist deterrence of future malfeasance, in contrast to the classical Greco-Judeo-Christian justification of punishment as the removal of a moral unbalance in the world due to the lack of retribution of past blameworthy actions. Most likely, the absence of such moral concepts as 'guilt,' 'repentance,' or 'retributive punishment' from the Three Teachings can be explained by the relative lack of cultivation in the Ancient Far East of the category of the morally autonomous person. (Fingarette, 1972)

Coda. Kant's basic idea that set off his Copernican Revolution in Philosophy was that our direct contact with the world is limited to a *sensible world* of phenomena that we perceive via our senses. To make sense of that phenomenal world we take it for granted that the sources of the phenomena we perceive are the real things-in-themselves, or *noumena*, of an *intelligible* world. To construct that intelligible world and its noumena, we interpret the phenomenal world in terms of two sets of *a priori* categories that inhere in our rational faculty. We use one set, which Kant called *pure theoretical reason*, to construct a natural/amoral realm of the intelligible world, whose noumena are natural objects governed by physical laws of determination. We use the other set, which Kant called *pure practical reason*, to construct a non-natural/moral realm, whose noumena are persons governed by moral laws of freedom. The two sets of *a priori* categories provide the basis for a theory of *epistemic dualism*, which can resolve the mind-body problem and the Paradox of Moral Responsibility.

ERASMUS OF ROTTERDAM (1466–1536)

Charcoal drawing by Albrecht Dürer (1520)

Chapter Eleven

Etiquette*

Manners. In Chapter 1, we adopted as the meaning of '*ethics*' the system of rules, or laws, devised for regulating human social behavior in conformance with the principles of right and wrong. We identified these principles with the set of categories of Kantian pure practical reason, designated collectively as '*morals*,' which includes duty, compassion, sacredness of the person, and free will.

There exists also another system of rules, known as '*etiquette*,' devised for regulating human social behavior, conformance with another set of categories of Kantian pure practical reason. That other set is referred to as '*manners*,' which includes such categories as *harmony*, *cultural coherence*, *beauty*, and *dignity of the person*. (Martin and Stent, 1990; 1992) Being concerned with neither moral responsibility nor free will, manners are not troubled by the Paradox of Moral Responsibility. Yet, hyperparadoxically, for that very reason etiquette plays only second fiddle to ethics, at least in the societies of the Western world.

Manners form part of the basic beliefs, wants, and interests that bring order to our social relations, just as do morals. In view of the considerable overlap between the aspects of the human condition to which morals and manners pertain, they do not represent two entirely different, conceptually clearly separable components of the ensemble of our fundamental beliefs, wants, and interests inherent in Kantian pure practical reason. Nonetheless, manners do differ from morals in at least two basic aspects:

1. Their domains of concern. Whereas morals tend to be concerned with social situations that involve matters of potentially grave consequences for life, limb, and property, manners tend to be concerned with situations of potentially less grave offenses against personal dignity, ritual, and the aesthetic sense.

*A substantial part of this chapter is based on the paper *I Think; Therefore I Thank*, by J. Martin and G. S. Stent (1990).

175

2. The psychological consequences of their violations. Whereas awareness of a violation of morals tends to engender feelings of *guilt* in the sinner, awareness of a violation of manners tends to arouse feelings of *shame* in the boor.

Origins of Etiquette. Archeological and historical records do not provide very clear indications as to just when etiquette first arose as a system of explicit but not legally binding rules intended to implement the innate categories of manners inherent in pure practical reason. It seems most likely, however, that the articulation of explicit rules of etiquette, just as the articulation of explicit rules of ethics, dates back some ten thousand years to the dawn of civilization. As we noted in Chapter 2, there would have been no need for the articulation of explicit rules of social intercourse before the agricultural-urban revolution of the late Stone Age before sedentary civilizations with their large settlements first arose in southwestern Asia. No doubt, prior to this change in the human condition there had already existed *some* rules that guided mannerly social relations, just as there had already existed *some* laws in conformance with the categories of morals. But as long as the horizon of human social life did not extend beyond the narrowly circumscribed group of the hunter-gatherer clan, these rules of proto-etiquette would have been tacitly known to and understood by all members of the clan.

Once people began to live in large urban settlements, however, and began dealing with strangers from a variety of clannish backgrounds, they would have encountered a diversity of systems of rules of social behavior. Though in isolation each system might have served the innate categories of manners, the resulting farrago of rules from different systems would most likely have been dysfunctional. So the need arose for an explicit codification of a single, consistent system of etiquette rules (as well as moral laws) regulating the social interactions of all the members of an urban community.

Noble Savage. Kant's eighteenth-century contemporary, the Geneva philosopher, Jean-Jacques Rousseau, interpreted the connection between the development of codified rules of social behavior and the rise of civilization in a way very different from that presented in the preceding paragraphs. As Rousseau saw it, the change in the human condition brought about by the agricultural-urban revolution had disastrous social consequences. According to him, human nature is intrinsically virtuous and mankind conducted itself admirably from the standpoint of morals and manners in its pre-civilization, 'natural' hunter-gatherer condition, when people were still 'noble savages.' To rephrase Rousseau's argument in the language of Kantian critical idealism, Rousseau asserted that mankind's naturally noble categories of pure practical reason became corrupted by the non-natural conditions of civilization. Hence Rousseau advocated that human virtue be restored to its original, pre-lapsarian state by abandoning civilization and returning to mankind's natural condition of the noble savage. The appeal of Rousseau's call for restoring human virtue by returning to a state of nature was limited to the European and American Romantic movements of the nineteenth and twentieth centuries, but it had little influence on the mainstream of Western moral philosophy.

Yet Rousseau was not totally mistaken in claiming that the advent of civilization did bring on dramatic changes in the human condition. But the way in which these changes were accommodated was not by going back to the status of the noble savage, but by formulating the system of explicit rules of social conduct represented by ethics and etiquette. For there can be no such thing as civilized living in their absence. Even those people who have a well-developed intuitive feeling for morals and manners cannot navigate through a complex civilized society by untutored social instinct alone, that is, by reliance on their 'human nature.'

History of Etiquette. In predynastic Egypt and archaic Greece, etiquette was certainly in place by the fortieth century BCE. Yet, even though rules of mannerly conduct are of high antiquity, their designation as 'etiquette'—whose etymological origin is the Old French verb *estiqu(i)er* (to stick)—dates back only to the seventeenth century court of Louis XIV at Versailles. There the Sun King frequently changed the rules of courtly behavior, to shame those nobles who did not trouble to come to Versailles often enough to keep up with the *comme-il-faut comportement du jour*, by figuratively sticking an *étiquet* (sticker) on them that labeled them as unmannerly country bumpkins.

The essential differences in the social roles of these two parallel systems—ethics and etiquette—were not explicitly emphasized by the ancient Mediterranean and East Asian sages at the dawn of moral philosophy, whom we considered in Chapter 3. Insofar as Socrates, Plato, or Aristotle paid any attention to this distinction, they regarded etiquette of much lesser importance for the guidance of social behavior than ethics. The ancient Greeks managed to bequeath their lack of interest in etiquette to our postmodern, be-yourself-and do-your-own-thing Western societies.

The distinction between ethics and etiquette seemed to be of equally little interest to the Athenians' coeval Chinese philosopher, Confucius. However, in contrast to the Greeks, Confucius' interest was focussed more on etiquette than on ethics, since he considered morals of lesser importance than manners in the regulation of social behavior. For unlike the way personhood is perceived from the Greco-Judeo-Christian viewpoint, Confucianism does not regard the person as sacred by virtue of her possession, within herself and independently of other persons, of a piece of the divine, namely an immortal soul. Instead, the central concern of Confucianism is the blossoming of humanity in its ceremonial acts. Confucius managed to pass on his relative lack of interest in ethics to present-day East Asian societies. (Fingarette, 1972) We will consider Confucius' views on etiquette in more detail after we have clarified our present understanding of the philosophical standing of manners.

Changing Rules of Etiquette. It seems odd that in view of Socrates' evergreen question 'How should one live?' Western philosophers have shown so little interest in etiquette. [The 150-page index of the 8-volume, 4,000-page *Encyclopedia of Philosophy* edited by Paul Edwards and published in 1967 contains no entry under either rubric of 'etiquette' or 'manners.'] As heirs of the Greek founders of moral philosophy, one might have expected Western philosophers to remain concerned with the quest for the virtuous life, where 'virtuous' refers to good social behavior in general and not merely righteous moral conduct.

This lack of attention to etiquette by Western philosophers is regrettable. Being a complex system requiring contextually dependent judgments rather than a set of simple, rule-ordained routines, etiquette is a subtle discipline. Moreover, the work of an etiquette expert is never done, because the rules of etiquette keep on changing. Usually, those changes occur slowly, since etiquette is essentially conservative, as are the law, religion and language—all of which must take into account the inertia of the beliefs of their constituencies due to emotional ties to tradition. But sometimes changes in the rules of etiquette are very abrupt, especially when radically novel social philosophies are installed.

Such abrupt changes did occur at the times of the American and French Revolutions, when the etiquette of the Court of St. James and of the *Ancien Régime* at Versailles intended for aristocratic courtiers was obviously unsuitable for their republican successors. Thus, the Founding Fathers of the United States faced some (still unresolved) problems about the design of etiquette suitable for a democratic society. These problems arise from the tensions inherent in such antithetical desiderata of manners as dignity and obeisance, ceremony and efficiency, or comfort and good taste. The questions that the Founding Fathers had to address included the following:

1. Is obeisance to distinction by personal achievement any less offensive than obeisance to distinction by birth?
2. How can rules of conduct in the workplace acknowledge the professional hierarchy, from apprentice to master, without implying subservience?
3. Must the lowest, crudest styles of conduct necessarily serve as the norm, or can one aim at a higher, more refined general standard of deportment?

Etiquette as a Regulative System. How do etiquette and law differ as systems for the regulation of social behavior? Both systems prescribe conduct in the interest of community harmony. But while the law addresses violations of ethics, the first purpose of etiquette is to reduce personal antagonisms and thus to avert conflict, just as the first purpose of diplomacy is to avert war. Thus the law handles conflicts threatening life or property that etiquette has failed to avert. In accord with this division of labor, the law dispenses fierce sanctions for violations of its rules, such as fines, corporal punishment, imprisonment and loss of life. Meanwhile, etiquette handles all those conflicts that can be controlled by restraints for which voluntary compliance is usually obtainable without the threat of fierce sanctions.

That is why etiquette restricts freedom of expression more than does the law. Much of what people would say if they expressed their thoughts and feelings indiscriminately would be highly provocative to others and the cause of social disharmony. It is within my legal right to tell you that you are ugly, or that your baby is, but such locution is likely to lead to ugly—which is to say, dangerous—behavior. Etiquette rejects the latter-day encounter group, rap-session theory of social harmony, which seeks to clear the air by frankly expressing one's every thought and feeling. Instead, by proscribing the voicing of offensive, albeit sincerely held opinions, etiquette reduces the need for lawsuits charging slander and libel.

The only sanction available to etiquette for non-compliance with its rules is *shame*. In that regard, etiquette resembles international law, which, like etiquette, depends on voluntary compliance (by sovereign states rather than individuals) and, in case of non-compliance, can only resort to shame as its sanction, short of retaliation by acts of war. Even shame is merely a voluntary sanction, since it requires the collusion of righteous shamers and self-effacing shamees. In fact, etiquette may even demand *not* invoking the only sanction available to it, as set forth in the Golden Maxim of Manners promulgated in the sixteenth century by the Dutch humanist, Erasmus of Rotterdam, in his *De Civilitate* (one of the few etiquette books ever written by a philosopher). According to Erasmus, "It is part of the highest civility if, while never erring yourself, you ignore the errors of others."

The breadth of the general subscription to manners is demonstrated by the fact that even people most devoted to lawlessness—those with the least developed sense of law and order—still believe that others should treat *them* courteously. For instance, it is not unusual on Los Angeles freeways for motorists to shoot at strangers in other cars. To justify their mayhem, the gunslingers cite violations of traffic etiquette by their targets as sufficient provocation (not responding promptly to a signal requesting permission to pass, or not ceding the right of way, or forcing the assailant to slow down by pulling in front of his car). Thus they plead that they were merely upholding the standards of highway etiquette by punishing its violators.

Social Regulation of Smoking. Changes in the social regulation of smoking exemplify the historical give-and-take between etiquette and the law. The task of separating smokers from non-smokers used to be accomplished quite satisfactorily by the rules of etiquette. In addition to such devices as smoking rooms and smoking jackets to protect non-smokers from exposure to smoke there was a smoking ban during dinner. After dinner, the non-smokers (a.k.a. ladies) repaired to the drawing room, while smokers (a.k.a. gentlemen) enjoyed their cigars. But when smoking became com-

GUIDANCE OF HUMAN SOCIAL BEHAVIOR

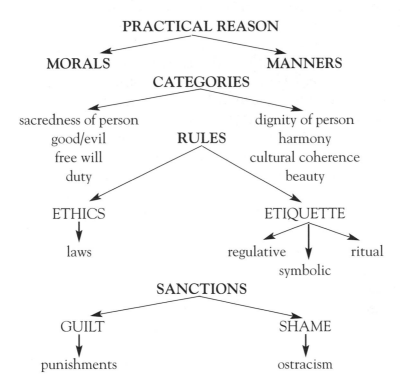

PRACTICAL REASON

MORALS   MANNERS

CATEGORIES

sacredness of person   dignity of person
good/evil   RULES   harmony
free will   cultural coherence
duty   beauty

ETHICS   ETIQUETTE

laws   regulative   ritual

symbolic

SANCTIONS

GUILT   SHAME

punishments   ostracism

mon to both sexes, etiquette turned uncharacteristically lax and allowed the will of the smoking majority abrogate the rights of the non-smoking minority. Not only did the rules change to permit smoking almost everywhere, but also they even required that the formal table setting include little cigarette urns and ashtrays for the diners' *ad libitum* use.

Only recently have non-smokers managed to change the rules back, so that it has again come to be considered rude to smoke near non-smokers without first seeking their wholehearted agreement. However, a declining recognition of the need to obey etiquette when it goes against one's personal wishes made enforcement of these rules difficult. Smokers who refused to comply voluntarily with the new rules incensed non-smokers, not only because of the involuntary continued exposure of non-smokers to smoke, but also because of the galling refusal of smokers to observe the new etiquette. The offended non-smokers began to treat the offending (rude) smokers rudely in turn, abandoning other rules of etiquette that forbid insulting others, criticizing their personal habits, and announcing that they are about to die. It was at this impasse that the law took over from etiquette, because medical findings that smoke inhaled indirectly by non-smokers may be injurious to their health made the conflict sufficiently serious to merit the law's attention. More and more laws restricting the freedom of smokers were passed, regulating (or forbidding altogether) smoking in virtually all public places, such as aircraft, restaurants, and offices. Smoking in the private realm remains an unregulated grand melee, however.

Etiquette and the Administration of Law. The example of smoking shows that the law can be said to exist to compensate for the failure of etiquette. If we had perfect obeisance to etiquette, we would not need the law. So one might suppose that once the law takes over, etiquette should retreat gracefully from the scene.

Wrong! The law cannot be administered justly without etiquette. The etiquette of jurisprudence, governing proper behavior in the courtroom, is extremely strict, just as it is in other professions that must deal with strongly felt conflicts—parliament, the military, the Church, athletics. In all of them, strict adherence is required to rules that specify how one dresses, when and where one sits or stands, how one moves, and how one acknowledges superiors. Such rigor is necessary because the more orderly the form of a social structure, the more conflict it can support. Etiquette requires participants in adversary proceedings to present their opposing views in a restrained manner, to provide a disciplined and respectful ambience in which to settle conflicts peacefully. Everybody knows what is meant by the statement "My distinguished colleague seems to be unfortunately misinformed," but this polite circumlocution permits the proceedings to continue, rather than to have them interrupted by a fistfight set off by direct locution ("You're lying, you bastard!").

The dependence on etiquette of the just administration of law was demonstrated dramatically in the 1960s, at the trials of the Chicago Seven and the Black Panthers. Here the defendants deliberately defied the rules of courtroom etiquette—addressing the judge by his first name, wearing judicial robes, putting their feet on tables and chairs, speaking out of turn, shouting, swearing, and not behaving very nicely in general. The judges sought to establish order in the courtroom, using the weapon of contempt of court, ordering the defendants manacled and gagged, and having them removed from the courtroom altogether. But these judicial remedies, in turn, violated the judges' explicit Constitutional commitment to conducting a fair trial, at which the defendant has the right to be present and in a condition that is not prejudicial to the jury's findings.

Which is more important, we may ask, the defendants' constitutional right to attend their own trial or mere courtroom etiquette? On appeal, the United States Supreme Court found in favor of etiquette: A misbehaving defendant may be removed from the courtroom. From this ruling it does not follow, of course, that etiquette is more important than the Constitution. But adherence to etiquette is a prerequisite for any aspect of civilized life, including jurisprudence.

Etiquette as a Symbolic System. Along with its regulative functions, etiquette serves as a system of symbols, whose meanings provide predictability in social relations, especially among strangers. Examples of the symbolic function include the rules governing greeting, eating, dressing, and restraining bodily functions. Some detractors of etiquette ground their disdain for it in the commonsense notion that a rule of etiquette is silly if it cannot be directly, obviously, logically, and functionally justified. (An example of such an allegedly silly rule is that which requires an RSVP to be composed in the third person if the invitation addressed the invitee in the third person). But inasmuch as the essence of a symbolic system is that its symbols refer to something other than themselves and that the relation between a symbol and the thing that it stands for is more often than not arbitrary, many rules of etiquette cannot be given a direct functional justification). Hence the rules of etiquette are not simply a matter of common sense. They have to be learned rather than deduced from first principles.

Once learned and correctly interpreted, the symbols of etiquette allow one person to recognize such essential attributes of other persons as their intentions, status, friendliness, or hostility, and thus to deal appropriately with a wide range of social situations and relationships. It is essential, therefore, that children be taught the meaning of the symbols of etiquette (rather than telling children simply to 'act naturally'), so that they will know what to expect of others and how their own behavior is going to be interpreted. The child who grows up taking literally a statement such as 'Please make yourself at home,' or using the same language and attitude towards teachers as towards playmates, is going to have a rough life.

Another reason for the demand of strict etiquette in the law courts, in the military, and in the Church and athletics is that compliance with the rules of conduct is taken to symbolize adherence to the particular values that these professions require, such as fairness, respect, obedience, valor, or piety. Such symbolic expressions of adherence to shared values may be insincere, of course, since it is possible to lie just as well by means of non-linguistic symbols as by means of words. There is no incentive like the desire to get a job or a verdict of 'not guilty' for making people recognize the wisdom of following the conventions of dress and behavior rather than their personal choices or 'natural' inclinations. The well-dressed, soft-spoken grandmother is a more effective anti-war agitator than the unkempt, obscenity-spouting youth.

People benefit their society by a mannerly symbolic affirmation of their adherence to shared social values. This should be contrasted with the damage done by those social misfits who take it onto themselves to violate a rule of etiquette because they have their own good reasons for ignoring what they consider a piece of nonsense or deny that they have reason to do 'what's done.' Such violations of the rules of etiquette give offense, because they are necessarily interpreted as overt defiance of, or an indifference to, or an antagonism toward, the interests of the community. The person who disregards her hosts' expectations about what time or in what kind of attire she will arrive for a party is signifying disdain for their standards as much as the person who refuses to stand up when the national anthem is sung.

There is ideologically motivated civil disobedience of etiquette just as there is of law. But people who mean to change the values of the community for its own supposed benefit by such actions must be prepared to accept the punitive consequences of their defiance. They would be well advised to violate only the rule that offends them, carefully adhering to other conventions, if they do not wish to have their protest interpreted as a general disdain for other people.

Etiquette as a Ritual System. There can be few people left nowadays, even among hard-core materialists, who would deny that mankind cannot live by bread alone. Not many people would question the legitimacy of the sacred and its aesthetic as a means to satisfy those spiritual needs that make us distinctly human and transcend the physical needs that we share with the animals. Nevertheless, it is not widely appreciated that in our own enlightened industrialized societies ritual still plays a central role in the satisfaction of those spiritual needs. Many people have nothing but scorn for their own, familiar rituals, which they reject as silly. At the same time, they wax enthusiastic about preserving the integrity of the strange customs and folklore of the jungle dwellers of the Upper Amazon, which they find full of wonderful significance. Or, while they may adore the rain dance of the Hopi Indians, they may refuse to participate in their parents' holiday dinner traditions. It is in its role as a system for the codification of ritual in the service of the sacred that etiquette has yet a third function, in addition to its regulative and symbolic functions.

By way of two examples of etiquette's codification of ritual, we may consider funerals and weddings. Rather than leaving it to individuals as a do-it-yourself project to work out how to come to terms with their chaotic feeling on such momentously emotional social occasions, the ritual codified in etiquette facilitates this process and, additionally, provides for a sense of social cohesiveness and sharing of our humanity.

In the lives of most people, even of those who do not usually trouble themselves with good manners, a wedding is one occasion at which they acknowledge a desire to do 'what's done.' This leads them to buy etiquette books, hire wedding consultants, and accept etiquette advice from such wedding-industry tradespeople as caterers and photographers. Sometimes conflicting customs cause difficulties in fitting the circumstances of the families of bride and groom into the general pattern of the marriage ritual. Yet there derive obvious emotional benefits from the use of a traditional wedding ceremony to ease accommodation to the strange idea that two people and their families who have been strangers hitherto suddenly become relatives.

The problem posed by death—how can someone whom one knew only yesterday as a living person is today no more than a hunk of decaying organic tissue?—remains as deep an existential puzzle as ever. Yet funeral rites, in contrast to the extravagantly elaborate wedding rites, are now often improvised. As a reaction against nineteenth-century conventions of mourning, which restricted the clothing and behavior of a large circle of mourners long after the demise of the deceased and regardless of the depth of their emotional bereavement, mourning etiquette has been largely abandoned. With no outward signs (such as black garments, black wreaths on doors, or black-bordered writing paper) to warn others of the mourner's vulnerability and no customs of seclusion from society, the bereaved are unprotected against the demand of normal social life, which they may be unable to handle. Indeed, the bereaved are often encouraged to plunge into social situations where joviality is expected—and yet, just as often, are deemed heartless when they succeed in behaving as if nothing had happened. Etiquette's codifying behavior under bereavement allows a period of readjustment safe from prying judgments of others, as well as from normal social expectations.

Natural and Positive Etiquette. Two different kinds of etiquette rules can be distinguished. One kind are 'natural' rules and the other kind are 'positive' rules—just as the philosophy of law distinguishes between a 'natural law' and a 'positive law.' The rules of natural etiquette and natural law *could not be* otherwise, while the rules of positive etiquette and positive law are conventional, or arbitrary, and *could be* otherwise. For instance, a rule of natural (traffic) law is: 'Vehicles moving in opposite directions travel on *opposite* sides of the road.' This rule is 'natural' because its contrary ('Vehicles moving in opposite directions travel on the *same* side of the road') would lead to traffic chaos. Another version of this rule ('All automobiles travel on their driver's *right* hand side of the road') is a 'positive' rule because its contrary ('All vehicles travel on their driver's *left* hand side of the road') works perfectly well in England, except for visitors from the Continent.

[It should be noted that in this section the term *'natural'* is used in a sense different from that in which it is used in all other parts of this essay, where it denotes 'being in accordance with the laws or ordinary course of nature.' This confusing divergent semantic use of the same word is regrettable but unavoidable since the terms 'positive law' and 'natural law' are standard locutions in the philosophy of law.]

A natural rule of ritual etiquette is 'Behave respectfully in a sacred place of worship.' This rule is natural because its contrary (that is, 'Feel free to behave disrespectfully in a sacred place of worship') would be incompatible with having any sacred places of worship, and hence irrational. Two mutually incompatible (and hence obviously conventional) positive transforms of this natural rule are 'Uncover your head when in a place of worship' (man in church) and 'Cover your head when in a place of worship' (man in synagogue).

By way of another example, let us consider the 'ladies-first' rule of symbolic etiquette. It is often assumed that this rule, which contemporary feminists find offensive and seek to relegate to the trashcan of outdated customs, has always existed as a non-negotiable tenet of European (as opposed to Asian) etiquette. But it is only one of the rules of positive etiquette, not of natural etiquette, and therefore subject to gradual change. In fact, the 'ladies-first' rule did not always exist and, from the women's point of view, was a great improvement over its fifth-century Greek predecessor, 'ladies-never.' Moreover, the rule applies only to the private world, where the differences between ladies and gentlemen may be highly relevant for their activities, and not to the workaday world, where rational business practice demands not making gender distinctions. Precedence in the workaday world is by professional standing, not gender. The new rule is 'CEOs-first,' rather than 'ladies first.' We are now slowly headed toward a new system of positive rules of precedence in the private world, according to which age, rather than gender, is likely to be the determinative factor. This would resolve the conflict between the regulative and the symbolic functions of the 'ladies-first' rule in favor of the former.

Is Etiquette a Social Evil? Some people believe that etiquette is frivolous, or snobbish, or repressive—unworthy of serious attention except perhaps as a social evil. One reason for that belief appears to be the demand of etiquette for hypocritical concealment of one's true feelings towards others. That is to say, by asking people to pretend to have higher moral qualities than they actually have, etiquette is perceived as a subversive force that subverts the Kantian categorical imperative of truth telling. But, as we already noted, despite their dignity and plausibility, the categorical imperative does not generate rules that can be universally applied to all situations without conflict. Here is another self-referential paradox:

> There is only one rule that *never* has to yield precedence to any other rule to reach a valid moral judgment, namely the rule that there is no such rule.

For instance, there is no *a priori* reason why, to reach the greater Good in some social situations, the imperative of truth telling should not yield to etiquette's imperative of hypocritical conduct, if the promotion of justice and of harmonious personal relations is at stake. There are many people who feel morally justified by the imperative of truth telling to make remarks that etiquette has always categorized as insults ('You're too fat'; 'You ought to get married'). But few of the targets of such remarks would agree that these insults represent the correct choice between the conflicting virtues of truth telling and mannerly behavior.

Another reason for the belief in etiquette as a social evil is the idea that it is used mainly as an instrument of oppression—a tool of elitism. This view should not come naturally to many philosophers, among whom, ever since Plato, the ideal of an intellectual elite has ever been popular. Thus Erasmus pointed out in his *De Civilitate* that it is exactly the people risen to leadership, thanks to their own intellectual merit, who ought to set the highest standards of social conduct.

General rudeness, or the lack of obeisance to etiquette, is much more of a burden to the poor than to the rich, who can usually pay for special treatment and buy their way out of any trouble caused by their own rude behavior. The Duc de Lévis' 200-year-old injunction

noblesse oblige!

expresses etiquette's demand that the rich not only avoid taking advantage of the poor, but that the rich actually treat the poor more considerately than their own peers. One of the most heinous crimes known to etiquette is being rude to a subservient person, such as an employee, who is not in a position to respond in kind. Etiquette considers such behavior far more reprehensible than rudeness toward a peer or superior.

Ethics and Etiquette as a Continuum. The sets of imperatives derived from morals and manners for the sake of bringing order into our existence are not the totally separate systems for the regulation of social relations that some philosophers make them out to be. In fact, there seems to be little point in trying to draw the line of demarcation between them. Ethics and regulative etiquette form a continuum of imperatives whose metric is the gravity of the consequences of their willful violations. Ethics lies towards that end of the continuum where the consequences of violations, such as murder, are most grave. Many imperatives of ethics are embodied in laws established by authority of a sovereign legislator, with severe, usually formally stipulated penalties as sanctions and retributions provided for violations. A highly structured judicial system exists for administering the law and resolving cases where the legal system leads to conflicting imperatives.

Symbolic etiquette lies towards the other end of the continuum, where the consequences of violations, such as disgusting others by one's way of eating, are least grave. Many imperatives of etiquette are part of an oral tradition and usually owe their definitive formulation to writers of etiquette books. There are no formally stipulated penalties for violation, with shame and social ostracism as the only sanctions. There is no formal system for administering etiquette, and the resolution of conflicts arising from its rules is in the hands of self-appointed arbitrators who also decree new rules of etiquette. Nevertheless, it is as true for etiquette as it is for ethics (and the law) that in the long run, its rules can prevail only with the consent of the governed—that is, the rules must be rationally connectable with the *a priori* categories of morals and manners. Between these extremes of the continuum, in its middle range, where the consequences of violations, such as offending the dignity of a person, are of an intermediate gravity, there is a broad region where ethics and etiquette overlap.

Confucianism and Etiquette. As noted in Chapter 3, Confucianism is a secular prescriptive system of rules for the establishment of harmonious social relations. Confucius was concerned not merely with communal order but also with human dignity, as well as with a culture that was founded in a sense of the beautiful, the noble, and the sacred as distinctive dimensions of the human existence. The guiding principle that leads to the attainment of these harmonious relations is a Sacred Way of Life, the *Tao of Humanism*. It is concerned with the political order and the practical life of the person and deals with the problems inherent in human social relationships, by demanding adherence to man-made (rather than divinely ordained) social norms and moral precepts.

[It should be remembered that, according to a parallel Chinese tradition, there is also another Sacred Way of Life, namely, the *Tao of Nature* of Lao Tzu's Taoism, whose main function is guidance of the peoples' inner lives rather than of their social relations. Since its precepts are based on the fundamental premise that mankind is part of nature and that, therefore, its life must follow the way of natural phenomena, it has little relevance for any discussion of etiquette, except by way of serving as a counterexample.]

The Confucian *Tao of Humanism* may be regarded as a combination of the two kinds of categories of pure practical reason—morals and manners—whence the rules of both ethics and etiquette are derived. This analogy is strengthened by the constant recurrence in the Confucian *Analects* of two themes related to the *Tao of Humanism*. One theme is *li*, often rendered in English as a combination of 'etiquette' and 'ritual,' since it specifies the manners, social graces, and show of sympathy that promotes harmony in interpersonal relations. Thus the *Analects'* exposition of *li* anticipated by six centuries the Christian Gospels' Golden Rule (Matthew 7:12) in quoting Confucius as having said

"What you do not want done onto yourself, do not do unto others."

According to the *Analects*, formally correct conduct is honorable only if it is the result of a sense of virtue inculcated by observing suitable models of deportment, such as those provided in theatrical performances, rather than having been compelled. Thus, *li* appears to be a rough equivalent of the category of manners.

The other theme frequently mentioned in the *Analects* is *jen*, which is usually rendered as 'virtue' and would appear to be the equivalent of the category of morals. The identification of *jen* with morals is further supported by the *Analects'* subdivision of *jen* into two further components, namely *chung*, which is usually rendered in English as 'conscientiousness,' and *shu*, which denotes obligations entailed by familial-social relationships.

This then is the essence of Confucius' perspective of *li*:

> I see you on the street; I smile, walk toward you, and put out my hand to shake yours. And behold—without any command, stratagem, force, special tricks or tools, without any effort on my part to make you do so, you spontaneously turn toward me, return my smile, raise your hand toward mine. We shake hands spontaneously.

Coda. Ethics and etiquette form a single, albeit highly complex—and by no means contradiction-free—system of rules of regulation of social conduct. Despite the prevalence of rule conflicts in actual situations, the imperatives of ethics and etiquette all take the unconditional form characteristic of the Kantian categorical imperative, namely, 'you ought to do Y.' This is the case because the reason-giving force of the oughts of etiquette, no less than that of the oughts of ethics, devolves rationally from fundamental normative wants and interests to which we subscribe simply because we are human beings. In view of its source, the ethics-etiquette system is essential for the practical and spiritual aspects of civilized life. Were morals and manners to fall by the wayside, civilization would disappear.

KONRAD LORENZ (1903–1989)   JEAN PIAGET (1896–1980)

Chapter Twelve

—⟫◆⟪—

Evolutionary and Genetic Epistemology*

Pure Reason and Nietzsche's Will to Power. Kant's critical idealism presents us with a puzzle. How can it be that the intelligible world with its noumena of our own construction seems to provide us with such a fabulously workable understanding of the phenomena of the sensible world, if the categories of pure reason existed in our mind *a priori*? After all, there are so many dysfunctional notions that our pure reason *might* have brought to the sensible world *a priori*. Space might have been one-dimensional; time might have been multidimensional; and things might change without cause. So it seems like a miracle that everything has been working out so well for us. Admittedly, if we follow Kant all the way and accept his argument on behalf of the existence of God, we might be satisfied with a simple, non-natural answer. It was He who had arranged for that concordance of our pure reason with the world that He made when He created us in His image.

But just in case we are *not* satisfied with such deistic handwaving, we could consider an alternative natural explanation that Friedrich Nietzsche offered in the latter part of the nineteenth century. (Nietzsche, 1883). He proposed that pure reason is simply a product of our mode of existence, and that our mind's origin can be accounted for in terms of what he believed to be a fundamental principle driving the evolution of the species. According to that principle, the salient traits of any species arose as stratagems for facilitating that species' dealings with the world.

And *how*, in the course of evolution, did we acquire our salient trait of pure reason and its *a priori* categories? According to Nietzsche, it was by inheriting a *will to power* from our ancestors, which drives us to acquire knowledge about the world. And how did our ancestors acquire *their* will to power in the first place? They acquired it *a posteriori* from their interactions with the phenomenal world. Did they acquire it by the natural se-

*A substantial part of this chapter is based on Chapter 9 of *Max Delbrück's Mind from Matter?* Stent, G.S., et al., editors (1986).

lection mechanism that Darwin proposed in 1859 in his *Origin of Species* twenty-five years before Nietzsche developed his theory of the will to power? No, not according to Nietzsche, who was of the opinion that Darwin greatly exaggerated the role of natural selection in evolution. What Darwin did not realize—so Nietzsche claimed—was that the essential thing in life processes is precisely the 'creative force' (that is, the will to power), working from within us, which *utilizes* and *exploits* (rather being *determined* by) external circumstances. Thus, according to Nietzsche's argument, the *a priori* categories that our pure reason brings to the sensible world arose *a posteriori* as a *direct* and *heritable* cognitive acquisition by interaction with the phenomena of the sensible world. Nietzsche's view of the origin of hereditary variation in evolution was therefore Lamarckian (that is, based on the erroneous thesis of Kant's French contemporary and original founder of the theory of evolution, Jean Baptiste Lamarck, that evolution was driven by the inheritance of acquired traits).

Evolutionary Epistemology. It took another sixty years after Nietzsche's proposal until a truly Darwinian explanation was provided for the baffling origin of our Kantian *a priori* categories of pure reason. By what seems like an uncanny coincidence, this explanation was presented in 1944 as the subject of the inaugural dissertation of a successor of Kant to the Chair of Philosophy in the University of Königsberg (of which Kant had been the first incumbent). That successor was Konrad Lorenz, one of the founders of the evolutionarily based study of animal behavior. The bottom line of Lorenz's explanation was "what is *a priori* for the individual is *a posteriori* for his species" (Lorenz, 1944), reminiscent of Nietzsche's much earlier Lamarckian solution but grounded in more modern evolutionary and genetic principles.

Lorenz proposed that the worldly success of our *a priori* categories of pure reason is simply another product of the Darwinian natural selection process that guided our entire evolutionary history. According to Lorenz, any early hominids whose hereditarily determined cerebral neuronal network happened to generate *a priori* such categorical ideas as before coming later than after, or near being more remote than far, or changes having no causes, left no descendants to whom to pass on such dysfunctional notions. Lorenz's Darwinian explanation of the origins of the Kantian categories gave rise to a discipline at the interface between biology and philosophy styled *evolutionary epistemology*. (Campbell, 1974; Vollmer, 1975)

Brain Evolution. Let us grant then, that, as supporters of Aristotelian monism would have it (and as supporters of Kantian epistemic dualism would have no reason to deny), mental states *are* brain states. Then it would follow that, in line with the dogma of evolutionary epistemology, the human brain is hereditarily endowed with the set of innate mental states representing pure reason. One subset of the innate mental states of pure reason would include the categories of pure theoretical reason that were selected by evolution for providing the construction of the noumena of the natural/amoral realm of material objects of the intelligible world. Another subset of the innate mental states of pure reason would include the categories of pure practical reason that were selected by evolution for providing the construction of the noumena of the non-natural/moral realm of human subjects of the intelligible world.

Accounting for the evolutionary origins of the human brain poses no greater conceptual difficulties than accounting for the evolutionary origins of any other organ of the human body, say of its liver. The human brain is obviously an elaboration of the brain of some ancestral species of fish that lived a hundred or so million years ago. That fish's brain, in turn, was an elaboration of the nervous system of an ancestral jellyfish which lived about five hundred million years ago. That ancestral jelly-fish's nervous system was already capable of performing such basic brain functions of interpreting signals taken in by sensory receptors from the environment and commanding movements that are appropriate responses to environmental changes.

The brain of vertebrate animals became more and more elaborate in the course of its evolutionary history. It came to be composed of more and more nerve cells and the network linking these cells became more and more complex. As a result, the brain of vertebrates gained the capacity to perform more and more sophisticated functions, culminating in mankind's well-known fabulous intelligence. In line with Darwinian principles, this evolutionary development towards an ever-more complex brain would have been driven by natural selection, which allowed ever-cleverer animals to be fruitful and multiply in previously vacant ecological niches.

Macrocosm, Mesocosm, and Microcosm. The sensible realm of the world of phenomena, to which our mental states became adapted in the course of human evolution, represents but a tiny sliver of the whole world. It merely comprises those phenomena in the ecological niche of *Homo sapiens* whose dimensions in time and space make them accessible to our direct sensory perception and, moreover, are commensurate with phenomena manifested by our own bodies. This domain of the phenomenal world is referred to as the *mesocosm*. Its scales of time and length range roughly from the 1-second human heartbeat period to the 100,000 second day/night cycle and from the 0.1 mm thickness of a human hair to the 10,000,000 mm distance to the horizon of a human observer standing at the seashore. Beyond the mesocosm lie the *macrocosm*, extending outward to the stars and their galaxies, and the *microcosm*, extending inward to the atoms and their subatomic particles. (Vollmer, 1984). Mankind became aware of the macrocosmic and microcosmic domains of the phenomenal world only upon the rise of modern science. And that rise took place merely during the last 0.1 percent of the approximately 100,000 years that lapsed since the first appearance of *Homo sapiens* on the terrestrial scene.

The terms 'macrocosm' and 'microcosm' actually date back to Pre-Socratic Greek philosophers of the sixth century BCE, who used them with a meaning rather different from that adopted by the evolutionary epistemologists of the twentieth century CE. By 'macrocosm' the Pre-Socratics meant the world as a whole and by 'microcosm' the ensemble of elements (including living creatures) of which the macrocosm is composed. According to the Pre-Socratics, the structure of the elements of the microcosm reflects, or mirrors, the structure of the macrocosm. The Pre-Socratics did not use the term 'mesocosm,' which, from our present perspective, encompasses what *they* called 'macrocosm' *and* 'microcosm.'

When, in the waning years of the nineteenth century, astronomers and physicists began to study phenomena that lie outside the mesocosmic domain, an incredible fact came to light. It turned out that some of the categories of Kantian pure theoretical reason fail us when we address phenomena in the microcosmic and macrocosmic domains. On second thought, however, this failure of our categorical intuition *outside* the mesocosmic domain is accounted for by evolutionary epistemology just as well as is its success *within* it.

Thus, according to the doctrine of evolutionary epistemology, it is the phenomena of the mesocosm with which our sensory organs and our reason cope and to the verbal description of which our language, as well as our Kantian pure theoretical reason, is adapted. So it should not come as a total surprise that we have to discard, or at least modify drastically our categorical intuitions of pure theoretical reason when our scientific studies move beyond the mesocosm to the microcosmic or macrocosmic domains. This is the case, of course, when we seek to fathom the structure of the tiny atom and its function or of the vast universe and its history. In other words, our innate Kantian categories of pure theoretical reason do not serve us all that well, or may even be fundamentally inadequate, when we apply them to the microcosmic and macrocosmic domains.

Classical Physics. From the beginnings of science in classical antiquity until the turn of the twentieth century it was assumed tacitly—and asserted explicitly by Descartes in his *Principles of Philosophy*—that the natural world has the same structure throughout the Universe. In particular, it was taken for granted that the invisible microcosm of the atoms (postulated by Democritus in the fifth century BCE) and the visible macrocosm of the stars are governed by the same natural laws as the mesocosm. Although this assumption seemed eminently reasonable, by the turn of the twentieth century it had been shown to be wrong. As it turned out, the structures of the macrocosm and microcosm have some properties that make them qualitatively (and not merely quantitatively) different from structures in the mesocosm.

Kant was (excusably) unaware that it is only for the phenomena of the mesocosmic domain of the sensible world that the *a priori* categories of pure theoretical reason provide such a remarkably serviceable explanatory account. That is why he had (mistakenly) declared that the seventeenth-century physics of Isaac Newton (whose strict validity is limited to the mesocosm) is a *universal* truth and that the geometry of Euclid (which is only one of several possible geometries) reflects the *true* structure of space. The physics that were developed to account for the phenomena of the mesocosm came to be known as '*classical physics,*' of which Galileo's *and* Newton's theories are the paradigmatic examples.

Relativity Theory. One of the first contraventions of classical physics was Albert Einstein's development in 1905 of his *relativity theory*, which tampered with the categories of time and space of Kantian pure theoretical reason. The point of departure of Einstein's relativity theory was a then recent, to physicists very surprising, discovery by Albert Michelson and Edward Morley. They had found that the speed of propagation of light is the same [namely 3×10^8 m/sec] for all observers, regardless of their own motion relative to the light flow. Einstein attributed the inconsistency of this fact with our intuitive concept of relative motion to our evidently false intuition that the flow of time is absolute, i.e. independent of how it is observed. So he developed a theory of relative motion—later designated as the *'special theory of relativity'*—which does not invoke the concept of an absolute flow of time. Instead, Einstein's theory posits that the time of occurrence of an event depends on the frame of reference of the event's observer, so that there does not exist just one universal, or pancosmic time, but many times, to each observer his own. Einstein thus dissolved the intuitive conceptual independence of space and time.

In 1916, Einstein presented another counterintuitive theory, which he called the *general theory of relativity* and whose purpose was to fathom the nature of gravity. Here Einstein actually replaced a counterintuitive idea of *classical* physics; namely that gravitational attraction is a force that acts instantaneously at a distance in three-dimensional space, by another, even more counterintuitive idea. According to Einstein's general theory of relativity, a massive material body produces a curvature in a *four-dimensional* space (for which *time* provides the fourth dimension). That curvature is the equivalent of a gravitational field, in that the path taken by a moving object is determined by the field's curvature.

When Einstein announced his general theory of relativity, the physics community generally rejected it, because it seemed impossible to fathom the counterintuitive concepts on which the general theory depended, such as space characterized by four dimensions and by non-Euclidean geometric relations. (A geometry is designated as 'non-Euclidean' if it omits or modifies one or more of the axioms of Euclidean geometry, such as the axiom that disallows the intersection of parallel lines or the axiom that disallows the existence of triangles whose angles sum to more than 180°.) In Chapter 14 we will encounter some other examples of counterintuitive theories in the microcosmic domain of atomic physics, such as the existence of energy as discrete (rather than infinitely divisible) packets, or *quanta,* and the wave-particle duality of the electron.

Visualizability. The counterintuitive nature of some propositions and theories about the structures and phenomena of the macrocosmic or microcosmic domains of the phenomenal world impairs our ability to *visualize* (that is, to form a mental picture of) some of the noumena of the intelligible world of our own construction. Fortunately, *some* of the structures and phenomena in macrocosmic or microcosmic domains *are* visualizable. For instance, the general features of our solar system, which extends well beyond the mesocosmic spatial domain, can be visualized by scaling down its spatial dimensions a hundred-millionfold, resulting in a *virtual* mesocosmic object, such as a planetarium with a diameter of about one meter. Similarly, the spatial configuration of chemical molecules can be visualized by scaling them up a hundred-millionfold, resulting in a *virtual* mesocosmic object, such as a wooden ball with a diameter of about one meter. Even the mechanical model of the atom devised at the turn of the twentieth century by the British physicist, Ernest Rutherford, can be visualized, since its mini-planetary-system-like properties are mesocosmically representable.

Yet many, if not most structures outside the mesocosmic domain *cannot* be visualized by simply scaling them up or down to the mesocosmic dimensional scale. This includes the neutron stars and black holes of the macrocosm and the protons and electrons of the microcosm, since they have properties that are utterly different from any mesocosmic structure of our direct experience. The classical physics of Galileo and of Isaac Newton are visualizable because they are based on our innate categories of space and time of Kantian pure theoretical reason. As pure theoretical reason has it, both space and time are absolute and independent realities that can be measured separately by use of yardsticks and clocks. But this basic tenet regarding space and time had to be abandoned at the turn of the twentieth century upon the emergence of Einstein's relativity theories.

There are four general principles regarding the role of visualizability in the evaluation of scientific theories.

First, the impossibility of visualizing a theory, whether it is derived from mathematics, or from physics, or from any discipline whatsoever, does not necessarily imply that the theory is not correct. On the contrary, any theory dealing with microcosmic, subatomic particles that *can* be readily visualized by a dimensional transformation to the mesocosmic scale is likely to be wrong.

Second, if visualizability is neither a necessary nor a sufficient criterion of truth, and if visualizability is not even a *guide* to truth, then we have to depend on non-visualizable, or abstract arguments for demonstrating truths. This explains the prominent role of mathematics in the progress of modern science. This role derives not only from the provision by mathematics of precise, quantitative formulations of linguistically vague and non-quantifiable ideas, but also from its ability to remodel the structure of the intelligible world in terms of counterintuitive concepts that are not amenable to visualization. Though mathematics itself does not yield any direct knowledge about the world, it puts at our disposal various abstract structures that can be helpful for probing the truth of non-visualizable propositions in the description of nature, such as the four- (or more) dimensional and non-Euclidean geometrical aspects of space.

Third, the impossibility of visualizing some abstract objects does not imply that they cannot be *understood*. We may claim that we understand a theory if we know, at least qualitatively, what the theory does and does not say. This shows that the reach of reason is farther than that of intuition of thought farther than that of visualization, of concepts is farther than that of sensation, and of calculations is farther than that of images. Modern physics is non-intuitive and could not be otherwise if it is to extend beyond the mesocosm. Yet, it is not incomprehensible.

Fourth, the two worlds of Kantian critical idealism—the sensible world of phenomena and the intelligible world of noumena—are not coextensive. Whereas our direct sensory experience of phenomena is limited to the sensible world of the mesocosm, the intelligible world of noumena transcends the mesocosm and reaches out into the micro- and macrocosm, of whose strange properties Kant did not have and could not have had any inkling.

Antinomies Revisited. The four general principles regarding the role of visualizability in the theoretical evaluation of scientific propositions account for Kant's (forgivable) error in concluding that theses as well as antitheses of his first and second antinomies are *false*. [Thesis and antithesis of the first antinomy assert that the world is finite (respectively infinite) and that it has a beginning (respectively no beginning) in time and limits (respectively no limits) in space. Thesis and antithesis of the second antinomy assert that every (respectively no) composite thing in the world is made up of simple parts.] For when in his argumentation Kant referred to 'things of which we have experience' he obviously meant the *visualizable* things of the *mesocosm* of which we do have *direct* experience. However, the first antinomy, being concerned with the macrocosmic spatial and temporal limits of the Universe, and the second antinomy, being concerned with the microcosmic (atomic) compositional elements of matter, far transcend the dimensional limits of the mesocosm of our direct experience, and hence *cannot* be visualized.

200

Kant erred in his judgment that both theses and antitheses of his first two antinomies are false. But he was remarkably prescient with his over-arching epistemological conjecture that reason inevitably falls into contradiction with itself whenever it ventures beyond experience and tries to think about the intelligible world as a whole.

Genetic Epistemology. Characterization of the categories of Kantian pure reason as *a priori* for the individual does not necessarily mean that they are present already full-blown at the time of the person's birth. To us latter-day Wisenheimers with our wisdom of hindsight, it seems strange that this obvious epistemological platitude was not recognized by Kant himself or by any of the advocates or opponents of his critical idealism. A plausible explanation for this odd historical fact is that philosophers—not excepting even Kant—discussed epistemology only as the capacity for knowing possessed by the *adult* human mind. They did not take into account that the *origins* of adult cognitive faculties lie in the mind of the infant.

Kant's contemporary, the Genevese philosopher Jean-Jacques Rousseau, provided the exception that proves the rule of the general pre-twentieth-century philosophical neglect of the development of the cognitive capacities of the infantile mind. Rousseau *did* declare that "nature wants children to be children before being men.... Childhood has its own seeing, thinking, and feeling." In his philosophical novel, *Emile*, Rousseau (1762) put forward the idea, taken up by almost all later theoreticians of cognitive and moral development, that young people pass through an age-related sequence of stages in reaching maturity. Rousseau listed five stages: *infantile* (birth to three years), *sensory* (four to twelve), *ideational* (thirteen to puberty), *sentimental* (puberty to age twenty), and *nuptial-socially-responsible* (onwards from twenty-one).

It was only at the beginning of the twentieth century that psychologists, especially the American, James Mark Baldwin, began to make a systematic assessment of the cognitive capacities of the infantile mind and of the process by which it matures to its adult condition. In the middle years of the twentieth century, the psychologist, Jean Piaget (1932; 1954; 1964),—a Genevese like Rousseau—extended Baldwin's pioneering studies.

Piaget's work showed that the Kantian categories, though they are *immanent* in the mind, arise postnatally during childhood, as a result of an interaction between the developing infantile mind and the sensible world. This interaction proceeds gradually by a process that Piaget named *genetic epistemology*. (In the context of Piagetian studies, the adjective 'genetic' means '*ontogenetic*' or 'developmental,' rather than 'hereditary.') Yet, even after Piaget had taken up this line of investigation, another quarter century had to pass before his findings would have any significant impact on philosophy. Finally, it was appreciated that the study of the cognitive development of children is a virtual gold mine for epistemological explorations. It still seems puzzling, though, why philosophers overlooked this gold mine for millennia, when all the while children were readily available as observational subjects.

Piaget began his studies while designing IQ tests to be given to French school children. He had noticed that children are consistent in the sort of *incorrect* answers they give to certain questions. Their answers are not randomly wrong but show a systematic, age-related error profile. Piaget inferred from this unexpected finding that the observed consistency of errors must be attributable to a stereotyped, progressive evolution of the mental structures present during the infantile cognitive development. To account for that development, he rejected the idea that the mind is a *passive* device that processes sensory input according to some fixed mental program of analysis. Instead, Piaget postulated that the infantile mind *actively* explores the pattern of sensory input from the sensible world by subjecting it to a series of tentative exploratory transformations. In performing this exploratory process, the immature mind passes through succession of distinct cognitive *developmental stages* on its way to the mature adult mind. As did Kant, so did Piaget regard the function of human reason as the active construction of an intelligible world by processing the sensory input to the mind from the phenomena of the sensible world.

Invariance, Assimilation and Accommodation. One of the most striking of Piaget's findings was that although the age at which individual children reach one or another of these distinct cognitive developmental stages can vary greatly, the *sequence* of stages is invariant. Piaget interpreted this to mean that the beginning of one stage presupposes the completion of the developmental goals characteristic of all preceding stages. Moreover, he inferred that each stage is integrated within itself, according to an *equilibrium* that comprises the child's cognition. Here Piaget did not use the word 'equilibrium' in its usual mechanical or chemical sense.

Instead, he intended the word to convey the idea of a dynamic steady state between the two major antithetical aspects of cognitive performance, namely *accommodation* and *assimilation*.

Accommodation to novel situations means changing an existing mental or behavioral technique to adapt it to the specific characteristics of novel objects and novel relationships, thus taking into account novel aspects of reality. Thus accommodation is a way of being realistic, taking life as it comes. Assimilation, the counterforce to accommodation in the equilibrium, means fitting novel aspects of reality into old behavioral and cognitive schemes rather than changing them. It is a way of being autistic, or of shaping reality according to one's own preconceived notions.

For instance, according to a very simple example of this equilibrium, infants have a method of grasping objects. If given a novel object to grasp, they perform assimilation, by including the object in the mental class of things that are graspable, as well as accommodation, by modifying their grasping technique to suit the novel object. It is the particular state of the equilibrium between the two antithetical cognitive forces that characterizes each stage of cognitive development. The equilibrium becomes upset in play, dreams, and make-believe, where autistic assimilation occurs without accommodation to reality. In the upset of the equilibrium during these activities, objects may be commanded to do certain things, which leads to symbolization: one bends the object playfully to represent something that it is not. The equilibrium also becomes upset during imitation, but in the opposite direction: imitating a model is nothing other than accommodation of the mind to the reality of the world. This also applies to imagery, since a mental image is an internalized representation of reality.

Piaget did not concern himself very much with the extent to which the postnatal development of cognitive structures proceeds autonomously (that is, driven by hereditary determinants) or heteronomously (that is, driven by experience or parental training). In any case, for our present discussion of the development of the infantile mind, it is unimportant whether our adult notions about the world and us are determined by our genes or implanted in our minds by experience. It suffices to recognize that our Kantian cognitive categories constitute a set of mental adaptations to the phenomenal world. That phenomenal world is the mesocosm of middle dimensions, constituted of things that are more-or-less directly accessible to our sensory perception.

Development of Pure Theoretical Reason. According to Piaget, the maturation of the infantile mind begins with the development of Kantian categories of pure theoretical reason, with particular categories arising in the immature mind during the sequence of distinct developmental stages.

The first stage is the *sensorimotor stage* (from birth to age 2 years), during which the infant's mind acquires the categories of object, space, and time and develops hand-eye coordination. The infant can move its arms willfully, but it does not yet appreciate that the hand it sees is its own. The grasping reflex is already present, i.e. the infant's reaching out for an object triggered by the appearance of that object in its visual field. The infant's hand will not usually aim directly at the object, though it may eventually get there by locating the object by trial and error. By the end of the first stage, tactile, visual, acoustic, and kinesthetic spaces have been coordinated, and the infant can perform target-directed movements.

The initial object concept of infants is clearly not what adults think of as an object. At the outset of the sensorimotor stage, infants consider an object to be a thing that has a permanent place. A particular object becomes a different object when it is moved from one place to another, and it ceases to exist as soon as it disappears from view. Accordingly, for the early infant objects do not persist. The next step in the development of the object concept is the beginning of the infants' capacity for remembering objects while they are out of sight, and by the end of the first year infants come to believe in their continued existence.

By this sequence of steps infants gradually acquire the notion of a permanent object with continued existence and identity under various transformations. Finally, by the end of the sensorimotor stage, the concept of the permanent object has been formed. This sequence constitutes a mutual assimilation of tactile and visual spaces. It is succeeded by the coordination of sight and sound and by the ability to follow a moving object. Once infants have acquired the belief in the persistence of objects, they are able to search for objects that are not in view. They can form mental images of objects and fathom their complex, even invisible, spatial displacements.

The second stage is the *preoperational stage* (age 2 to 5 years), during which the child's thought processes begin to use symbols. These symbols take either the form of mental images, whose source is imitation, which become more and more internalized, or the form of words, as symbolic representations of objects and events. Children also begin to reason from memory and analogy during this stage. But they are not yet able to understand the notion of the equivalence of sets. For instance, they are not yet able to order sticks of varying lengths according to length, although upon being asked to do so, they may produce some kind of fictitious (though clearly not random) ordering.

The third stage is the *concrete operational stage* (age 5 to 10 years) during which children gain the ability to carry out mental operations on objects, such as counting them and classifying and arranging them as orderly ensembles. It should be noted that the development of the number concept has nothing to do with learning to recite strings of numbers in their proper order. Rather, acquisition of the number concept consists of getting hold of the idea of the equivalence of sets. Once that equivalence idea has been grasped children are able to pair two sets containing the same number of elements, such as sets of pennies and candies, or of vases and flowers, without being distracted by the disparate features of their elements.

Numbers. Early in the concrete operational stage children still lack the concept of relative sizes of sets. For instance, if a child is given three yellow flowers and three flowers of colors other than yellow and asked which set is greater—the set of flowers or the set of *yellow* flowers—the child will reply "they are the same size," even though the whole set contains six items and its subset only three. For the child cannot as yet quantify class-inclusion relations, that is, appreciate that the whole is the sum of its parts. Later in the concrete operational period, however, there comes a moment at which the child realizes that a set contains more items than its subset.

By this time the child understands the numerical equivalence of sets, such as the equivalence of sets containing five elements as distinct from sets containing seven elements. This understanding allows the child to master the concept of *cardinal number*. Cardinal numbers denote particular classes of numerically equivalent sets, without, however, implying a serial relation between them, such as that 'seven' comes after 'five.' The task of serially ordering sets is served by the concept of *ordinal number*, which can arise only after the concept of cardinal number has been grasped, since ordinal numbers are not entailed logically by cardinal numbers. Thus children pass through a stage at which they have no notion that when one goes from one cardinal number to another, one must pass all intervening cardinal numbers. For instance, that in going from 'five' to 'seven' one must pass through 'six.'

At this point the child has gained the ability to handle hierarchical structures, that is, sets comprised of subsets, such as the set of 'flowers,' which includes various *kinds* of flowers. Upon gaining the ability to conceive hierarchical structures, children also have access to the notion of ordinal number. They are now equipped with the two most powerful conceptual tools for dealing with the quantitative aspects of the phenomenal world.

The fourth and last stage is that of *formal operations* (age 10 to 14 years) during which intelligible world is conceived as a subset of possible worlds. Propositional thinking, with assertions and statements that can be true or false, has become intellectually possible.

Time and Space. The categories of time and space do not arise automatically in the infantile mind. The notion that the whole world is embedded in one all-pervading universal flow of time is reached only at a comparatively late stage of development. This is the case also for the notions that an all-pervading space provides unique places for the world's objects and that motion consists of an object's change from one place to another in the universal flow of time. The inability of children to grasp these notions is illustrated by the following experiment. Suppose a child still in the preoperational stage is confronted with two objects that start and stop moving at the same time and at the same speed and is asked: (1) Have the objects started at the same time? (2) Have they moved at the same speed? (3) Have they moved the same distance? (4) Have they stopped at the same time?

The child will generally respond correctly to all these questions. But if the test is repeated with one of the objects moving faster than the other, the child will still respond correctly to questions 1, 2, and 3 but will reply incorrectly to question 4. It will say that the faster moving object stopped later, despite answering correctly questions 2 and 3 that the faster moving object moved at a greater speed and for a longer distance. Piaget concluded from this finding that, at the preoperational stage, speed is an intuitive primary kinetic category based on the ordinal succession of points traversed in space and time, without separate consideration of the actual distances moved or time intervals taken. At this early stage, intuition about time, especially about the notion of simultaneity, is derived from, rather than underlying, the assessment of speed. Thus at the preoperational stage children are unable to conceive that two objects might start at the same time and stop at the same time, while one of them has traversed more space. They can focus on the different displacements of the two objects, but they cannot embed those displacements in a common time frame.

How does the child develop the concept of space? The branch of mathematics concerned with spatial relations is geometry; and the objective of most geometric analyses is to demonstrate the equivalence of shapes. Mathematicians first grasped the *metric* aspects of space in the fourth century BCE, upon the development of Euclidean geometry. Metric geometry depends mainly on the concepts of length of a line and width of an angle. Here the equivalence of figures is based on an equality of their contours with regard to these parameters. For example, two circles of equal diameter are metrically equivalent (that is, congruent).

The *projective* aspects of space were grasped next, in the nineteenth century. Projective geometry depends mainly on the concept of the straight line as the basis of spatial relationships. Here the equivalence of figures is based on the notion of perspective, or on the possibility of transforming one figure into another by projecting its contour onto the contour of another via a set of straight lines. For example, any two circles are projectively equivalent.

The *topological* aspects of space were grasped last, in the twentieth century. *Topological* geometry depends mainly on the identification of qualitative features inhering in shapes, such as continuity as opposed to separation and openness as opposed to closure, as well as on counting the number of such features present. Here the equivalence of figures is based on the notion of *homeomorphy*, that is, the possibility of transforming one figure into another by a simple continuous deformation of its outline without any tear or overlap. For example, a circle and a square are topologically equivalent.

The results of his studies led Piaget to conclude that the order in which children acquire spatial concepts during their cognitive development is exactly the reverse of the order in which mathematicians acquired them historically: Children grasp topological aspects of space first, projective aspects second, and metric aspects last.

Causality. Piaget also studied the genetic epistemology of another crucial category of Kantian pure theoretical reason, namely causality.

Causality had been the subject of vigorous philosophical debate since antiquity. And onwards from Newton, the epistemological foundation of causality became a topic of concern also to physicists, because Newton's postulation of forces acting at a distance, such as gravitational attraction, seemed to run counter to the intuitive notion that a cause and its effect ought to be contiguous. The role of the causality concept in physical theory became more controversial still with the advent of modern physics, particularly, as we shall soon see, upon the appearance of the relativity and quantum theories early in the twentieth century. By causality we mean that there is a necessary, although often hidden, connection between an earlier event and a later event, between cause and effect. This idea is closely tied to the notion that the entire universe is embedded in a common space and time. Whence does this idea come? Early in the eighteenth century, David Hume declared that the idea of such a necessary connection between cause and effect arises from our feelings rather than from our reason, because *logical induction*, i.e. the extrapolation from past experience to the future, cannot be rationally justified. For instance, just because every morning the Sun rose in the East and every evening set in the West, it does not follow logically that the Sun will do so again tomorrow.

Hume's epistemological criticism of the rational basis of the causality concept was addressed by Kant, who argued that causality, though not of demonstrable logical validity, is another of the *a priori* categories, like time, space, and object, that are a precondition of all experience. Thus, since the causality category is used for creating experience (that is, transforming phenomena into noumena), the concept cannot be acquired by, or inferred from, experience. We simply take the validity of induction for granted because, according to Kant, the human mind simply cannot conceive a world in which the future is *not* determined by the past. The Kantian view of causality was inspired by Newtonian physics and its application to celestial mechanics, whose success made it seem obvious that the world is governed by determinate laws: given the initial conditions and Newton's laws of motion, the trajectories of the celestial objects are uniquely determined.

This viewpoint was to be dealt a blow by Einstein's development of the special theory of relativity, because in situations to which that theory applies, notions of what is past and what is future must be modified. Here the finding by one observer that event A preceded event B is ambiguous, since a second observer moving relative to the first might find that event B preceded event A. Accordingly, the first observer might infer from his measured order of these events that A is the cause of B, whereas the second observer might infer from *his* data that B is the cause of A. However, in this case both observers would be wrong, since, according to the special relativity theory, an inversion of the order of two events can be registered only if they are *not* causally connected. This follows from the (seemingly incontrovertible) proposition that if the earlier event A is the cause of the later event B, some signal must be exchanged between A and B. Because the signal—whatever be its nature—cannot propagate faster than light, the minimum measurable time interval between A and B is zero, which would be registered by an observer himself traveling at the speed of light from A to B. All other observers would find that the cause preceded its effect.

What can Piaget tell us about the genesis of the idea of causality in the infantile mind? He argues that the notion of cause and effect arises during the first, or sensorimotor stage and has two roots. The first root Piaget identified as *dynamism*, or *efficacy*, which means that children are vaguely aware that their own intentions and volition are somehow responsible for what happens. They discover that in order to make a rattle rattle, they must move themselves in some way, such as wriggling, although they are not aware of just how they cause the effect. All that they are aware of is that there exists some connection between their wish for the noise of the rattle and its occurrence.

The second root of the idea of causality Piaget identified is a consistent linkage between events of which one always follows the other, such as the mother's unfastening of her dress and the availability of milk. Such awareness of the connection between events that are contiguous in time (but not necessarily in space) is reached much earlier than the development of the space concept. The child's notion of causality is peculiarly different from that of an adult, and continues to be weird from the adult's point of view well into its concrete operational stage. Children think that anything can cause anything, whether the requirements of the adult notion of causality, such as continuity of cause and effect in time and space, are met or not. Thus, the notion of a complete (eighteenth-century Laplacian) determinism in the external world, is not yet present in the child's mind at the third or concrete operational stage.

The connection in the infantile mind between will and event, where the will can be mine or thine or that of gods or demons, is often carried over into adulthood. Under that view of causality there is no need for a physical connection between will and event, as there is not in the case of the cause-effect relation commonly designated as 'magic.'

By way of an example of the development of causal explanations of physical phenomena in the infantile mind, we may consider the uniform, straight-line motion of an object. According to the principles of Aristotelian physics, such motion requires a continuously acting motive force. If the force ceases to act, the object stops moving. According to the principles of Galilean physics, however, only a *change* in velocity of the object requires the action of a force, since the object's *momentum* (a concept of which Aristotelian physics is innocent) perpetuates its motion in the absence of any force. Both explanations envisage a determinate world (that is, that there is one and only one straight-line motion in a given context), but Aristotelian and Galilean theories make different assignments for the cause that is necessary to produce the same phenomenon.

The decision regarding which is the more reasonable theory—the Aristotelian or the Galilean—has to be based on evidence gathered in the particular context of the phenomenon. A motile bacterium would certainly believe in the Aristotelian theory, since it lives in a world where viscous forces dominate inertial forces by an enormous factor. That is to say, the drag exerted on the bacterium by the viscosity of the water through which it moves vastly exceeds any momentum that the bacterium may have while moving. Admittedly, a bacterium swims at high speed in relation to its body size, covering 30 times its body length in 1 second (which, on the scale of an automobile, would correspond to a speed of about 300 miles/hour). Yet its forward motion stops within a distance that is a fraction of its body length (say within a foot or so, on the automobile scale), as soon as its flagella stop beating. Thus, the empirical evidence would lead the bacterium to conclude that continuing motion requires a continuously acting force.

To probe their capacity to provide a causal explanation of uniform linear motion, Piaget asked children between the ages of 4 and 10 what makes clouds move. He reported that, on the basis of the answers he received, he was able to distinguish definite stages in the development of causal thought. In the first stage children think that as people walk, the clouds move with them; in other words, the motion of the person causes the clouds to move in some magical manner. In the second stage, reached by the age of 5 or 7, children think that clouds are moved by the sun and moon, that is, by command rather than physical force. Finally, 8-year-olds usually think that the wind moves the clouds, and the wind is in turn created by the clouds.

Development of Pure Practical Reason. Just as Piaget had been the first to investigate methodically the development of Kantian pure *theoretical* reason in children, so was he also the pioneer of the empirical study of the childhood development of Kantian pure *practical* reason. Insofar as there had been any interest prior to Piaget in the problem of how morally naïve children grow up into morally cognizant adults, the process was generally attributed to passive learning under the tutelage of parents and other adults. The morally most pernicious of the theories invoked in early twentieth century to account for such learning was the doctrine of *connectionism*, which tried to explain all learning in terms of conditioned reflexes, as manifested by Ivan Pavlov's dogs.

Piaget, however, considered the childhood development of pure practical reason as essentially similar to that of the development of pure theoretical reason: Both processes occur by way of a reciprocal interaction between the gene-directed maturation of the infantile nervous system and the phenomenal world. So, to fathom the way children develop their practical reason for making morally responsible judgments, Piaget discussed stories and played games with them. His findings led Piaget to conclude that, following an initial *premoral stage* (lasting for the first three to four years of life), at which the child has little awareness or understanding of ethical rules, the genetic epistemology of pure practical reason passes through two further distinct developmental stages.

During the first of these two post-premoral stages—designated as the *heteronomous stage* and lasting from 4 to 8 years of age—morals of constraint obtain. At the onset of the heteronomous stage the child first becomes aware that controls are being imposed on its behavior by rules. The source of these rules is adults, whose authority the child considers as sacred and whose rules it regards as unchangeable and applicable, whatever the circumstances. To do right means acting in conformance with the adult-imposed rules, and to do 'wrong' means defying them. Moral responsibility for actions devolves from conformance with moral rules rather than from the intentions of the agent. Though the child is generally able to identify what the rules require or prohibit, it does not yet fathom their underlying justification.

During the second of the two post-premoral stages—designated as the *autonomous stage* and lasting from 8 to 10 years of age—the child's concept of morals becomes reorganized. The onset of the autonomous stage marks the emergence in the child's mind of the concepts of reciprocity and equality. Once the child has reached the autonomous stage, it no longer regards rules as immutable or sacred. Instead, it now views the rules as products of mutual agreement (and thus as changeable) and as beneficial guides for reciprocal cooperation rather than as autocratic edicts ordained by the sacred authority of adults. Moral responsibility for actions has been transferred from simple conformity of actions with rules ordained by powerful adults to the freely willed intentions of autonomous child-persons.

Between the 1960s and 1970s the Harvard psychologist, Lawrence Kohlberg (1969, 1976) modified and extended Piaget's studies of moral development in children by interviewing them regarding their reactions to made-up stories Kohlberg told them involving moral dilemmas. Like Piaget, Kohlberg interpreted moral development as a progression through stages characterized by different ways of understanding moral rightness and wrongness. He extended Piaget's three-stage system to constitute a more finely divided six-stage system. The major modifications made by Kohlberg in his staging system were that at the earliest post-premoral stages, the child's moral judgments are based, not as envisaged by Piaget on respect for authority and rules, but on a fear of punishment. Later the child's judgments become oriented towards the maintenance of the rules and laws of the social system. And at their most advanced developmental stages moral judgments are autonomous and based on principles of justice.

Just as Piaget claimed for the stages he identified, so did Kohlberg claim for his that their sequence is invariant and universal. Children progress through his system without skipping any stages or ever regressing from a higher to lower stage. The sequence applies to all individuals in all cultures, although different individuals may go through the stages at varying speeds and some may stop at a particular stage and not progress further. Each stage involves a unified way of thinking, a distinct 'moral logic,' rather than a set of separate attitudes toward specific situations. Thus particular judgments that occur at a given stage share a general framework for organizing and interpreting moral concerns.

Kohlberg's student, Eliott Turiel, agreed with Piaget's and Kohlberg's general conceptions of moral development as a process that passes

212

through a sequence of distinct, culturally invariant, and universal stages. Turiel criticized his elders, however, for exaggerating the role of social convention and fear of punishment in infantile moral development. In line with Kantian critical idealism, Turiel asserted that young children can make autonomous moral judgments on the basis of *a priori* categories of their pure practical reason without resorting to adult *idées recues*. On the basis of his own, non-interventive observations of children playing in a Kindergarten, he wrote, "in the moral domain the existence of a social regulation is not necessary for a child to view an event as a transgression. If, for example, one child hits another and thereby causes physical harm, a third child's perception of that event as a moral transgression would stem from features intrinsic to the event (e.g. from a perception of the consequences for the victim)." (Turiel, 1980)

Coda. The philosophical importance of the development of evolutionary and genetic epistemology in mid-twentieth century still awaits its full appreciation at the start of the twenty-first. Admittedly thus far, this development has contributed little to the resolution of the deep paradoxes generated by pure theoretical and pure practical reason that trouble the human mind. But it *has* led to an explanation for why, as Kant had asserted, man is made out of timber so crooked that from it nothing entirely straight can be built.

Actually, Kant's choice of the metaphor of crooked timber was not altogether felicitous. The timber from which man is made is not all that crooked. It is insufficiently *plastic*, however, to be able to adapt in a timely manner to the secular changes in the phenomenal world that arise largely because of mankind's own activities. Thus, while by now, many philosophers are aware of the gist of evolutionary epistemology, fewer of them appreciate that natural selection has adapted pure reason to yesterday's rather than today's world.

THE RIGHTE HONOURABLE
S.ʳ Francis Bacon, knight.

FRANCIS BACON (1561–1626)

(Engraved by Frances Holl, after an old print by Simon Tuss)

Chapter Thirteen

⮚◆⮘

Scientism

Francis Bacon and the Rise of Scientism. In his books, *The Advancement of Learning* and *Novum Organon,* the seventeenth century English statesman and philosopher of science, Francis Bacon, praised the virtue and dignity of scientific research. Bacon considered science not merely an academic or intellectual exercise intended to increase our knowledge of nature. He thought that its more important goal was to give mankind *mastery* over nature, since the practical applications of the results of scientific research were bound to improve the quality of the human condition. In fact, Bacon gave his life for the advancement of useful scientific knowledge. One cold winter's day he went out to stuff a dead chicken with snow, to see how long the freezing temperature would preserve the raw meat. While performing this experiment, Bacon caught a cold and died from bronchitis a few days later.

Bacon, who saw no conflict between religion and science, died just a few years before the Roman Catholic Inquisition forced Galileo in 1633 to renounce his belief in the heretical, heliocentric Copernican planetary system that has the Earth moving around the Sun. As it turned out, in not worrying about the Church's hostility to science, Bacon was not all that far off the mark. In the long run, conflicts between science and religion were always resolved in favor of science, as was also true in Galileo's case. By the middle of the eighteenth century this ever-repeating pattern of initial religious criticism of some scientific advance, followed by its eventual vindication and religious acceptance, had inspired a new creed that came to be called '*scientism.*' (The adjectival form of 'scientism' is '*scientistic,*' but—inconveniently for our discussion—there is no noun in English, or, as far as I know, in any other language, denoting its True Believers.)

According to the creed of scientism, the positive methods and insights of science are valid not only for the entire sphere of human interests, but they are the *only* authentic source of true knowledge. These interests include morals and the management of social affairs, of which scientific ignoramuses, such as priests and politicians, have always made such a mess in the past. Yet, despite the widespread tacit acceptance of scientism in modern society, the term 'scientistic' has become an invective that, like 'reductionist,' people apply only to the views of others but never to their own. [In his book, *Scientism*, Tom Sorell (1991) provided an excellent overview of the subject.]

In considering the scientistic approach to morals and to the management of social affairs, it is useful to distinguish between two different grades of scientism. One is *hard-core scientism*, whose adherents hold that moral norms and values *must* be justifiable on scientific grounds. The other grade is *soft-core scientism*, whose adherents allow that valid moral values may be justified on nonscientific grounds, but they still insist on the primacy of science as a guide to the optimal implementation of moral values. (Stent, 1976a)

The Evolutionary Origins of Morals. To clarify the nature of the scientistic approach to morals, we may consider an application of scientific principles and methodology to moral problems that on first sight does not seem to *be* scientistic. This example concerns the evolutionary origins of morals. It qualifies for the predicate 'scientific' rather than 'scientistic' because its intent is the presentation of a *descriptive* theory of how morals arose in human history rather than of the development of a *prescriptive* set of rules for how people *ought* to live.

In our earlier discussion of evolutionary epistemology in Chapter 12 we accounted for the origins of the natural/amoral categories of Kantian pure *theoretical* reason (such as space, time, and causality) in terms of their Darwinian fitness in the course of mankind's biological evolution. So it requires no great leap of the imagination to fathom the evolutionary origins of also the non-natural/moral categories of Kantian pure *practical* reason (such as virtue, vice, sacredness, and free will) as products of the natural selection process that drove the evolutionary history of *Homo sapiens*. That is to say, any early hominids whose hereditarily determined cerebral neuronal network happened to generate categorical ideas according to which vice is preferable to virtue, free will is wholly subject to determinism, and human life is not sacred, left no descendants in the long run to whom to pass on such socially dysfunctional notions.

216

As seen from the biological perspective, *Homo sapiens* is just one of the many social species belonging to the class of mammals in the vertebrate phylum. So it seemed plausible that a comparative study of the social behavior of our relatives in the animal kingdom should reveal significant clues about the evolutionary origins of our own social behavior. For just as evolutionary biologists can ask how there arose the intricate and superbly adapted facet eye of the honey bee by Darwinian natural selection, so can they ask how it was possible for natural selection to give rise to the intricate and superbly adapted society of the beehive or to the hierarchical social structure in bands of social mammals such as canines and primates.

Despite Darwin's full awareness of the importance of social behavior for his theory of descent by heritable variation, it was only in the 1930s that the evolutionarily oriented study of the social behavior of animals really got under way. One of its Founding Fathers was none other than Konrad Lorenz, the main originator of evolutionary epistemology and holder of the Chair of Philosophy in Königsberg of which Kant had been the first incumbent. By the 1950s, Lorenz's line of study had become an established academic discipline under the name of *ethology*. There can be little doubt that the ethological approach to social behavior has greatly enhanced our understanding of the animal world. For that contribution Lorenz was awarded the 1973 Nobel Prize in Physiology or Medicine.

However, Lorenz's ethological approach to the origins of morals did turn out to be scientistic after all, because it soon transpired that his goal was not merely a *descriptive* account of the natural origins of morals. What he really had in mind was the provision of a *hard-core scientistic prescriptive* account of the moral values that govern, or *ought to govern*, the social behavior of our species. So Lorenz assigned *moral virtue* to those righteous features of human behavior, such as altruism, mother-love, and marital fidelity, for which analogs can be found in the animal world and for whose functional role in nature, credible ethological explanations can be put forward. Contrariwise, Lorenz assigned *moral vice* to those depraved features of human behavior that animals seem to avoid in the wild and exhibit only under the socio-pathological conditions of captivity.

Lorenz's ethological studies came to be used for the scientistic rationalization of moral values traditionally justified on religious grounds. An — undoubtedly unintended—caricature of this approach was provided by Wolfgang Wickler (1971) in his *Biology of the Ten Commandments*.

However, in a not quite so trivial reversal of Lorenz's scientistic rational-izations, the ethological vindication of conventional morals was stood on its head by Desmond Morris (1967). Morris bestowed the predicate 'vir-tuous' on some features of human behavior normally regarded as wicked, such as aggression and marital infidelity, on the grounds that animals ex-hibit them in nature, for evolutionarily accountable reasons.

Hard-core Bioscientistic Definition of Moral Virtue. In mid-twenti-eth century, concurrently with Lorenz's development of ethology, two prominent British biologists, Julian Huxley (1943) and C. H. Wadding-ton (1960), provided another example of hard-core scientistic argumen-tation. They asserted that evolutionary theory provides a secure basis for an objective assessment of moral values. According to them, moral virtue can be attributed to those features of social behavior, such as mother-love, marital fidelity and economic cooperation, for which it can be rea-sonably argued that they promote the Darwinian fitness of *H. sapiens* in the evolutionary epic of natural selection. Conversely, moral vice can be attributed to other features of human behavior, such as cannibalism, murder, and incest, for which it can be reasonably argued that they im-pair the Darwinian fitness of our species.

Waddington, whose political sentiments were distinctly left wing, had to deal with one, for him, very troublesome predecessor in the scientistic grounding of moral values in Darwinian evolutionary concepts. That predecessor was Herbert Spencer (1892), the late-nineteenth century, politically right wing English apostle of the hard-core scientistic doctrine of Social Darwinism. Spencer asserted that the concept of virtue could be identified with human progress, which is driven by the forces of natural selection in social evolution, just as it is in biological evolution. Accord-ing to Spencer, *laissez-faire* capitalism is morally virtuous because, like nature (which, according to Alfred Tennyson, "is red in tooth and claw"), it is the optimal context for assuring social progress. Socialism, by contrast, is morally vicious because it stifles progress by interfering with the natural selection of the economically fittest people and pampering the ne'er-do-wells.

In line with the politically correct rejection of Social Darwinism by mid-twentieth century, Waddington wrote that Spencer's ethical "theo-ries have been so completely discredited at this time that little further needs to be said about them." So Waddington did say nothing further about them. He merely presented his own variant of Spencer's hard-core scientistic ethics, claiming that although the notion of moral virtue cannot be simply identified with 'progress,' a particular set of moral values can be judged to be virtuous if it promotes *anagenesis*, or evolutionary improvement. The general metaphysical idea underlying Waddington's anagenesis argument is evidently that, from a moral viewpoint, the condition of our planet has been improving all the time, as more and more complex forms of life, and finally wonderful, wonderful *H. sapiens*, made the scene. But Waddington did not spell out to what kind of evolutionary improvement, or anagenesis, he was looking forward. In any case, his natural idea of moral virtue was even more remote from our normal, intuitive understanding of that concept provided by Kantian's pure practical reason than was Spencer's. Moreover, Waddington seemed to have been unaware of an essential feature of the 'fitness' concept of Neo-Darwinian evolutionary theory. According to that feature, natural selection can favor only those variant genotypes in a population that give rise to a higher differential reproductive rate in the *here-and-now*, but not if they merely promote anagenesis, that is, provide benefits at some future time.

Naturalistic Fallacy. On first sight, these efforts to develop a hard-core scientistic foundation for morals would seem to fail on logical grounds. For the authority of science and the claims for authenticity of its knowledge are based on the belief that scientific propositions are objective and value-free. In view of that belief, it would be clearly invalid to derive value-laden moral conclusions from the value-free propositions of biology. This logically invalid procedure, to which David Hume first drew attention in the early eighteenth-century, came to be epitomized by the mantra "an 'ought' cannot be inferred from an 'is.' " At the turn of the twentieth century, the Cambridge philosopher G. E. Moore designated the inference of a moral-value-laden 'ought' from a value-free 'is' as the *'naturalistic fallacy,'* the name under which this invalid procedure is generally known nowadays.

Thus the scientistic project of establishing objective criteria for moral virtue would fail because no moral values can possibly be inferred from objective and value-free ethological findings regarding the behavior of animals in their natural setting. For that same reason, the derivation of virtue from the evolutionary 'fitness' concept would fail because the primary value judgment on which the evolutionary ethic depends, namely that evolution is progressive, cannot itself be inferred from any set of objective and value-free statements about the paleontological record.

It follows, therefore, that hard-core scientistic morality cannot, in fact, be based wholly on the objective propositions of biology and must base its authority on unstated premises with hidden values. In the case of ethology-derived ethics, the source of those unstated, value-laden premises is not hard to identify. It is the Bible, to which the evolutionary ethicists resort even more fundamentally than do their stout adversaries, the Protestant Christian Fundamentalists. Rather than taking their ethics directly from God's ten explicit commandments of Exodus 21:23, as do the Fundamentalists, ethological ethicists go back to the basics of Genesis 1, 2, and 3 and its account of His creation of the world and the First Couple's expulsion from the Garden of Eden. It is evidently from this account that biologists derive the idea that the natural behavior of animals provides a moral baseline, because before the Fall, Adam and Eve, still naked and nameless, lived beyond good and evil, like all the other animals. The idea that the course of evolution has been progressive, culminating in the appearance of mankind, is evidently derived as well from Genesis 1:27, which has God making us in His own image as the crowning act of the sixth day.

On second sight, however, the derivation of moral value from biological propositions may not be invalid after all, and the dismissal of the 'naturalistic fallacy' on logical grounds may itself be a fallacy, albeit for reasons that can give little comfort to the adepts of hard-core scientism. According to some latter-day philosophers, such as Thomas Kuhn and Paul K. Feyerabend, the kind of objective science on behalf of which authority is claimed for scientism is only a myth and does not, in fact, exist in the first place. Since the practitioners of science are human beings rather than disembodied spirits, since they necessarily interact with the phenomena they observe, and since they use ordinary language to communicate their results, they are really part of the problem rather than part of the solution. That is to say, scientists lack the status of autonomous observers external to the world of phenomena, a status they would have to have if their scientific propositions could justly claim to be truly objective.

This lack of conceptual autonomy of scientists vis-à-vis their working materials is particularly evident in the case of biologists. As the evolutionist Ernst Mayr has pointed out, in speaking about their findings, biologists cannot avoid terms that imply functions, roles, and values. For example, ethological investigators of insect societies resort to such words as 'queen,' 'worker,' 'soldier,' 'slave,' and 'caste' to describe the objects of their studies. It would be unreasonable to demand of them for the sake of objectivity to replace these value-laden metaphors by an ostensibly value-free vocabulary, such as referring not to 'queen' but to 'type 248,' or not to 'caste' but to 'social subset MNO.' After all, it is precisely in the perception of a functional typology that any study of social behavior has its starting point. The typology both defines the phenomenon that is to be explained and already comprises within it part of the eventual explanation.

Another example of such linguistic contamination with value of a presumably value-free scientific term is provided by 'fitness,' the central concept of Darwinian selection theory. In ordinary English discourse, 'fitness' connotes value, and it was that value-laden quality of the term that gave meaning to the slogan 'survival of the fittest' in the context of Spencer's Social Darwinism. In their politically correct rejection of Social Darwinism, contemporary biologists charge Spencer with having misunderstood the technical meaning of 'fitness,' which is meant to represent a value-free algebraic parameter that indicates the contribution made by a particular hereditary determinant to the differential reproduction rate of a creature. Thus Darwinian 'fitness' itself implies nothing about 'progress.'

However, the semantic problem posed by 'fitness' is more complicated than this rough-and-ready dismissal of Spencer would imply. Geologists seek an understanding of the physical evolution of the Earth, and, just as do evolutionary biologists, they try to account for the history of our planet in terms of the laws of nature. But there is an important difference between these two callings. Although in the course of the Earth's history geological forms have come and gone—just as have biological forms—geological theories put forward to explain this succession of forms do not resort to any concept equivalent to 'fitness.' There is no need for such a concept because geologists do not think of geological evolution as progressive. Since the presently existing continents are not perceived as an 'improvement' over Pangea, (the single continental mass from which they evolved by plate tectonics), no explanation positing progress is called for. But for biologists it would require an act of intellectual self-denial to view biological evolution in any light other than that of progress. Not only does the truth of the Biblical idea of mankind as the crowning achievement of creation seem self-evident, but also it is even difficult to deny that the swift, sharp-eyed hawk represents an improvement over lumbering, deservedly extinct *Archaeopteryx*. Thus, if the Darwinian concept of fitness were really purged of all value content, it would lose its explanatory power for the deep question in want of a credible answer. That question is not "how did evolution happen?" but "what has made evolutionary progress possible?"

If it were really the case that the propositions of science, and especially those of biology, are not value-free, then there would be no inherent logical error—no naturalistic fallacy—in deriving moral value from them. Accordingly, ethological and evolutionary ethics would not have to fail on logical grounds. But the idol of the uniquely authentic, wholly objective scientific knowledge that inspires the hard-core scientistic project of universalizing the scientific perspective in the first place would turn out to stand on feet of clay.

Sociobiology. In the 1960s William Hamilton (1964) brought a novel approach to ethology that was more quantitative and more sharply formulated than Lorenz's original, rather qualitative evolutionary reasoning. Hamilton's most important contribution was the development of his *kin selection* theory, according to which the Darwinian fitness of a particular social behavior pattern does not derive solely from the extent to which it promotes the reproductive success of an *individual* animal who displays it. Kin selection takes into account, as well the extent to which that behavior pattern augments, also reproductive potential of an individual animal's close relatives, a parameter that Hamilton named *inclusive fitness*.

The conceptual advance represented by inclusive fitness led to the development of an ethological subdiscipline styled 'sociobiology,' dedicated specifically to the evolution of the *social* behavior of animals. Of that subdiscipline a treatise by E. O.Wilson (1975) entitled *Sociobiology* provided the first comprehensive account. Admittedly, there exist differences in opinion among biologists regarding the achievements of sociobiology, but regardless of whether sociobiology has or has not any substantial achievements to its credit, it would be downright cranky for any biologist to deny that the professed general scientific goal of sociobiology is not intrinsically worthwhile. Yet, the publication of Wilson's scholarly treatise caused a tremendous ruckus in the late 1970s. Wilson became the subject of both laudatory feature stories in the news media as well as the target of invective, and even physical assault, from political activists. For he argued in his final chapter that the methodology and findings of sociobiology are applicable not only to insects and other lower orders but also to the social behavior of our own species, H. sapiens. Wilson claimed that sociobiology can provide for the human social sciences, such as anthropology and sociology, the objective scientific basis that they lacked hitherto.

Much of the virulent criticism directed against Wilson was not, however, based on the grounds that the naturalistic view of morals embodied in his sociobiology is philosophically mistaken. Most of Wilson's ideological (mainly Marxist) critics actually shared his fundamental (Aristotelian) viewpoint that moral behavior is to be viewed as a strategy for optimizing human welfare. No, their criticism was based on a fervid rejection of the scientific premise fundamental to sociobiology, namely that human behavior is genetically determined. Contrary to Wilson, his adversaries believed (inspired mainly by one—but not the only possible—interpretation of dialectical materialism) that human social behavior is determined by the environment and not by human genes.

It may seem that the question whether human social behavior is determined by genes or by the environment ought to be susceptible to an objective, empirical resolution, just as it was shown that human eye color —blue eyes or brown eyes—is genetically rather than environmentally determined. But there lies a fundamental difficulty in the way of an empirical resolution of the problem of the genetic determination of human social behavior. For the very notion of the genetic determination of complex features of living creatures, and not just of social behavior, is an elusive concept. As we noted in our earlier discussions of evolutionary and genetic epistemology, the most reasonable explanation of the Darwinian origins of the Kantian *a priori* categories of pure reason is that these complex mental structures develop in the course of our postnatal development. This development is mediated by a dialectical-materialist interaction between our genes and our infantile environment.

Selfish Gene. Thus, if there is to be effective criticism of the claims of sociobiology with regard to the biological basis of morals, it has to be made on philosophical rather than scientific grounds. In fact, it is not difficult to show that Wilson and his fellow sociobiologists are misusing the locutions and categories of moral discourse. To illustrate this semantic deficit of sociobiological theories dealing with morals, we may examine the concepts of 'altruism' and 'selfishness,' which were the central focus of Richard Dawkins' (1976) popular and widely discussed book, *The Selfish Gene*. Dawkins epitomized the sociobiological viewpoint of mankind by saying that we are machines created by our genes. These genes have managed to survive in a highly competitive world only by virtue of their ruthless selfishness.

This argument has little philosophical merit because it resorts to the rhetorical slight-of-hand known as 'metaphorical slippage.' Dawkins applies the terms 'selfishness' and 'altruism' metaphorically as *indirect* (or target) meanings to objects (that is, genes), while their *direct* (that is, source) meanings refer to the moral praiseworthiness and blameworthiness of human subjects. (In ordinary, morally relevant discourse, the direct meaning of *selfishness* denotes disregard by one person for the interests of another, whereas the direct meaning of *altruism* denotes regard for the interests of others.) The use of metaphors is not objectionable in itself in scientific discourse. On the contrary, it enriches the language. For instance, if Dawkins had identified a gene which he believed to be involved in the development of morally selfish behavior in people, it would have been semantically legitimate (but maybe not advisable) for him to refer to it as a 'selfishness gene.' But this is not the indirect meaning that Dawkins intended to imply. What he did intend to imply (and *needs* to imply for his sociobiological account of the evolutionary origin of moral behavior in accord with the inclusive fitness theory) is that the gene acts selfishly on its *own* behalf.

Thus Dawkins slipped his metaphors by attributing the moral quality 'selfish' of the metaphor's direct meaning, (which refers to a moral subject), to an amoral object (the gene). Evidently not wholly unaware of the questionable legitimacy of his procedure—how can genes, not being persons, have regard or disregard for the interests of persons?—Dawkins put forward his own idiosyncratic and wholly unconventional, value-free definitions of the moral categories of selfishness and altruism. According to him, an 'entity' is altruistic if it behaves in such a way as to increase another entity's welfare at the expense of its own, with 'welfare' being defined as 'chances of survival.' Selfish behavior has exactly the opposite effect. Thus Dawkins' idiosyncratic definitions of altruism and selfishness are beyond good and evil, since they concern consequences for survival rather than regard for the interest of others, and they pertain to 'entities' rather than persons.

By contrast, the conventional, morally relevant meanings of altruism and selfishness apply only in the context of interpersonal relations. And, as we previously noted, according to Pierre Abelard and Kant, *intent* rather than *consequences* is the necessary and sufficient criterion for these morally relevant meanings. For instance, if little Jack takes away chocolate from little Jill because he wants to eat the chocolate himself, Jack is morally selfish. However, since Jack has thereby lowered for Jill and raised for himself the chances of dental caries, Jack's morally selfish act is at the same time sociobiologically altruistic. (Stent, 1977)

Dawkins argues that an apparently altruistic behavior, such as the alarm call of birds, is really selfish after all. For according to the principle of kin selection, the selfish genes of the alarmist bird have actually increased the welfare of their own informational replicas in the other birds of the flock. It ought to have been obvious that such sociobiological playing with the words 'altruism' and 'selfishness' is unlikely to contribute very much to our understanding of morals, especially not to connecting the non-natural categories of Kantian pure practical reason with the natural noumena of the intelligible world. Yet, some sociobiologists proclaimed that, thanks to their alleged insights into the evolutionary origins of moral principles, we would finally be able to rid ourselves of our antiquated metaphysical baggage. This argument is reminiscent of Sigmund Freud's claim that neurotics will be able to rid themselves of disabling mental obsessions once psychoanalysis has uncovered their psychogenetic origins. Thus even if, in accord with evolutionary epistemology, Kantian pure practical reason *did* provide Darwinian fitness to our caveperson ancestors, we have no longer any need for it, and these days it just causes us no end of trouble.

Star Wars. Since soft-core scientism does not claim to justify moral norms or values on scientific grounds, it escapes the logical dilemma of hard-core scientism. It is this version of scientism that is often encountered among philosophically more sophisticated scientists. They recognize the epistemological shortcomings of hard-core scientism, but nevertheless cannot help but believe that the scientific method praised by Francis Bacon, which proved of such tremendous help in allowing us to gain mastery over nature, ought to be of equal help in the successful management of human social affairs.

One of the many literary examples informed by soft-core scientism was provided by the science fiction tale *The Voice of the Dolphin*, written by the Hungaro-American physicist (and sometime molecular biologist) Leo Szilard (1961). Szilard himself was no stranger to the management of human affairs. In 1939, he had counseled Einstein to write the letter to President Roosevelt that induced the U.S. government to embark on the project for developing the atomic bomb, and in the immediate post-War years, Szilard played a leading role in the efforts to bring atomic energy under civilian control. In *The Voice of the Dolphin*, which he wrote in 1969 during the coldest days of the Cold War, Szilard envisaged the founding in Vienna of an International Biological Research Institute. Contrary to their chartered scientific duties, the fabulously brilliant young molecular biologists staffing the Vienna Institute intervened in world-wide economic, political, and military affairs and thus saved the world from the then seemingly imminent U.S.-Soviet nuclear holocaust. Szilard wrote his story to show that the same kind of clear thinking that cracked the genetic code will get us out of the messes that the woolly-headed politicians are always getting us into.

Now, with the wisdom of several decades of hindsight, it would appear that scientists *did* play a critical—albeit inadvertent—role in bringing about the end of the Cold War and averting a nuclear holocaust. For by persuading President Reagan to adopt the extremely expensive and probably ineffective 'Star Wars' Strategic Defense Initiative, his scientific advisors bankrupted the Soviet Evil Empire, whose equally woolly-headed leaders felt obliged to follow suit.

The more restricted claim of soft-core scientism for the primacy of science as a guide to management of human affairs also fails, however, if not on logical then on empirical or practical grounds. For it seems to be impossible to consider moral issues touching on science while minding the underlying moral values that have an other-than-scientific basis. By way of an example of this fundamental difficulty, we considered in Chapter 5 the conference held in Paris in 1975, at which an international panel of biologists and biomedical scientists had been convened to define the stage in human fetal development at which life can be said to begin. For prior to that stage there could be no moral objection to abortion. Not surprisingly, this scientistic discussion turned out to be entirely futile because the actual question at issue was "when does the fetus gain the status of a person and thus fall under protection of the moral law that forbids the killing of persons?" Evidently, that question can be dealt with only in the non-natural context of the moral metaphysics of personhood and not in the natural context of human biology.

Utility of Objectively False Beliefs. One of the, on first sight reasonable, tenets of soft-core scientism is that the implementation of moral aims is necessarily impeded by acts that are motivated by objectively false beliefs. Indeed, a more extreme version of this proposition claims that a society is doomed if it bases its organization on scientific falsehoods. This claim is itself a false belief because one can point to many societies that operated in a successful and stable manner while making value judgments based on witchcraft, astrology, prophecy, and other practices which we now know to be scientifically unsound. The reason why objectively false beliefs can promote the realization of worthy moral aims is that social relations are complex, multicausal phenomena and that any social aim can only be regarded as an optimization rather than a maximization of a set of values.

This fact has been well known to the Chinese since the days of Confucius in the sixth century BCE. And in the West it has been generally recognized by cultural anthropologists ever since Bronislaw Malinowski pointed out early in the twentieth century that the function of myths and rites is to strengthen the traditions that help to maintain a social way of life. For instance, the false belief of the Hopi Indians that they can bring about rain by dancing may have been harmful for their agriculture. But the rain dance fostered a communal cohesion whose benefits may have outweighed the potential gains in crop yield which abandonment of that false belief might have produced.

Heredity and Intelligence. The unwillingness to admit the possibility of deriving social benefits from holding objectively false beliefs is at the root of the ongoing, mainly demagogic, dispute in the United States and

Britain about research on the hereditary basis of intelligence. The battles regarding this controversy have been fought at two different levels. At the first level, the question to be addressed is whether the statement that intelligence has a hereditary basis is a genuine proposition in the first place, i.e. whether it is capable of being true or false. Those who deny propositional status to the assertion of a hereditary basis of intelligence usually claim that, absent an objective, context-free definition of the concept of intelligence, the assertion can be neither true nor false. This argument has little force, however, since it *is* possible to design tests that do provide a meaningful and stable measure of intelligence, at least insofar as that concept applies to the capacity to succeed in the society in whose contextual setting the tests are given. Moreover, it is an empirical fact that there exist significant, stable differences in test scores between different individuals, as well as between homogeneous social and racial subgroups. (Bodmer and Cavalli-Sforza, 1970)

At the second level, the question to be addressed is whether the proposition of a hereditary basis of intelligence is actually true or false. And it is at this level that the problem is extremely difficult to resolve empirically, especially when the differences in intelligence between social and racial subgroups are at issue. The reason for this is that intelligence, however defined in any practically significant way, is obviously a multicausal phenomenon, in whose postnatal development both genes and environment play determinant roles. Moreover, the relative contributions of genes and childhood environment in this developmental process, from infancy to adulthood, of normal individuals who are not mentally defective is bound to be subject to such large individual variations that the data are unlikely to lead to many practically useful conclusions.

Yet, both opposing sides in this dispute appear to accept the validity of the soft-core scientistic proposition that if there *were* a significant variation in the genetic contribution to intelligence between individuals, or between racial groups, then this factor ought to be taken into account in the organization of society. Since, to the opponents of such research, the mere consideration of the notion of hereditary determinants of intelligence, let alone taking it into account in social action, is a morally inadmissible underpinning of racist ideology, they deny outright the possibility of any connection between heredity and intelligence.

The proponents of research on the hereditary determination of intelligence, on the other hand, are convinced that the failure to give due recognition to the existence of hereditary differences in intelligence has pernicious social consequences. Hence they insist that no effort should be spared to try to identify the genetic basis of intelligence in a scientifically valid manner. This conclusion is not, however, rationally self-evident. Suppose that there really *were* a hereditary contribution to intelligence. Now consider Society A, which falsely believes that there is no such hereditary contribution and utilizes its educational resources less efficiently than Society B, which 'tracks' its pupils according to a scientifically valid familial or ethnic prognosis (that is, if such a prognosis were really possible). Cultural anthropologists might easily conclude under these circumstances that Society A is better off than Society B. For they could very well argue that whatever pedagogic losses are sustained by Society A due to its scientifically falsely based educational system are more than offset by the greater communal cohesion fostered by the (false) belief in an innate equality of human intelligence.

It ought to be noted in this connection that the implementation of social practices based on an objectively false belief can foster greater communal cohesion only if that false belief is actually shared generally among the members of the community. This was presumably the case for the belief in the meteorological efficacy of rain dancing among the Hopis, but would not likely to be the case for the belief in an innate equality of human intelligence among *politically incorrect* modern Europeans and Americans.

Limits of Scientism. The most serious deficiency of scientism, however, derives from its habitual overestimation of the power of science to provide an authoritative understanding of just those phenomena that are most relevant for the social sphere. That is to say, scientism fails to appreciate the difference in explanatory power between theories of the physical sciences and of the social sciences. The physical sciences, whose explanatory propositions are the most solidly validated, have the least bearing on the realization of moral aims. By contrast, the propositions in the social sciences, which have the most bearing on the realization of moral aims, are conspicuously deficient in objective validation. Biology occupies an intermediate position between these two extremes with respect to both the validity and the moral relevance of its propositions. Although this difference between the laws of physics and sociology is, of course, generally recognized, the deeper epistemological reasons why the physical sciences are 'hard' and the human sciences 'soft' are less widely appreciated.

In fact, there not only still arise so many troublesome conflicts between science and morals that the credibility of the Baconian creed of salvation through science is itself losing ground in its Western heartland. Some of this loss of faith in mankind's salvation through science was set off by the misuses of science in war and peace. The misuses commonly mentioned include the killing and maiming of defenseless civilians by nuclear weapons, the control and exploitation of subject peoples by their electronic surveillance, and the despoilment and pollution of the Earth by the technological fruits of modern research. Scientists deplore these misuses as much as do the critics of science. But scientists tend to point out that it is wrong to blame science only for mankind's problems while ignoring its contributions to mankind's welfare. According to them, the way to avert these misuses is not to stop doing science but to remedy the misuses politically and scientifically. Anyhow, how will we ever be able to feed the hungry of the world and to cure cancer if we turn away from science now?

Machiavelli. These discussions rarely consider a class of deeper causes of the latter-day decline of the Baconian creed, which is philosophically more troublesome than the misuses of science, inasmuch as it has no remedy, even in principle. That category comprises some projects, which, even though they are far from being intended to kill or enslave people or to destroy nature, are sincerely meant to augment human welfare. Yet, these projects are perceived as having sinister implications. It is to this troublesome, paradoxical category of causes responsible for the decline of the Baconian creed that some of the present and proposed applications of human biology belong, such as cloning and other manipulations of human genes, as well as mood-control by psychoactive drugs. Despite their overtly benevolent intent, these applications seem monstrous and evoke the specter of Doctors Frankenstein and Strangelove.

The surprising overarching conclusion that can be drawn from the moral dilemma posed by benevolent science (in contrast to its malevolent applications) is not merely that science sometimes conflicts with ethics. It is also that the growth of scientific knowledge and the power that sprung from it has made it evident that the ensemble of Western metaphysics and morals that spawned science in the first place is inherently paradoxical.

As we noted briefly in Chapter 1, this troublesome character of the Western moral tradition was discovered, or at least was first plainly stated, by the sixteenth century Italian statesman and political theorist, Niccolo Machiavelli, a century before Galileo even opened the door to modern science. According to the British philosopher Isaiah Berlin (1971), it is one of the great enigmas of Western letters why scholars have argued for centuries about just what it was that Machiavelli meant to convey in his two famous books, *The Prince* and *The Discourses*. Berlin's proposed resolution of the great enigma was that Machiavelli—who (unlike Immanuel Kant) was a highly lucid writer—presented a most disturbing insight, which no Utopian visionary of the future of mankind can accept. For Machiavelli showed that the ensemble of our social aspirations is paradoxical. Hence the belief that the correct, objectively valid solution to the question of how men should live can in principle be discovered is itself, in principle, not true.

By publishing his insight Machiavelli managed to incur an ecumenical and everlasting hatred of people representing the entire spectrum of Western religious, philosophical, and political thought. Catholics and Protestants, autocrats and democrats, reactionaries and revolutionaries, all despised him. Different visionaries may disagree about the felicity of their respective visions, but they all share the same fervent belief that such a thing as an ideal society can exist. No wonder that Machiavelli's subversive message that no such thing is possible has made him appear as the Devil incarnate, a.k.a. (as Machiavelli's namesake) 'Old Nick.'

Thus Machiavelli drew attention to the two incompatible systems of ethics that form part of the Western cultural heritage. One of these systems, which Berlin termed 'Christian,' regards morals as being based on ultimate values sought for their own sakes—values recognition of which alone enable us to speak of crimes or morally to justify and condemn anything. The other system, which Berlin terms 'pagan' derives it authority from mankind's being social creatures that live in communities. The pagan system knows no ultimate values, only communal purposes, and its moral judgments are relative rather than absolute. Or, more simply stated, the two mutually incompatible aims and values projected into the

Utopian society are freedom and justice for the individual, on the one hand, and law and order for the body politic, on the other.

What is the source of the 'Christian' belief in ultimate values in the first place? Berlin identifies it as the doctrine that in one version or another has dominated Western thought since Plato "that there exists some single principle that not only regulates the course of the sun and the stars, but prescribes their proper behavior to all animate creatures." Central to this doctrine (brought to Christianity, as we noted earlier, by St. Augustine in the fourth century) is the notion of God, or His atheistic equivalent, Eternal Reason. Its power "has endowed all things and creatures, each with a specific function; these functions are elements in a single harmonious whole and are intelligible in terms of it alone. This unifying pattern is the very heart of traditional rationalism, religious and atheistic, metaphysical or scientific, transcendental or naturalistic, which has been characteristic of Western Civilization. It is this rock upon which Western beliefs and lives have been founded, that Machiavelli seems, in effect, to have split open."

To illustrate the moral contradictions to which he called attention, Machiavelli provided some concrete examples from politics, statecraft, and warfare of classical antiquity and Renaissance Italy. Other examples are provided in our own modern times, which illuminate the troublesome and equivocal ethical role of science—one of the crown jewels of Western Civilization. As Machiavelli noted, no Utopia can be achieved on Earth, not because of the frailties and imperfections of mankind, but because every conceivable ideal society is meant to satisfy mutually incompatible, that is, paradoxical, goals.

Evolutionism vs. Creationism in the Schools. It had long seemed that the controversy regarding the teaching of Darwinian evolution in American public schools had been settled judicially in favor of modern science at the Scopes Monkey Trial held in Tennessee in the 1920s. But, as it turned out, the controversy still festered in the 1970s. At that time, the Curriculum Commission of the California State Board of Education reconsidered whether the Biblical account of Creation ought not to be presented in the officially approved high school biology textbooks on an equal footing with Darwinian evolutionary theory. At hearings held in response to demands by some Christian Fundamentalist groups, much of

232

the argument was devoted to the question whether the Darwinian theory is merely an unproved speculation, as alleged by the Fundamentalists, or a solidly documented scientific proposition, as claimed by the biologists. The deeper matter at issue, however, was not scientific truth but religious freedom. For the Fundamentalists claimed that a Christian child attending a tax-supported school has as much of a right to be protected from the dogmas of atheism as an atheist child has to be protected from prayer. Hence, it would follow that the classroom teaching of Darwinism as the only explanation of biocosmogeny is an infringement of the religious freedom of Christian parents to raise their children in the faith of their choice.

In the light of the citizen's rights guaranteed by the US Constitution, the Fundamentalist's argument seemed sound. And the Fundamentalists rightly rejected as irrelevant the pro-Darwinist testimony by liberal apologist clergymen that one can be a devout Christian without taking the biblical account of Genesis all that literally. After all, the Fundamentalist faith *is* to take the Bible literally. But the practical inference that flows from admitting the justice of the Fundamentalist claim is not that secondary-school biology texts should give the Genesis story equal time with the Darwinian theory. Rather, what follows is that no public school system can operate effectively in a heterogeneous social setting without having its curriculum prejudice the minds of its students against the cherished beliefs of some of their parents. In other words, to be practicably workable, the Constitution (just as the Bible, in fact) cannot be interpreted in a wholly literal way. Rather, the Constitution's judicial interpretation must (and usually does) take into account the complex contextual situation in which its articles are to be applied and seek an optimal, albeit imperfect solution. As for the textbook case, it has been recognized in most (but by no means in all) American jurisdictions that the ultimate Judeo-Christian (Western) moral aim of freedom and individual rights has to give way to the pagan (Confucian) aim of mounting a pedagogically effective society.

A concrete example of the metaphysical gulf that still separates Western and East Asian approaches to nature and her laws was provided by the Reverend Hogen Fujimoto (1972) at the biology-textbook revision hearings of California Curriculum Commission. Fujimoto spoke as a representative of the Buddhist Churches of America, and just as the Darwinist biology teachers, he too voiced his opposition to the inclusion of the *Genesis* story in the biology textbooks. But his opposition was based on ideological grounds that were entirely different from those represented by the scientist witnesses. Reverend Fujimoto objected to the inclusion of the Biblical account because it is contrary to Buddhist epistemology, which holds, according to his testimony, that "in the complexities of causes and subcauses one cause cannot be isolated, and is hidden within the myriad of subcauses and conditions. For this reason, a one-cause concept such a Divine Creation cannot be accepted by the Buddhists."

Although Reverend Fujimoto did not seem to object to the retention of the Darwinian account of evolution in the textbooks, he ought to have done so. For the same, and from the East Asian perspective, naïve ideas informed both the Torah and the *Origin of Species*, namely that single causes *can* be isolated and that from their isolation devolves an explanation of the universe. Whether one believes that the cause of present life forms was God's will or natural selection is, as the East Asian remove from Western doctrines, a comparatively inconsequential detail. Hence Buddhist children in California schools ought to be spared exposure to the simplistic notion that it is given to mankind to explain the phenomena of the world by rational thought, be it of the Biblical or the Darwinian variety. Reverend Fujimoto concluded his testimony with the observation that the "the question of the beginning is beyond human intellect to grasp and, therefore, should not be incorporated into the school curriculum."

Coda. The deeper cause for the latter-day decline of the Baconian creed is philosophically more troublesome than the misuses of science, inasmuch as it has no remedy, even in principle. That cause stems from the moral difficulties that arise from some applications of science which, far from being meant to kill or enslave people or to destroy nature, are intended to augment human welfare and which nevertheless have sinister implications. It is to this troublesome paradoxical category that some of the present and proposed applications of human biology belong. As stated, despite their overtly benevolent intent, these applications seem monstrous and evoke the specter of Doctors Frankenstein and Strangelove. The surprising, overarching conclusion that can be drawn from the moral dilemma posed by benevolent science (in contrast to its malevolent applications) is not merely that science sometimes conflicts with morals. The growth of scientific knowledge and the manipulative power it provided for mankind has made it evident also that the ensemble of Western metaphysics and morals that spawned science in the first place is inherently paradoxical.

Niels Bohr (1885–1962)

Chapter Fourteen

Complementarity*

Paradoxes of Quantum Physics. In our discussions of Kantian epistemic dualism we considered the paradoxical relation between pure theoretical reason (with its value-free, natural categories, such as space, time, causality, and object) and pure practical reason (with its value-laden, non-natural categories, such as good and evil, sacredness, free will, and personhood). These discussions led us to the insight that our interpretation of persons' actions can be very different when we encounter them in a natural/amoral context or in a non-natural/moral context. In a natural/amoral context—especially in a scientific or medical setting—we regard persons as *objects*, whose actions are determined heteronomously by the laws of nature and for which they bear no moral responsibility. But in a non-natural/moral context—especially in a social setting—we regard persons as *subjects*, whose actions are determined autonomously by their free will and for which we *do* hold them morally responsible.

We had noted briefly, moreover, that epistemological paradoxes arise not only *between* the two realms of the intelligible world—the natural realm and the non-natural realm created by pure theoretical reason and by pure practical reason, respectively—but also *within* the natural realm. We thus saw that we encounter paradoxes *within* pure theoretical reason when we address phenomena in the microcosmic domain of the phenomenal world. For the tiny dimensions of that microcosmic domain situate its phenomena outside the mesocosmic domain of our direct experience to which our innate categories of pure theoretical reason are evolutionarily adapted.

To conclude our discussion of the limits of human rationality, we now turn to one particular set of—as yet not fully resolved—paradoxical phenomena of nature that physicists encountered in the first half of the twentieth century. These paradoxical phenomena arise from the existence of energy as discrete (rather than infinitely divisible) packets, or *quanta*, and from the wave-particle duality of some basic (microcosmic) constituents of

*A substantial part of this chapter is based on Chapter 17 of *Max Delbrück's Mind from Matter?* Stent, G.S., et al., editors (1986).

matter. They confront us with the kind of 'deep truth' of which Niels Bohr had said that its opposite also contains deep truth.

Exchange of Energy between Light and Matter. The scientific study of light began in the Renaissance and, by the seventeenth century, Isaac Newton and Christian Huygens had put forward antithetical theories about its nature. According to Newton, light consists of fast-moving particles flying through space. According to Huygens, however, light consists of transverse waves propagated as oscillatory disturbances of a hypothetical 'ether' supposed to permeate all space, just as ocean waves are propagated as oscillatory disturbances of seawater. By the beginning of the eighteenth century, Newton's particle theory had fallen into disfavor, after it was found that light manifests the phenomena of *interference* and *diffraction* characteristic of waves but not of particles. [Interference diminishes the amplitude of two waves of equal wave length upon their encounter if they oscillate out-of-phase and augments it if they oscillate in-phase. Diffraction changes the direction of propagation of a wave when it encounters an obstruction, such as an edge or a small hole.]

By the 1870s James Clerk Maxwell had succeeded in unifying electricity, magnetism, and light, by demonstrating that all three phenomena consist of waves propagated as oscillatory disturbances of an electromagnetic field. Maxwell's conception of light as an electromagnetic wave encouraged physicists to try to account for the exchange of energy between light and matter. That problem had arisen as a result of efforts to explain the commonplace observation that as a body, such as a bar of iron, is heated to higher and higher temperatures, it emits light waves of higher and higher intensities and frequencies (that is, oscillations per second). At low temperatures, light is emitted in the low frequency range of the (for us invisible) infrared and at low intensity. Then, as the bar becomes hotter and hotter, the light it emits turns red, then yellow, then blue (a.k.a., 'white heat'), and finally the (for us again invisible) ultraviolet, all the while becoming more and more intense. This process can be represented by a series of graphs, on which the intensity of light $\rho(v)$ [that is, the flux of radiant energy per unit volume] emitted at the frequency v is plotted against v—with each graph representing the intensity-distribution curve at a given temperature, T.

As seen in the graph of an intensity-distribution curve such as that presented here, the light intensity, $\rho(v)$, rises with increasing values of v, until it reaches a maximum at v_{max}. After that point, $\rho(v)$ declines again and falls to zero at very high values of v. The value of v_{max} corresponds to the frequency of the perceived color of the light emitted at the temperature T. Additional graphs of intensity-distribution curves measured at a series of temperatures T would have shown that with increasing values of T, the position of the curve's v_{max} shifts to the left (i.e. to higher values of v), in a manner such that the ratio T/v_{max} remains constant. This relation was discovered by Wilhelm Wien and is known as 'Wien's law.' The additional graphs would have shown also that the *total intensity of light emitted over the entire range of frequencies* [that is, the area under the $\rho(v)$ distribution curve] at any given T increases proportionally with the fourth power of T. This relation is known as the 'Stefan-Boltzmann law.'

Rayleigh's Distribution Formula. By 1900, the British physicist, Lord Rayleigh, had developed a theory intended to account for the $\rho(v)$ intensity distribution curve of light emitted by hot bodies. His theory was based on three ideas, in addition to Maxwell's conception of light as an electromagnetic wave. One idea was to formulate the problem in terms of a hollow box filled with light waves, whose interior temperature is T and whose black interior walls absorb from the box and reemit into its interior all light waves that strike them. A second idea was to regard each light wave in the box as the equivalent of a gas molecule. And Rayleigh's third idea was to apply to the (conceptually molecularized) light waves the thermodynamic law known as the '*equipartition principle.*' According to that principle, the total, evenly shared heat energy available to an ensemble of n molecules is nkT (where k denotes Boltzmann's constant, having the value of 1.3805×10^{-16} erg/degree/molecule, and T denotes the absolute temperature in degrees Kelvin).

On the basis of these three ideas, Rayleigh derived a formula that relates the light intensity $\rho(v)$ emitted at a light frequency v (of dimension sec^{-1}) to the temperature T.

$$\rho(v) = (8\pi\, v^2/c^3)kT$$

In this formula the letter c denotes the velocity of light (3×10^8 m/second) and the factor $8\pi\, v^2/c^3$ represents n, the number of light wave "molecules" of frequency v per unit volume, according to Maxwell's theory of electromagnetic radiation.

As is evident from the plot shown here, the light intensity $\rho(v)$ at a given temperature T *predicted* by Rayleigh's formula increases rapidly with increases in the light frequency, ν. For low values of ν, such as that characteristic of lukewarm iron bars glowing in the infrared, Rayleigh's formula is in reasonable agreement with both Wien's law and the Stefan-Boltzmann law. In fact, Rayleigh's formula gives a satisfactory account of the experimentally observed intensity distribution $\rho(\nu)$ as long as the values of ν are below ν_{max}.

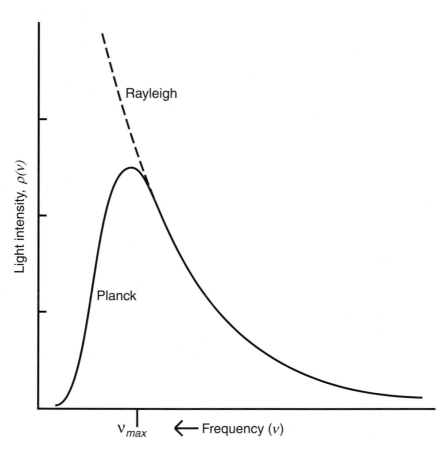

Distribution of the intensity, $\rho(\nu)$, of light of frequency ν emitted at a given temperature T. The Rayleigh distribution formula correctly describes the intensities emitted at low frequencies but diverges drastically from those actually emitted at high frequencies. The Planck distribution formula correctly describes the intensities emitted over the entire frequency range.

However, Rayleigh's distribution formula fails to account for the observation that the intensity distribution $\rho(v)$ reaches a maximum value at the frequency v_{max}, and it predicts counterfactually that $\rho(v)$ keeps on increasing ever more rapidly with increases in v. Hence Rayleigh's formula is in accord neither with Wien's law nor with the Stefan-Boltzmann law. The counterfactual prediction of Rayleigh's formula of ever-increasing values of the light intensity $\rho(v)$ at higher and higher light frequencies came to be known as the 'ultraviolet catastrophe.'

Planck's Distribution Formula and the Discovery of the Quantum.
In the same year of 1900 when Rayleigh had presented his inadequate formula, the German physicist, Max Planck, put forward a radically new, and, at the time, counterintuitive idea that would evade the counterfactual predictions inherent in Rayleigh's distribution formula. Planck proposed that the amount of energy contained by individual light waves is restricted to discrete values, rather than being capable of taking on any value whatever, as physicists had previously believed. According to Planck, the discrete amount of energy carried by an individual light wave is given by the product $h \times v$, where v is the wave's frequency (of dimension sec^{-1}) and h is a universal constant of nature, soon to become known as *Planck's constant*, having the value 6.624×10^{-27} erg sec. Thus the product hv represents the unit packet, or *quantum*, of energy that is carried by each wave of frequency v, and that it can exchange only *in toto* with matter.

Contrary to Rayleigh's assumption of energy equipartition among all the light wave "molecules" sharing the same black-walled box, Planck assumed that each wave in the box retains its energy quantum hv, which it contributes to the overall light-intensity distribution $\rho(v)$. Thus the quantized distribution of radiant energy among an ensemble of light waves would differ fundamentally from the equipartition of kinetic energies among an ensemble of gas molecules. Planck reckoned on statistical grounds that at a temperature T the relative abundance of waves in the ensemble with energy hv is $1/(e^{hv/kT} - 1)$. Thus the global light intensity of the whole ensemble at the frequency v would be

$$\rho(v) = 8\pi\, hv^3/c^3(e^{hv/kT} - 1)$$

At low values of the frequency ν, Planck's formula reduces to Rayleigh's formula $\rho(\nu) = (8\pi \nu^2/c^3)kT$. At high values of the frequency, ν, however, Planck's formula reduces to

$$\rho(\nu) = 8\pi h\nu^3/c^3 e^{h\nu/kT}$$

Planck's formula thus evades the ultraviolet catastrophe, since its denominator, $c^3 e^{h\nu/kT}$ increases more rapidly with the frequency ν than does its numerator $8\pi h\nu^3$. Hence unlike Rayleigh's, Planck's formula correctly accounts for the whole range of observed distribution of light intensities $\rho(\nu)$ and is in agreement with the laws of Wien and of Stefan-Boltzmann. (Planck, 1901)

Einstein's Wave-Particle Antinomy. Although quantum theory came into being in 1900, it took a quarter of a century before its full ontological implications were appreciated. Planck's postulation of the quantum was gloriously successful, but it soon led to a conceptual calamity for physicists when young Albert Einstein began his study of the *photoelectric effect*. (This is the name given to the phenomenon of emission of electrons from metal surfaces induced by their absorption of light.) Building on Planck's counterintuitive notion that a light beam composed of waves oscillating with frequency ν is an ensemble of quantized energy packets, each carrying an energy $h\nu$. Einstein showed in 1909 that light is not absorbed by the metal as waves, but as discrete lumps of energy, or 'photons.' According to Einstein, photons are massless particles (that is, objects without mass, which is yet another counterintuitive notion for us denizens of the mesocosm), with the radiant energy of each photon being $h\nu$, where h is Planck's constant and ν the frequency attributable to the wave-like aspect of the light. Thus Einstein resuscitated Newton's long-abandoned theory of the particulate nature of light and discovered that light has a dual nature, or to express it in terms of a Kantian antinomy.

Thesis:	*Antithesis:*
Light is a wave	Light is a particle
(Huygens, Maxwell)	(Newton)

When Einstein first made this proposal of the antinomial relation between the wave-like and the particle-like properties of light, it met with general rejection by the community of physicists. Even Planck would not accept it at first, so radical was its nature. But by 1921 the quantized photon had become a mainstream idea, and Einstein was awarded the Nobel

Prize in Physics for his work on the photoelectric effect (rather than for devising his relativity theories, which would make him the most famous scientist of the twentieth century).

Quantized Bohr Atom. The next stage in the development of quantum theory produced even more acute conceptual paradoxes. In the early years of the twentieth century, Ernest Rutherford had postulated that atoms consist of a *nucleus*, which comprises almost all of their mass and carries a positive electrical charge. Around the nucleus orbits a cloud of much lighter particles,—the *electrons*—, which carry a negative electrical charge. By 1913, however, Niels Bohr had realized that Rutherford's model of electrons orbiting the nucleus could not account for the fixed chemical properties of atoms. So Bohr modified Rutherford's atomic model by postulating that the electrons move in a *discrete, quantized subset* of the continuously varying range of orbits that would be theoretically possible according to classical Newtonian mechanics. Bohr proposed, furthermore, that the orbiting electrons jump from one quantized orbit to another by absorbing or emitting quanta of light. The idea of quantized electron orbits was very offensive to many physicists, especially to those whose data Bohr took the liberty of reinterpreting in terms of his model. Bohr's atomic model may have offended some people, but it was tremendously successful and led to a much deeper understanding of the chemists' periodic table of the elements.

Uncertainty Principle. Efforts during the period 1913–1925 to give Bohr's quantized atomic model a quantitative formulation culminated in two independent theoretical breakthroughs: the wave equation of Erwin Schrödinger and the matrix mechanics of Werner Heisenberg. Schrödinger's wave equation was based on Louis de Broglie's recent conjecture that, just as photons, electrons also have wave-like properties. De Broglie's conjecture that electrons, authentic particles possessing a measurable mass, have also the properties of waves, [and hence Schrödinger's wave equation based on that conjecture], was even less palatable for the physics community than Einstein's earlier inference of the wave-particle duality of the massless photon.

As for Heisenberg's matrix mechanics, it seemed an even greater assault on rationality than de Broglie's attribution of wavelike properties to the electron. For when Heisenberg's formulation was restated by Paul Dirac in terms of an algebra whose variables represent the positional coordinates (p) and momenta (q) of electrons, supposedly real quantities measurable with rods and clocks, it transpired that these variables do not obey the law of '*multiplicative commutability*.' [According to that law, it is true for all ordinary quantities a and b encountered in everyday life that $a \times b$ is equal to $b \times a$. But it is *not* true for the positional coordinates and momenta of electrons that $p \times q$ is equal to $q \times p$.]

Heisenberg's 'uncertainty principle' brought further disorder into this conceptual chaos. This principle asserts that the variables p and q represent quantities that cannot in principle be measured jointly to any arbitrary degree of accuracy in a single experiment or have their exact magnitudes inferred from successive experiments. For it inheres in the nature of these experiments that when an experimental arrangement is set up that is designed to measure the magnitude of one of these variables, information is necessarily lost concerning the magnitude of the other. The product of the uncertainties, Δp and Δq, in the measure of both p and q is never smaller than $h/2\pi$ (where h is Planck's constant) as seen in Heisenberg's uncertainty principle.

$$\Delta p \times \Delta q > h/2\pi$$

Complementarity. It had not escaped Bohr's notice that the parade of counterintuitive findings that turned up in the development of the quantum theory confronted physicists with deeply troubling epistemological problems. The problems had begun to turn up upon Planck's discovery of the quantum and continued with Einstein's discovery of the wave-particle duality of the photon and Bohr's own discovery of the discrete character of the electron orbits around the atomic nucleus. And they culminated in de Broglie's conjecture of the wave-particle duality of the electron [soon to be vindicated by the demonstration that, like photons, electrons too, are subject to *diffraction*] and in Heisenberg's Uncertainty Principle. By 1927, Bohr had realized that all these strange phenomena could be traced to a common epistemological root, which he called '*complementarity*.'(Bohr, 1928)

In his use of the term complementarity Bohr did not refer to its ordinary, everyday meaning, namely the aspects of two different parts of an entity that make it a whole, as the two 'complementary' polynucletoide chains make the DNA double helix a whole. Rather, Bohr gave 'complementarity' a special, esoteric meaning, namely the relation between two *rationally* irreconcilable (or in Kantian terminology, *antinomial*) descriptions of the world whose *factual* irreconcilability no experiment can ever demonstrate. Bohr's prime example of complementarity was the description of electrons in terms of *both* waves and particles. The irreconcilability of these two antinomial descriptions is not experimentally demonstrable, because a critical test of either the wave or of the particle nature of the electron demands mutually exclusive observational arrangements.

Bohr pointed out that the mutually exclusive experimental arrangements needed for the study of complementary aspects turn out to be responsible for a fundamental limitation of our analysis of natural phenomena. For in a physical measurement it is never possible to take into account the interaction between object and measuring instruments. Or, as Bohr put it, "the instruments cannot be included in the investigation while they are also serving as means observation." But the admission of such a fundamental limitation of empirical knowledge inhering in Bohr's complementarity puts in doubt our intuitive idea—usually referred to as 'realism'—that phenomena exist independently of the means by which they are observed.

That this is bad news for those scientists (namely, the majority of them), for whom realism is the unquestioned metaphysical foundation of their vocation in the first place, was clearly exposed by Donald McKay (1957, 1974). After all, if phenomena do not exist independently of the means by which we observe them, then as far as reality is concerned, there would be no "there" there, as Gertrude Stein once said of her hometown, Oakland, California.

Conspiracy of Nature. The furthest-reaching epistemological consequence of Bohr's complementary concept, however, was that far from *having* both properties of wave and particle, an electron takes on one or the other property only as we are observing it under one or the other of mutually exclusive observational setups. To illustrate this point, Bohr developed a thought experiment whose apparatus consists of a gun that shoots a beam of electrons at a wall. The wall has two small holes through which some of the electrons impinging on the wall may pass and then hit a backstop at some distance behind the wall. Either hole can be opened or closed. [The following four panels are taken from R. Feynman, R. B. Leighton, and M. Sands, *The Feynman Lectures on Physics*, Volume III. Addison-Wesley, Reading, MA. 1965.]

In panel **A**, we see a gun shooting bullets at random at the wall. There are two holes, 1 and 2, in the wall, spaced at equal distances from the intersection with the wall of a perpendicular line projected to the wall from the point at which the gun is positioned. Either hole may be opened or closed. Behind the wall is a backstop with a moveable bullet detector.

The detector measures P, the frequency with which (and hence the probability that) bullets that pass through one of the holes in the wall and strike the backstop at a distance x from the projection to the backstop of the midpoint between the two holes. When only hole 1 or only hole 2 is open, the detector registers the bullet frequency distributions designated respectively as P_1 and P_2. When both holes are open the distribution P_{12} registered is the sum of the distributions P_1 and P_2 that are observed with either hole open alone. That is to say, in this setup, $P_{12} = P_1 + P_2$.

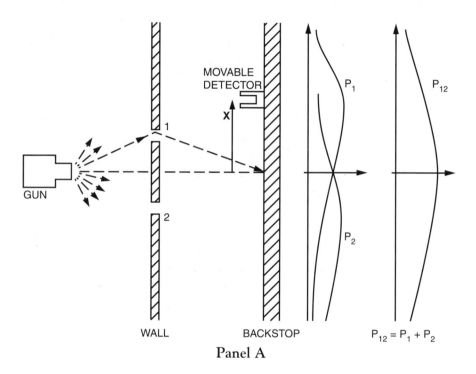

Panel A

In panel **B**, the setup is immersed in water. The gun has been replaced by a source of water waves (such as stones dropping into the water). The backstop has been replaced by an absorber (that is, by a non-reflector) of the waves and a wave detector that measures the intensity I of the waves reaching the absorber at the distance x from the midpoint has been substituted for the movable bullet detector. Here the 'intensity' is defined as the square of the absolute value of the mean amplitude $|h|$ of the waves absorbed at x, averaged over the whole duration of the experiment. When only hole 1 or only hole 2 is open, the wave detector registers the intensity distributions designated as I_1 and I_2 respectively, where $I_1 = |h_1|^2$ and $I_2 = |h_2|^2$. When both holes are open, the distribution I_{12} registered is *not* the sum of the distributions I_1 and I_2 observed with either hole open alone. Instead we see a distribution with crests and troughs, or 'fringes,' due to the following relation.

$$I_{12} = |h_1 + h_2|^2$$

The difference between the results shown in panel **A** and panel **B** is attributable to interference at the absorber of parts of the same wave that passed through both open holes in the experiment of panel **B**. In the experiment of panel **A**, the bullets do not show interference at the backstop, since any given bullet can pass through only one of the two open holes.

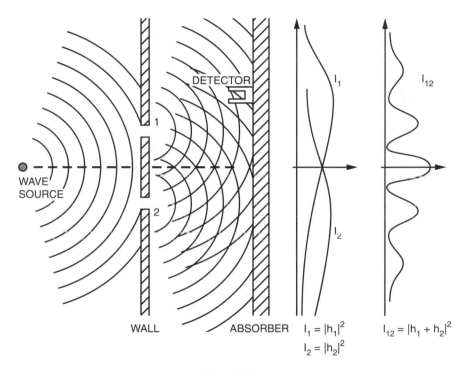

Panel B

In panel **C,** the setup is in a vacuum chamber. The gun is an electron gun, which emits an electron beam in random directions. The electron detector at the backstop is an electronic device connected to a loudspeaker. Each electron that strikes the detector is heard as a distinct click, thus demonstrating that the electrons strike the backstop as particles, just as do the bullets in panel **A**. When only hole 1 or only hole 2 is open, the detector registers the electron frequency distributions P_1 and P_2 respectively. But when both holes are open, the observed frequency distribution P_{12} is not the sum of P_1 and P_2. Rather, just as in the case of the water waves, P_{12} manifests the results of interference at the backstop. Loudspeaker clicks notwithstanding, each electron behaves as if it had reached the backstop by traveling through *both* holes, that is, like a water wave rather than a bullet. Thus at x there are two mean amplitudes, ϕ_1 and ϕ_2, associated with parts of the electron waves having traveled through either hole, so that $P_1 = |\phi_1|^2$, $P_2 = |\phi_2|^2$, and $P_{12} = |\phi_1 + \phi_2|^2$. This uncanny result is obtained, even if the electron gun is firing so slowly that each electron has reached the backstop before the next electron has been released, thereby eliminating the possibility that the interference pattern represented by P_{12} is the result of interactions between several electrons.

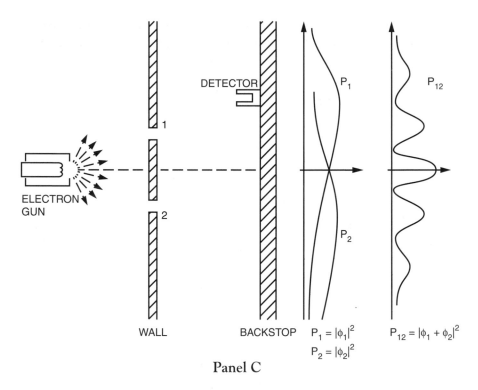

Panel C

The setup shown in panel **D** is similar to that of panel **C**, except that it includes an additional feature that can tell us whether an individual electron that produced a distinct click in the loudspeaker had actually passed through hole 1 or hole 2. This feature consists of a strong light source placed behind the wall between the two holes, as well as a device that registers the direction in which light was scattered by passage of an electron. It is thus possible to know on which side of the light source proximal to hole 1 or to hole 2, each electron has traveled. Here it is found that, as would be expected of a particle, when both holes are open, each click is associated with transit of an electron through one or the other of the two holes, but never through both. But in this case the distribution P_{12} is characteristic of bullets rather than waves, namely that $P_{12} = P_1 + P_2$: That is to say, the interference phenomenon observed in the setup of panel **C** has disappeared: The inclusion of the additional feature in the experimental setup that demonstrates the particulate character of the electron has eliminated its wave-like character. This result leads to the even more uncanny inference that a single electron goes through both holes only when we are not watching through which hole it actually went. It is uncanny, but not inconsistent, as it would have been had the device had shown that any given electron goes through only one of the two open holes and yet that the electron distribution at the backstop is still that characteristic of an electron wave.

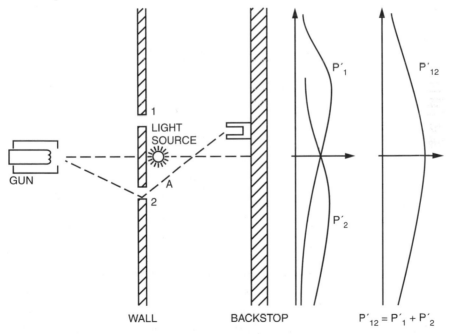

Panel D

Maybe the result obtained with the setup of panel **D** is not all that strange, because, after all, the quanta emitted by the light source of the additional feature do disturb the electrons. Thus we can at least console ourselves with the thought that in setup **D** something is being done to the electrons that is not being done in setup **C**. To remove any residual complacency, let us therefore consider a fifth setup (which is not shown here). That setup is again similar to that of panel **C**, except that the wall with the holes is now mounted on wheels riding on a track running parallel to the backstop. The wall is thus free to move back and forth, due to the recoil imparted to the wall by the momentum of individual electrons that are colliding with the edges of the holes. Thus it should be possible to infer from the direction in which the wall moves whether an electron passed though hole 1 or hole 2. In this setup nothing extra is done to the electrons, since they cannot help but collide with the edges of the holes. Should not their wave-like character, and hence the interference phenomenon, be preserved under these conditions? The answer is that we cannot tell, because we are unable to observe the interference pattern, even if the wave-like pattern *were* preserved.

There is a good reason for this frustration of our earnest efforts to infer from the direction of the movement of the wall which hole an electron has passed through. This reason arises from the necessity of measuring with very high accuracy both the momentum imparted to the wall and the positions of the two holes before and after passage of the electron. But the experimental arrangement needed for measuring the momentum of the wall with high accuracy introduces an uncertainty, or wiggle, in the positions of the two holes. This procedure generates an error in the measurement of the distance Δx from the midpoint at which an electron released by the electron gun in a given direction actually strikes the (stationary) backstop. This error causes a corresponding error ΔP in the electron distribution P measured by the detector, which, in accord with Heisenberg's uncertainty principle, is sufficiently large to smear out the crests and troughs of the interference pattern $P_{12} = |\phi_1 + \phi_2|^2$, if any interference *did* occur.

We thus reach another stage in the torturous development of quantum theory. The eerie fact is that the uncertainty principle and the complementarity of mutually exclusive measurements protect the conceptually paradoxical elements of quantum theory from being shown up by any experiment. Every observational act of ours entails an element of subjectivity, since we must make an arbitrary choice of where and how to make the conceptual cut between the instruments of observation to be used and the objects to be observed. The observational setup has to be described in the terms of classical (i.e. non-quantum, or mesocosmic) physics, so that the observers can report to others (as well as making clear to themselves) in unambiguous terms the exact experimental setup and the results obtained.

In Bohr's thought-experiment, for example, we can choose a wall fixed in position relative to the electron gun and the backstop. This setup permits a determination of the wavelengths of the electrons on the basis of their interference patterns, but not of the identity of the hole through which any given electron went. Or we can choose a wall that is free to exchange momentum, but with an uncertain position, by mounting the wall on wheels. This setup permits a determination of the momentum exchange between wall and electrons, and hence an identification of the hole through which each electron went. However, any information regarding the wavelength of the electrons is lost. These two setups are clearly mutually exclusive, since the wall cannot be both fixed and yet free to exchange momentum. If the wall is fixed, it is part of the observational apparatus with which we seek to define the wave character of the observed object (the electron). If the wall is free to move, and its momentum is measured before and after the collision with the particle, then the wall is itself an object of observation rather than part of the observational apparatus.

Bohr's thought-experiment shows that complementarity amounts to a fiendish conspiracy of nature (or of God) to keep us from attaining an objective description of reality. She (or He) ties observer and object together so that, in the microcosmic realm of applicability of quantum mechanics, no sharp line that can be drawn in any experimental setup would demarcate where the 'observer' ends and the 'object' begins. Thus, according to Bohr, in the drama of existence, we play the dual role of actor and observer. It seems ironical, indeed bizarre, that a conclusion so subversive for the metaphysics of materialism should have been forced on us by twentieth-century physics.

Criticisms of Complementarity. The proposition that the complementarity concept is universally applicable to physical reality and is the crux of quantum phenomena was hotly debated for the twenty years following

Bohr's first presentation of the concept. The most prominent among Bohr's critics was Einstein, who was unwilling to admit any such conspiracy of nature and would not accept quantum mechanics as a complete description of physical reality. He felt that quantum mechanics is *incomplete*, in the sense that it fails to account for some quantities that are 'physically real.' He believed that it should be possible to develop a more adequate theory, which would provide a fully determinate, or *complete* account of all real phenomena.

Many attempts were made to find loopholes in Bohr's complementarity argument, especially by designing clever thought-experiments that would circumvent the uncertainty principle. But all of these attempts failed, probably because the dictum of the Austrian philosopher Ludwig Wittgenstein, "whereof one cannot speak, thereof one must be silent" applies to Einstein's hoped-for complete and fully determinate description of all real phenomena in the microcosmic domain.

Lao-Tzu and Bohr. In a lecture that Bohr presented in Bologna in 1937, he likened complementarity to the philosophy of Lao-Tzu, the founder of Taoism. As we noted in Chapter 3, Taoism provided the philosophical fountainhead for the development of Chinese science, even though Taoism distrusts the powers of reason and regards the workings of nature inscrutable for the theoretical intellect. Taoism turned out to be wrong, of course. But it turned out to be wrong only in the short run: The workings of nature are not all *that* inscrutable. Provided that the questions one asks of nature are not too deep and the phenomena under study not too remote from our direct experience, rationally coherent answers can usually be found. But Taoism turned out to be right in the long run. Once physicists began to address natural phenomena in the microcosmic—atomic or subatomic—domain, they encountered bizarre and totally surprising contradictions (*contraria*) that violate the *a priori* categories of pure theoretical reason that serve us so well in the management of our everyday affairs in the mesocosmic domain.

When shortly after World War II, King Christian X made Bohr a Knight of the Royal Danish Order of the Elephant, Bohr emblazoned his knightly coat of arms with the Taoist Ying/Yang device, under the motto "CONTRARIA SUNT COMPLEMENTA." Bohr had played a little joke on his sovereign, but like all good jokes, Bohr's joke embodied wisdom: Propositions and their antinomies (*contraria*) can both be true (*sunt complementa*), as are Ying and Yang.

Kant and Bohr. As we noted,—first briefly in Chapter 1 and later in more detail in Chapter 10—in his *Critique of Pure Reason*, Kant had anticipated Bohr by applying an analog of the complementarity concept of quantum physics to the mind-body problem. For in developing the epistemological theory to which we refer as "epistemic dualism," Kant had invoked two sets of categories—pure theoretical reason and pure practical reason—and identified the source of two unavoidable, albeit rationally irreconcilable, or *antinomial*, descriptions of persons. In a natural/amoral context, to which we apply the set of transcendental categories of pure theoretical reason, such as space, time, and causality, we describe persons as material objects. But in a non-natural/moral context, to which we apply the set of transcendental categories of pure practical reason, such as good/evil, sacredness, and free will, we describe persons as moral subjects. According to Kant, to be human means to live as a dualist in both realms of the intelligible world and struggle with the paradoxes that arise from their incompatibility. (Kant, 1949)

Thus we are confronted not only with a conspiracy of nature that keeps us from attaining an objective (i.e., observer-independent) description of reality but also with a conspiracy of existence, foisted on us by our joint dependence on the antithetical categories of theoretical reason and practical reason. Because of this conspiracy of existence, our descriptions of persons are bound to be conceptually irreconcilable (or complementary in Bohr's sense) when we observe persons either in a natural/amoral context or in a non-natural/moral context. Nevertheless, despite their being conceptually irreconcilable, both natural/amoral and non-natural/moral descriptions are needed for a complete account of the person.

Bohr made no reference in his philosophical writings to Kantian epistemic dualism of pure theoretical reason and pure practical reason, to which his ideas about complementarity as a dualistic epistemological theory are obviously analogous. (Stent, 1988). It seems surprising that Bohr failed to recognize this analogy, especially in view of his assertion in his 1933 *Light and Life* lecture that free will—a crucial category of Kantian pure practical reason—must be considered as *a trait peculiar to conscious life*.

Another indication of the affinity of Bohr's epistemology to Kantian critical idealism is implicit in his following statement. "In our description

PARADOXES OF FREE WILL

of nature the purpose is not to disclose the real essence of the phenomena but only to track down, so far as is possible, relations between the manifold aspects of our experience." (Bohr, 1934). Thus the electron, to which Bohr sometimes referred as a 'phenomenon,' is, *qua* phenomenon, part of the Kantian *sensible* world.

As Bohr knew only too well, to account for the electron's relations with the manifold aspects of our experience, that is, to bring the electron from the *sensible* world of phenomena to the *intelligible* world of noumena, the French physicist Louis de Broglie had applied to the electron the antinomial categories of 'wave' and 'particle.' And just as joint application to the same *moral* context (responsibility) of two antinomial categories— one (determinism) provided by pure theoretical reason and the other (freedom) provided by pure practical reason—leads to *moral* paradoxes, so does joint application to the same *physical* context (electron) of two antinomial categories provided by theoretical reason alone (wave and particle) lead to *physical* paradoxes. Thus, Bohr's dualism of complementarity is no more meant to represent the world *as it really is* than is Kant's epistemic dualism. What the paradoxes embodied in both Kant's and Bohr's dualist theories testify to is our inability to construct a wholly coherent intelligible world of noumena on the basis of the phenomena we perceive in the sensible world.

Bohr's not mentioning Kant in this connection can hardly be attributable to his not having heard of the Kant's Copernican Revolution in Philosophy and its principal manifesto, the *Critique of Pure Reason*. For Denmark's leading Kant expert, the philosopher Harald Høffding (1843–1931), was a close personal friend of Bohr's father, the physiologist Christian Bohr, as well as young Niels' philosophy professor in his first student years at Copenhagen University. In line with Bohr's failure to mention the analogous relation between his complementarity concept and Kant's epistemic dualism, Kant's name does not appear in such definitive Bohr biographies as those by Ulrich Röseberg (1985) and Abraham Pais (1991), nor in any of the 40 articles contributed to the Niels Bohr Centenary Volume edited by A.P. French and P.J. Kennedy (1985).

So it was not until the final years of the twentieth century that there began to appear writings that drew attention to the affinity of Bohr's ideas to Kantian philosophy. Several examples of such writings were presented in the collection of essays *Niels Bohr and Contemporary Philosophy* edited by Jan Faye and Henry J. Folse (1994). The topics covered by the sixteen authors of these essays included comparisons of Bohr and Kant's views on the use of language and symbolism and on the antinomial metaphysics of materialism and idealism, as well as the classification of Bohr's metaphysical views under the rubric of 'Pragmatic Kantian Realism.'

None of the essayists, however, pointed to the most striking parallel between Kant and Bohr's philosophies, namely their epistemic dualism. In Kant's case, his epistemic dualism consists of the two mutually incoherent domains of the intelligible world—the amoral/natural domain and the moral/non-natural domain—the former created by pure theoretical reason and the latter by pure practical reason. And in Bohr's case, his 'CONTRARIA SUNT COMPLEMENTA' dualism comprises the mutually incoherent descriptions of phenomena in the quantum world within the amoral/natural domain of pure theoretical reason.

There is a plausible explanation for the failure of Faye and Folse's sixteen essayists to mention the obvious epistemological parallel between Bohr's concept of complementarity and Kant's epistemic dualism: None of the essayists seemed to be familiar with (or interested in) moral philosophy and Kant's contribution to the clarification of its foundations.

Moreover, none of the essayists seemed to know—no more than did Kant or Bohr, of course–about the development of evolutionary epistemology in mid-twentieth century (let alone its anticipation by Nietzsche in the latter part of the 19th century). Thus they were unaware of the biological roots of the paradoxical aspects, or complementarity, of our transcendental categories when they are pursued *au bout de la nuit*. As we noted in Chapter 12, the mesocosmic domain of the sensible world of phenomena, for the verbal description of which our language, as well as our Kantian pure theoretical reason, became adapted in the course of our brain evolution, represents but a tiny sliver of the phenomenal world. That domain comprises merely those phenomena in the ecological niche of *Homo sapiens* whose dimensions in time and space make them accessible to our direct sensory perception. Beyond it lie the *macrocosm*, extending outward to the stars and their galaxies, and the *microcosm*, extending inward to the atoms and their subatomic particles.

Had the essayists been familiar with evolutionary epistemology, it would not have come as a surprise to them that our categorical intuition has to be discarded, or at least drastically modified, when our scientific studies moved beyond the mesocosm to the microcosmic and macrocosmic domains of very small and very brief, or of very large and very long-lasting

255

phenomena. Such a movement beyond the mesocosmic domain of middle dimensions occurs whenever we consider the structure of the tiny atom and its function, or of the vast universe and its evolution.

Biology and Complementarity. Bohr believed that complementarity is not restricted to the phenomena of atomic physics and would be applicable also to many other disciplines dedicated to the search for understanding the world. He thought, for instance, that one of these disciplines is biology, which he considered in his Opening Address of the International Congress of Light Therapy held in Copenhagen (Bohr, 1933). The title of Bohr's address was 'Light and Life,' and its purpose was to draw attention to the epistemological implications for the life science of the fundamental changes that the quantum theory has brought to the conception of natural law.

Bohr thought that these changes, which extend to the very idea of the nature of scientific explanation, were important not only for a full appreciation of the new situation brought to physics by the quantum theory. According to Bohr, these developments had created also an entirely new background for viewing the problems of biology, in the light of which serious consideration ought to be given to the possibility that the processes of life might not be reducible to atomic physics. He suggested that there might be a complementary relation between the physiological and physical aspects of life analogous to that obtaining for the wave and particle aspects of the electron. In that case there would exist a kind of Uncertainty Principle of Biology. This proposal was expressed in the following passage he presented at his lecture.

"We should doubtless kill an animal if we tried to carry on then investigation of its organs so far that we could describe the role played by single atoms in vital functions. In every experiment involving organisms there must remain an uncertainty with regard to the conditions to which they are subjected. The idea suggests itself that the minimum freedom that we must allow organisms in this respect is just large enough to permit it, so to say, to hide its ultimate secrets from us." Bohr thus suggested another conspiracy of nature. Bohr's suggestion made many biologists, especially biochemists, as uneasy as Heisenberg's uncertainty principle of quantum mechanics had made uneasy many physicists.

What novel insights into biology did Bohr think could be gained by taking into the account the concept of complementarity? First of all,

Bohr made clear what it was that he did *not* mean to imply: He did not wish to suggest that at the microcosmic quantum level we encounter phenomena that show a closer resemblance to the properties of life than do ordinary mesocosmic physical phenomena. On the contrary, at first sight the essentially indeterminate, statistical character of quantum phenomena is very difficult to reconcile with the highly structured organization of mesocosmic living creatures like ourselves, who have all the characteristics of their species implanted in tiny genes. It goes without saying that quantum theory applies to the chemical behavior of all atoms, be they part of living or non-living matter. But, so Bohr declared, regarding life as a chemical phenomenon will not explain it any better than had the ancient comparisons of life with fire, or the more recent comparison of living organisms with mechanical engines, such as clockworks. Rather, so Bohr said, "an understanding of the essential characteristics of human beings must be sought in their peculiar organization, in which properties that may be analyzed by the usual mechanics are interwoven with typically atomistic traits in a manner having no counterpart in inorganic matter." To illustrate this point, Bohr provided a brief and insightful discussion of the human eye and pointed out that the absorption of a single light quantum by the retina suffices to cause a determinate, macroscopic effect, namely a visual experience by the subject.

So the question at issue was not whether physics can explain some features of the function of living organisms, which it clearly can, "but whether some fundamental traits are still missing in the analysis of natural phenomena, before we reach an understanding of life on the basis of physical experience." Bohr hastened to point out that among those missing traits he does *not* include the mysterious 'vital force,' which some romantic biologists called on for the governance of organic life. He thought that "we all agree with Newton that the real basis of science is that Nature under the same conditions will always exhibit the same regularities. Therefore, if we are able to push the analysis of the mechanism of living organisms as far as that of atomic phenomena, we should scarcely expect to find any properties differing from the properties of inorganic matter."

What kind of missing fundamental traits did Bohr then have in mind? He was thinking of traits that are still unknown, because the conditions holding for biological and physical research are not directly comparable, since the necessity of keeping the object of biological investigations alive imposes a restriction on biological research that finds no counterpart in physical research. Because its ultimate secrets will remain hidden from us, Bohr suggested that "the existence of life must be considered as an elementary fact that cannot be explained. It has to be accepted as a starting point of biology, just as the existence of elementary [subatomic] particles and of [Planck's] quantum of action have to be accepted as starting points of atomic physics. The impossibility of a physical or chemical explanation of the physiological functions peculiar to life would in this sense be analogous to the insufficiency of a mechanical analysis for the understanding of atoms." But if the existence of life itself is to remain an unexplained elementary fact of biology, how are we going to find the missing fundamental traits that will allow us to come to terms with life on the basis of physical experience? Not, said Bohr, by embracing the doctrine of *vitalism*, which asserts that the processes of life are not explicable by the laws of physics and chemistry because they are driven by an occult '*vital principle*,' distinct from physico-chemical forces. Instead, Bohr proposed that the missing fundamental traits of life are likely to devolve from the *complexity* of the physico-chemical systems that govern the behavior of the living matter we encounter in biology. Compared to the traits of life, the properties of matter in non-living-forms that are the primary focus of interest in atomic physics, are relatively simple.

Bohr extended his considerations from the physiological aspects of life, which make living organisms appear merely as material objects, albeit highly complex ones, to its psychological aspects, which make human beings appear as *more* than material objects, namely also as mental subjects. He pointed out that the recognition of the epistemological limitation presented by mutually exclusive observational arrangements for the study of atomic phenomena is suited also for reconciling the apparently contrasting points of view that separate physiology from psychology. "Indeed, the necessity of considering the interaction between the measuring instruments and the object under investigation in atomic physics corresponds closely to the peculiar difficulties met within psychological analyses, which arise from the fact that mental content is invariably altered when attention is concentrated on any single feature of it." However, just as Bohr had warned that the extension of the complementarity concept from atomic phenomena to living organisms should not be regarded as supporting vitalism in the physiology of living organisms, so did he warn also that complementarity should not be regarded as supporting spiritualism in psychology. Bohr said that from this point of view, "the free will must be considered as a trait peculiar to conscious life. . . . Without entering into metaphysical speculations, I may perhaps add that any analysis of the very concept of an explanation would, naturally, begin and end with a renunciation of an explanation of our own conscious activity."

Niels Bohr's Last Lecture. Thirty years after his seminal Light and Life lecture in Copenhagen and a few months before his death in November 1962, Bohr (1963) spoke at the dedication ceremony of the newly founded Institute of Genetics at the University of Cologne. Bohr entitled his address, which was to be his last public lecture, 'Light and Life Revisited.' Aware of the explosive progress in molecular biology that had begun to take place in the meanwhile, he had reconsidered his one-time conjecture about the impossibility of reducing physiology to physics. Bohr now said:

> It appeared for a long time that the regulatory function in living organisms, disclosed especially by studies of cell physiology and embryology, exhibited a fineness so unfamiliar to ordinary physical and chemical experience as to point to the existence of fundamental biological laws without counterpart in the properties of inanimate matter studied under simple reproducible experimental conditions. Stressing the difficulties of keeping the organisms alive under conditions which aim at a full atomic account I therefore suggested that the very existence of life might be taken as a basic fact in biology in the same sense as the quantum of action is to be regarded in atomic physics as a fundamental element irreducible to classical physical concepts.

From the point of view of physics, the mysteries of life were indeed stark. Physiologists had discovered innumerable ways in which cells respond intelligently to changed environmental conditions. Embryologists had demonstrated the possibilities of such amazing feats as growing two whole animals from one embryo split into halves. The transgenerational stability of the gene and the algebra of Mendelian genetics suggested to Bohr that the processes underlying the phenomena were akin to quantum mechanics. The resistance of biologists to such ideas did not surprise Bohr. He had met resistance to the complementarity argument before among his fellow physicists.

But this time Bohr was wrong, because James Watson's and Francis Crick's discovery of the DNA double helix in 1953 did for biology what many physicists had hoped, in vain, could be done for atomic physics. It solved all the mysteries in terms of visualizable theories, without having to abandon our intuitive notions about truth and reality embedded in our natural Kantian *a priori* categories of theoretical reason.

Max Planck's Last Lecture. In the spring of 1947, when I worked for the U.S. Military Government in Occupied Germany, I went to hear a lecture given by the 89-year-old Max Planck on "Religion and Science" at the Bayer pharmaceutical plant in the Westfalian city of Elberfeld. I was super-excited by the prospect of listening to Planck. It would provide me not only with the historically unique opportunity to see the Founding Father of Quantum Physics, but I would also learn first hand the great man's views on a theologico-philosophical problem that I had endlessly discussed with my fellow graduate students at the University of Illinois. We were all agreed that the sole connection between religion and science consists of science having proven that religion is bunk, a proposition that seemed self-evident, hardly worth making a fuss about. I suspected that in his dotage, Planck might have forsaken scientific rationality and gone back to the irrationalities of religion, something that my colleagues and I had promised each other we would never do.

Planck, looking ancient and frail, walked very slowly down the center aisle of the auditorium, supported by his second wife, Marga. She helped him mount the speaker's podium, where he sat down on a chair facing the audience. Remaining seated, he read his lecture from a prepared manuscript in a barely audible voice. He began with the admonition that the belief in miracles, which he identified as one of the main pillars of support of religious teachings, is incompatible with science. It is not even admissible to hold the view that while miracles are impossible today, of course, Moses or Jesus might have worked some a long time ago. Planck then declared that, the impossibility of miracles notwithstanding, we do need a religion, but one that is devoid of all myths about "externalities." The beliefs of that religion must be confined to "essences," namely to the faith in the existence of an Almighty Rational Entity, who reigns over Nature. According to Planck, this faith is backed by the findings of science, which show that general laws govern all natural phenomena. These laws are valid over the whole realm of Nature, in which we humans on our tiny planet play only a negligible role. The laws are independent of the existence of mankind, and yet, insofar as they can be fathomed by our senses, we can formulate them in terms of purposeful actions. Thus far from having done away with religion, science provides its most secure rational support.

After having spoken for about 45 minutes, Planck suddenly slumped in his chair and fell silent. Greatly alarmed, several people rushed to his side and carried him out of the hall. This lecture turned out to be Planck's last public appearance. He died nine months later.

I felt lucky to have seen and listened to the great Max Planck, and I liked his insistence that the belief in miracles is incompatible with science. Yet, I suspected that in making his seemingly preposterous claim that the findings of science support, rather than disprove religious faith, he was merely trying to sneak discredited pious baloney back in through the rear door. But later that day I began to think that maybe there *was* something to Planck's thesis. Perhaps all those one-hundred percent rationally thinking, self-styled atheists (such as I was at the time) who take it for granted that all phenomena are governed by generally applicable natural laws, actually *have* to believe—as did the Sumerians,—in the existence of a Divine Legislator who made up all those laws.

Coda. Bearing in mind Bohr's insight that a fiendish *conspiracy of nature* lies at the root of physical complementarity, it becomes evident that Kant had the insight that a no less fiendish *conspiracy of existence* lies at the root of the free will paradox. For just as Bohr saw that mutually exclusive observational arrangements are required for the study of the complementary attributes of the electron, so did Kant see that resort to mutually exclusive realms of pure reason is required for dealing with free will. According to Kant, in any given social situation, free will can be viewed from the standpoint *either* of the categories of pure theoretical reason *or* of the categories of pure practical reason, but *never* from both standpoints simultaneously. Thus beastly and divine, natural and non-natural, pure theoretical reason and pure practical reason, all appear to be complementary, that is paradoxical, apects of human nature.

References

Aquinas, St. Thomas (1947). *Summa Theologia*. Translated by the Fathers of the English Dominican Province. Part One 'Free Choice'; New York: Benzinger Brothers.

Aristotle (1999). *Nichomachean Ethics*. Translated by Terence Irwin. Second edition. Indianapolis: Hackett.

Augustine, St. (1967). On the Free Choice of the Will. Books II and III. Macmillan reprinted in D. Pereboom's, *Free Will*. Indianapolis and Cambridge: Hackett Publishing.

Been, S.I. (1988). *A Theory of Freedom*. Cambridge: Cambridge University Press.

Bellamy, E. (1888). *Looking Backward 2000–1887*. Boston and New York: Houghton, Mifflin & Co.

Berlin, I. (1971). The Question of Machiavelli. *New York Review of Books, November 4, 1971*, pp. 20–32.

Bodmer, W.F. and L.L. Cavalli-Sforza (1970). Intelligence and Race. *Scientific American* (October 1970), 9–29.

Bohr, N. (1928). The Quantum Postulate and Recent Developments in Atomic Theory. *Nature* 121 (Suppl.) 580–590.

Bohr, N. (1933). Light and Life. *Nature* 131, 421–423, 457–495.

Bohr, N. (1934). *Atomic Theory and the Description of Nature*. Cambridge: Cambridge University Press.

Bohr, N. (1949). Discussion with Einstein on Epistemological Problems in Atomic Physics. In *Albert Einstein: Philosopher-Scientist*. Evanston: Library of Living Philosophers, Inc., V. 5, p. 199.

Bohr, N. (1963). Light and Life Revisited. In *Essays 1958–1962 on Atomic Physics and Human Knowledge*. New York: Wiley, pp. 23–29.

Bradley, F.H. (1927). *Ethical Studies*. London, New York: Oxford University Press.

Breasted, J.H. (1933). *Dawn of Conscience*. New York: Scribner.

Broad, C.D. (1925). *The Mind and its Place in Nature*. New York: Harcourt Brace.

Buechmann, G. (1884). *Geflügelte Worte*. Berlin: Handse und Spenersche Buchhandlung.

Campbell, D.T. (1974). Evolutionary Epistemology. In *The Philosophy of Karl Popper* (P.A Schilpp, ed.). The Library of Living Philosophers, Vol. 141. La Salle, IL: Open Court.

Chisholm, R.M. (1976). Person and Object. London: George Allen and Unwin.

Churchland, P.S. (1986). *Neurophilosophy*. Cambridge, MA: MIT Press.

Damasio, A.H. (1999). *The Feeling of What Happens*. New York: Harcourt, Brace & Co.

Dawkins, R. (1976). *The Selfish Gene*. Oxford: Oxford University Press.

Dennett, D.C. (1984). *Elbow Room. The Varieties of Free Will Worth Wanting*. Cambridge, MA: MIT Press.

Descartes, R. (1637). *Discourse on the Method* (translated by E.S. Haldane and G.R. Ross).

Descartes, R. (1650). *Meditations on First Philosophy* (translated by D.A. Cross), 4th ed. Indianapolis: Hackett (1998).

Edwards, J. (1957). *Free Will* (P. Ramsay, ed.). New Haven: Yale University Press.

Eliade. M. (1978). *A History of Religious Ideas*. Chicago: University of Chicago Press.

Faye, J. (1991). *Niels Bohr: His Heritage and Legacy*. Dordrecht: Kluwer Academic Publishers.

Faye, J. and H.J. Folse (1994). *Niels Bohr and Contemporary Philosophy*. Dordrecht: Kluwer Academic.

Ferm, V., ed. (1950). *Ancient Religions I*. New York: Philosophical Library.

Fingarette, H. (1972). *Confucius the Secular as Sacred*. New York: Harper & Row.

Fischer, J. (1982). Responsibility and Control. *J. Phil.* Jan. 1982. 24–40.

Flavius, J. (1987). *The Works of Josephus* (William Whiston, transl.). Peabody, MA: Hendrickson Publishers.

Frankfurt, H.G. (1969). Alternate Possibilities of Moral Responsibility. *Journal of Philosophy* 66, 829–839.

Frankfurt, H.G. (1971). Freedom of the Will and the Concept of the Person. *Journal of Philosophy* 68, 829–839.

French, A.P. and P.J. Kennedy (1985). *Niels Bohr: A Centenary Volume*. Cambridge, MA: Harvard University Press.

Freud, S. (1939). *Moses and Monotheism*. New York: Knopf.

Fujimoto, H. (1972). Statement distributed at the hearings of the California State Board of Education, Sacramento, October 31, 1972.

Gates, J.A. (1960). *The Life and Thought of Kierkegaard for Everyman*. Philadelphia: The Westminster Press, p. 145.

Goodman, M.F., ed. (1988). *What is a Person?* Clifton, NJ: Humana Press.

REFERENCES

Hamilton, W.D. (1964). The Genetical Evolution of Social Behavior. *Journal of Theoretical Biology* 7:1–16, 17–32.

Hart, H.L.A. (1951). The Ascription of Responsibility and Rights. In *Essays on Logic and Language*, First Series (A.G.N. Flew, ed.), Oxford.

Hart, H.L.A. (1968). *Punishment and Responsibility*. Oxford: Oxford University Press.

Heiberg, P.A., V. Kuhr and E. Torsting (1909). *Søren Kierkegaards Papirer*. Copenhagen: Gyldendal. Vol. IIA, p. 751.

Hobbes, T. (1651). *Leviathan*. Reissued by C.B. Macpherson. Harmondsworth: Penguin Books, 1968.

Hook, S. (1981). *Determinism and Freedom in the Age of Modern Science*. New York: Collier Books, p. 8.

Hume, D. (1740). *A Treatise of Human Nature*. Second revised edition (P.H. Nidditch, ed.). Oxford: Clarendon Press (1978).

Huxley, J.S. (1943). *Evolutionary Ethics*. The Romanes Lecture delivered in the Sheldonian Theatre, 11 June 1943.

Kant, I. (1784). Idee zu einer allgemeinen Geschichte weltbürgerlicher Absicht. In *Kant's gesammelte Schriften*. Berlin: Preussische Akdemie der Wissenschaften. Vol. 8, p. 23.

Kant, I. (1797). *The Metaphysics of Morals*, Pt. 11: The Metaphysical Principles of Virtue.

Kant, I. (1934). *Critique of Pure Reason* (N.K. Smith, translator). London: Macmillan & Co.

Kant, I. (1949). *Critique of Pure Practical Reason* (L.W. Beck, translator). Chicago: University of Chicago Press.

Kohlberg, L. (1969). Stage and Sequence: The cognitive developmental approach to socialization. In *Handbook of Socialization Theory and Research* (D. Goslin, ed.), pp. 347–480. Chicago: Rand McNally.

Kohlberg, L. (1976). Moral stages and moralization: the cognitive-developmental approach. In *Moral Development and Behavior: Theory, Research, and Social Issues* (T. Lickona, ed.), pp. 31–53. New York: Holt, Rinehart and Winston.

Lomasky, L.E. (1992). *Concept of Person*. In *The Encyclopedia of Ethics* (L.C. Becker and C.B. Becker, eds.). Garland, New York, pp. 950–956.

Lorenz, K. (1944). Kant's Lehre vom *a priori* schen im Lichte Gegenwärtiger Biologie. *Blätter für Deutsche Philosophie*, 15, 94–125. [English translation: Kant's doctrine of the *a priori* in the light of contemporary biology. In *General Systems* (L. von Bertalanffy and A. Rapoport, eds.), Vol. 7, pp. 94–125. Ann Arbor: Society for General Systems Research, 1962.]

Macdonald, C. (1989). Mind-Body Identity Theories. London. In *The Philosophical Works of Descartes*. Cambridge: Cambridge University Press (1981).

MacKay, D.M. (1957). Complementary Descriptions. *Mind* 66:390–394.

MacKay, D.M. (1974). Complementarity in Scientific and Theological Thinking. *Zygon* 9:225–244.

MacKay, D.M. (1978). Selves and Brains. *Neuroscience* 3:599–606.

McNeil, W.H. (1963). *The Rise of the West*. Chicago: University of Chicago Press.

Mandelbrot, B. (1963). New Methods in Statistical Economics. *Journal of Political Economy* 71:421S.

Martin, J. and G.S. Stent (1990). I Think; Therefore I Thank. A Philosophy of Etiquette. *American Scholar* 59 (2):237–254.

Martin, J. and G.S. Stent (1992). Etiquette. In *The Encyclopedia of Ethics* (L.C. Becker and C.B. Becker, eds.). Garland, New York, pp. 331–333.

Mercer, S.A.B. (1950). The Religion of Ancient Egypt. In *Ancient Religion I* (V. Ferm, ed.), pp. 27–43.

Morgenbesser, S. and J. Walsh (1962). *Free Will*. Prentice Hall.

Morris, Desmond (1967). *The Naked Ape*. New York: MacGraw Hill.

Murti, T.R.V. (1960). *The Central Philosophy of Buddhism*. London: George Allen and Unwin.

Needham, J. (1967). *The Grand Titration*. London: George Allen & Unwin.

Nietzsche, F. (1883). *The Will to Power* (trans. Kaufmann and Hollingdale). New York: Vintage (1987).

O'Connor, D.J. (1970). *Free Will*. Garden City: Anchor Books.

Pais, A. (1991). *Niels Bohr's Times, in Physics, Philosophy, and Polity*. Oxford: Clarendon Press.

Pereboom, D. (1997). *Free Will*. Indianapolis and Cambridge: Hackett Publishing.

Piaget, J. (1932). *The Moral Judgment of the Child*. Glencoe, IL: Free Press.

Piaget, J. (1954). *The Construction of Reality in the Child*. New York: Basic Books.

Piaget, J. (1964). *Child's Conception of Number*. Atlantic Highlands, NJ: Humanities Press.

Piaget, J. (1971). *Genetic Epistemology* (E. Duckworth, tr.). New York: Norton.

Planck, M. (1901). Distribution of Energy in the Spectrum. *Annalen der Physik* 4, 553–563.

Popper, K.G. and J.C. Eccles (1977). *The Self and its Brain*. Berlin: Springer International.

Radner, D. and M. Radner (1989). *Animal Consciousness*. New York: Prometheus Books.

Rank, Otto (1914). *The Myth of the Birth of the Hero*. Monograph No. 18 of *The Journal of Nervous and Mental Disease*. New York: Lippincott.

Rank, Otto (1930). *Seelenglaube und Psychologie*. Leipzig: Franz Deuticke.

Rawls, J. (1971). *A Theory of Justice*. Cambridge, MA: Harvard University Press.

266

REFERENCES

Röseberg, U. (1985). *Niels Bohr: Leben und Werk Eines Atomphysikers*. Berlin: Akademie Verlag.

Röseberg, U. (1994). Hidden Historicity. The Challenge of Bohr's Philosophical Thought. In *Niels Bohr and Contemporary Philosophy* (J. Faye and H.J. Folse, eds.), p. 336.

Rousseau, J.-J. (1762). *Emile*. New York: Dent (1911).

Ryle, G. (1984). *The Concept of Mind*. London. Hutchinson.

Schaer, R., G. Clayes, and L.T. Sargent (2000). *Utopia: The Search for the Ideal Society in the Western World*. Oxford: Oxford University Press.

Skinner, B.F. (1971). *Beyond Freedom and Dignity*. New York: Knopf.

Sorell, T. (1991). *Scientism. Philosophy and the infatuation with science*. London and New York: Routledge.

Spencer, H. (1892). *Principles of Ethics*. London: Williams and Norgate.

Stemberger, G. (1995). *Jewish Contemporaries of Jesus. Pharisees, Sadducees, and Essenes*. Minneapolis: Fortress Press.

Stent, G.S. (1975). Limits to the Scientific Understanding of Man. *Science* 187: 1052–1057.

Stent, G.S. (1976a). The Poverty of Scientism and the Promise of Structuralist Ethics. *Hastings Center Report* 6 (6):32–40.

Stent, G.S. (1976b). What are the aspects that make us regard an organism a human being? In *Biology and the Future of Man* (C. Galpérine, ed.). Universities of Paris: Paris, pp. 405–407.

Stent, G.S. (1977). You can take the ethics out of altruism but you can't take the altruism out of ethics. *The Hastings Center Report* 7(6):33–36.

Stent, G.S. (1983). Origin, Limits, and Future of Science. *Revista di Biologia* 76 (4):549–571.

Stent, G.S. (1986). Hermeneutics and the analysis of complex biological systems. *Proc. Am. Phil. Soc.* 130:336–342.

Stent, G.S. (1988). Light and Life: Niels Bohr's Legacy to Contemporary Biology. In *Niels Bohr: Physics and the World*. (H. Feshbach, T. Matsui, and A. Oleson, eds.). Chur: Harwood Academic Publishers, pp. 231–244.

Stent, G.S. (1990). The Poverty of Neurophilosophy. *Journal of Medicine and Philosophy* 15:539–557.

Stent, G.S. (1998). Epistemic Dualism of Mind and Body. *Proc. Am. Phil. Soc.* 142 (4):578–588.

Stent, G.S. (2001). Consciousness: One of the Last Unsolved Great Biological Problems. *Biology International* (41):53–57.

Stent, G.S. (2002). Epistemic Dualism. In *Mind as a Scientific Object: Between Brain and Culture* (D.M. Johnson and C. Ermeling, eds.). Oxford: Oxford University.

Stent, G.S., E.P. Fischer, W. Golomb, D. Presti, and H. Seiler. (1986). *Max Delbrück's Mind from Matter?* Palo Alto: Blackwell Scientific Publications.

Szilard, L. (1961). *The Voice of the Dolphin*. New York: Simon and Schuster.

Thorp, J. (1980). *Free Will*. Routledge and Kegan Paul.

Tu, W. (1980). The Moral Universal from the Perspective of East Asian Thought. In *Morality as a Biological Phenomenon* (G.S. Stent, ed.). Berkeley: University of California Press, pp. 109–123.

Turiel, E. (1980). The Development of Moral Concepts. In *Morality as a Biological Phenomenon*. G.S. Stent, ed. Berkeley: University of California Press, pp. 109–123.

Van Inwagen, P. (1975). The Incompatibility of Free Will and Determinism. *Phil. Studies* 75:185–199.

Van Inwagen, P. (1983). *An Essay on Free Will*. Oxford: Clarendon Press.

Volkenstein, M. (1980). About the Freedom of Will. *J. Social Biol. Struc.* 3:68–72.

Vollmer, G. (1975). *Evolutionäre Erkenntnistheorie*. Stuttgart: Hirzel.

Vollmer, G. (1984). Mesocosm and Objective Knowledge. In *Concepts and Approaches in Evolutionary Epistemology* (F.M. Wuketits, ed.). Amsterdam: D. Reidel, pp. 69–121.

Waddington, C.H. (1960). *The Ethical Animal*. London: Allen and Unwin.

Wickler, W. (1971). *Die Biologie der Zehn Gebote*. Munich: Piper Verlag.

Williams, B. (1985). *Ethics and the Limits of Philosophy*. Cambridge, MA: Harvard University Press.

Wilson, E.O. (1975). *Sociobiology: The New Synthesis*. Cambridge, MA: Belknap Press.

Glossary

ANALYTICAL METHOD	The procedures Descartes devised for solving complex problems by resolving them into their simpler constituent elements.
ANALYTIC PROPOSITION	A proposition whose truth is evident from the words it contains, such as 'no bachelor is married,' and whose negation, e.g., 'some bachelors are married,' is self-contradictory.
ANIMAL	Unless stated explicitly otherwise, in this essay the meaning of the term "animal" does not include the species *Homo sapiens*, which from a biological point of view is, of course, a member of the animal kingdom.
ANTINOMY	A pair of apparently equally valid principles or propositions that contradict each other.
A *PRIORI*-SYNTHETIC PROPOSITION	A proposition whose truth is evident *a priori* and yet not derivable from an analysis of the words it contains, e.g. 'every event has a cause.'
ATTRIBUTE	A property, like weight, that has no existence on its own and owes its existence to a SUBSTANCE.
AUTONOMOUS	Independent and self-directing; the opposite of HETERONOMOUS.
BCE	A date before the Common Era, formerly called 'BC' (Before Christ).
CARTESIAN	Belonging or pertaining to René Descartes.
CATEGORICAL IMPERATIVE	A moral obligation or command that is unconditionally and universally binding.

269

CATEGORY (KANTIAN)	One of the fundamental principles, or *a priori* concepts, of human reason, such as causation, that we bring to the SENSIBLE WORLD for construction of the INTELLIGIBLE WORLD.
CE	A date in the Common Era, formerly called 'AD' (Anno Domini, or After Christ).
COMPLEMENTARITY	The concept introduced by Niels Bohr, according to which some physical phenomena give rise to rationally irreconcilable alternative interpretations whose inconsistency can never be demonstrated empirically.
CRITICAL IDEALISM	The Kantian theory according to which human knowledge is limited to PHENOMENA, whereas NOUMENA are thinkable but not actually knowable.
DETERMINISM	The doctrine according to which event is an effect of a prior series of events necessitated themselves by even earlier events. Determinism implies that all future events are as fixed and as unalterable as past events.
DUALISM	The doctrine that mind and body are each a separate SUBSTANCE. The opposite of MONISM.
ENTAIL	Thing A entails thing B if A causes B or requires B as its necessary accompaniment.
EPISTEMOLOGY	The branch of metaphysics that deals with the nature of our Knowledge about the world.
ETHICS	The system of rules, or laws, devised for regulating human social behavior in accord with the CATEGORIES of MORALS.
ETHOLOGY	The evolutionarily oriented study of animal behavior.
ETIQUETTE	The system of rules devised for regulating human social behavior in accord with the CATEGORIES of MANNERS.
EVOLUTIONARY EPISTEMOLOGY	The discipline at the interface of biology and philosophy that seeks evolutionary explanations of the origins of the CATEGORIES of Kant's EPISTEMOLOGY.
EXEMPLAR	An ideal model or example.

270

GLOSSARY

EXPLICATION	A *description* of the meaning of a word, as distinguished from its *normative definition*.
EXPLICATUM	The meaning of the word to be explicated.
HETERONOMOUS	Subject to external influence or determination; the opposite of AUTONOMOUS.
HEURISTIC	Helpful for learning, discovery, or problem-solving.
IDEALISM	The theory about the world according to which its essential reality is TRANSCENDENTAL and exists only in our consciousness and reason. The opposite of MATERIALISM.
INTELLIGIBLE WORLD	The world of NOUMENA.
JUDGMENT	A proposition stating an authoritative opinion (or the opinion so stated).
LIBERTARIANISM	The doctrine according to which we are free to act in one way or another and make the future different from what it would have been otherwise, regardless of what happened in the past and given the present state of affairs.
MANNERS	A subset of tacitly held human intuitions, or categories, of PURE PRACTICAL REASON, including social harmony, cultural coherence, beauty, and dignity of the person, as distinct from MORALS.
MATERIALISM	The doctrine about the nature of the world according to which physical matter is its only essential reality and that all being and processes and phenomena can be explained as manifestations or results of matter; the opposite of IDEALISM.
MENTALIST	Pertaining to the mind.
MESOCOSM	The world of middle dimensions to which the human cognitive structures are evolutionarily adapted.
METAPHYSICS	The branch of philosophy which deals with the first principles of things, including such concepts as being, substance, essence, time, space, cause, and identity.
MONISM	The doctrine according to which mind is not a separate SUBSTANCE but an ATTRIBUTE of the body; the opposite of DUALISM.

271

MORALS	A subset of tacitly held human intuitions, or categories, of PURE PRACTICAL REASON, including good and evil, free will, duty, compassion, and sacredness of the person, as distinct from MANNERS.
NON-NATURAL	Transcending the laws or the ordinary course of nature.
NOUMENA	Things-in-themselves, which are thinkable by our reason but not directly knowable by our senses. [From the Greek *nooumenon*, that which is conceived], as opposed to PHENOMENA.
PARADOX	A proposition which seems reasonable on first sight but turns out to be self-contradictory. Or two paired propositions, either of which, when considered alone, is supported by apparently sound arguments, but which, when they are considered together, turn out to be mutually contradictory.
PHENOMENA	Things as they appear to our senses and are familiar to us in everyday experience. [From the Greek *phainein*, to show], as opposed to NOUMENA.
PHYSICALIST	Pertaining to the body.
PROPOSITION	A statement capable of being true or false.
PURE PRACTICAL REASON	The part of PURE REASON applied to the SENSIBLE WORLD that resorts to such NON-NATURAL categories as values, ends, and responsibility. Practical reason constructs an INTELLIGIBLE WORLD whose NOUMENA are human subjects governed by laws of freedom, as distinguished from PURE THEORETICAL REASON.
PURE REASON	Reasoning applied to the SENSIBLE WORLD that is based on *a priori* CATEGORIES and provides a unifying ground for its perception.
PURE THEORETICAL REASON	The part of PURE REASON applied to the SENSIBLE WORLD that resorts to such natural categories as space, time, and causality. Pure theoretical reason constructs an INTELLIGIBLE WORLD whose NOUMENA are natural objects governed by the physical laws of causal determination, as distinguished from PURE PRACTICAL REASON.

GLOSSARY

RES COGITANS	Descartes' term for mental SUBSTANCE (that is, the soul or mind).
RES EXTENSA	Descartes' term for material SUBSTANCE (that is, the body).
RETRODICTION	A rational account of the causes of a present event as an effect of past events; the opposite of 'prediction,' which is a rational forecast of a future event as an effect of present events.
SENSIBLE WORLD	The world of PHENOMENA.
SOCIOBIOLOGY	A subdiscipline of ETHOLOGY dedicated to the study of the evolution of the social behavior of animals.
SUBSTANCE	Something that can exist in the world on its own, independently of anything else, as distinct from ATTRIBUTE.
SYNTHETIC PROPOSITION	A proposition whose truth is evident from observation, such as 'no bachelor is happy,' and whose negation, e.g. 'some bachelors are happy,' is not self-contradictory.
TAO	The Way of virtuous conduct, according to Confucian moral philosophy.
TAOISM	Chinese mystical philosophy whose basic tenet is the conformance of human society with the natural order and the rejection of the restrictive influence of social norms, moral precepts, and worldly goals.
THEODICY	The paradox that arises from the belief that God is good, even though He permits evil in the world that He created.
TORAH	The Hebrew term designating (strictly speaking) the Five Boooks of Moses, or (more loosely speaking), all of those parts of the Bible that Christians refer to as *Old Testament*.
TRANSCENDENTAL	Referring to ideas or notions that we apply to rather than derive from our experience, of which God, love, and good and evil are examples.
UTILITARIANISM	The moral doctrine according to which pleasure and the satisfaction of desires is the sole human good.

Sources of Illustrations

Cover: The Copernican Revolution. Woodcut made in 1888, in imitation of the style of the early Renaissance. Copyright: Archiv für Kunst und Geschichte, Berlin.

Immanuel Kant. Döbler (1791). From J.H.W. Stuckenberg, *The Life of Immanuel Kant*. Macmillan and Co., London, 1882.

Søren Kierkegaard. Drawn by Niels Christian Kierkegaard (1840). From Joakim Garff. *SAK - En Biografi*. Gads Forlag, København, 2000.

Moses showing the Tables of the Law to the people. Rembrandt (1659). From H. Focillon and L. Goldscheider, *Rembrandt*. Phaidon Press, London, 1960.

Plato's Symposion. Anselm Feuerbach (1866). From H. Bodmer, *Feuerbach*. Wilhelm Goldmann Verlag, Leipzig 1942.

St. Augustine. Sandro Botticelli (1480). From G.C. Argan, *Boticelli*. Editions d'Art Albert Skira, 1937.

Aristotle Contemplating a Bust of Homer. Rembrandt (1663). From H. Focillon and L. Goldscheider, *Rembrandt*. Phaidon Press, London, 1960.

David Hume. Allan Ramsay, (1766). From D. F. Norton, ed. *The Cambridge Companion to Hume*. Cambridge University Press, Cambridge 1993.

Pierre Simon, Marquis de Laplace. Commemorative stamp issued by the French Postal Service in 1955.

Martin Luther. Lukas Cranach, the Elder (1520). From Martin Brecht, *Martin Luther; Sein Weg zur Reformation*. Calwer Verlag, Stuttgart, 1981.

René Descartes. Frans Hals (1649). From W.R. Valentiner, *Rembrandt and Spinoza*. Phaidon Press, London. 1957.

Title page of Kant's *Critique of Pure Reason*. First edition, 1781. From Norbert Weis, *Königsberg: Immanuel Kant und seine Stadt*. Georg Westermann Verlag, Braunschweig. 1993, p. 131.

Erasmus of Rotterdam. Albrecht Dürer, (1520). From Martin Brecht, *Martin Luther; Sein Weg zur Reformation*. Calwer Verlag, Stuttgart, 1981.

Konrad Lorenz. From *Wissenschaftliche Mitglieder der Max Planck Gesellschaft*. Part II. Drucker & Humblot, Berlin. 1998.

Jean Piaget. From Milton Schwebel and Jane Raph, eds. *Piaget in the Classroom*. Basic Books, New York. 1973.

Francis Bacon. From *The Works of Francis Bacon*, J. Spedding, R.L. Ellis and D.D. Heath, eds. Vol. I. London: Longman's & Co., 1872.

Niels Bohr. From *Biographical Memoirs of Fellows of the Royal Society*, 9, 37 (1963).

Index

Bodmer, W., and L. Cavalli-Sforza, 228
Bohr, Christian, 254
Bohr, Niels, 1, 3, 7, 10, 11, 16, 236, 238, 243, 244, 245, 251–259, 261
Bohr's last lecture, 259–260
Boltzmann's Constant, 239
Bradley, F.H., 116
Brain evolution, 195
Brain imaging, 147
Brain science, 12, 146
Brain states, 147, 195
Brainwashing, 101
Breasted, J.H., 25, 34
Broad, C.D., 149
Buddha, [Siddharta Gautama] 5, 49, 50, 57, 135, 170, 171
Buddhism, 48, 91
Buddhist doctrines of Four Noble Truths (*dharma*) and Five Precepts, 49
Buechmann, G., 128
Bush, President George, 147

California State Board of Education: Hearings before its Curriculum Commission, 232
Calvin, J., 111
Campbell, D., 15
Canaan, 33
Candide, 76
Carlyle, T., 121
Carter, President Jimmy, 97
'Cartesian,' 141
Cartesian coordinates, 142
Cartesian physiology, 143–145
Categorical imperatives, 55–57
Categorical propositions, 159
Categories of reason, 14
Causality, Aristotle, 210
Causation, prescriptive vs. descriptive, 114–115
Chaos, 118–121
Character traits (Humean), 100
Chicago Seven, 182
China, 5, 48, 52
Chinese science, 54
'Choice' and 'responsibility'; Absence from *Analects*, 104
Chomsky, N., 145

Chou dynasty, 50
Christian fundamentalists, 220, 232–233
Christian philosophy, 59
Christian X, King of Denmark, 252
Christianity, 8, 35, 109
Chung (conscientiousness), 51
Churchland, P.S., 13, 149
City of God (St. Augustine), 67
Civilization, rise of, 21, 65, 177
Clayes, G., 9
Cloning, 85–86
Coercion, 47, 48, 101, 130, 131
Compatibilists, 99, 111, 114–116, 122
Complementarity, 16, 237, 244, 251
Condorcet, Marquis de, 168
Confucianism, 48–52, 172, 189–190
Confucius, 5, 50–52, 57, 104–106, 227
Consciousness, 22, 147
Conspiracy of existence, 253
Conspiracy of nature, 245, 251, 253
Constantine the Great, 63
Constraints, 126
Copernican Revolution in Philosophy, 158, 171, 172, 178, 254
'Could-Have-Done-Otherwise,' 127–128
'*Couldn't* Have Done Otherwise,' 128–129
Counterenlightenment, 170
Counterexamples, limitations of, 132–134
Critical (Kantian) Idealism, 14, 15, 155–156, 158–160, 163, 170, 171, 177, 200, 253
Critique of Pure Reason, 155, 158, 162, 253, 254
Critique of Practical Reason, 161, 162
'Crooked timber of humanity,' 164, 213
Cuneiform script, 28

D'Alembert, 169
Damasio, A.H., 147
Darwin, C., 133, 193, 194, 217
Dawkins, R., 224, 225
Dawn of Conscience, 25
Dead Sea Scrolls, 62
Decade of the brain, 147
De Civilitate, 180, 188
Deep Blue Chess Program, 163
Deep truths, 1, 3

Flood (Myth), 30
Folse, H.J., 254
Foreknowlege of the future, 8
Form (of the Good), 6, 7, 8, 44
Forms (Platonic), 6, 7, 14, 19, 79, 97, 138
Frankfurt, H., 81, 82, 91, 129–134
Frankfurt's counterexample, 129
Free will, 1, 3, 12, 13, 62, 67, 69, 96, 110,
    112, 113, 116, 138, 141, 150, 155,
    159, 162, 170, 175, 259
Freedom of action, constraints on,
    125–127
French, A.P., 254
Freud, S., 2, 34, 36, 112, 225
Fujimoto, Reverend Hogan, 233–234

Galen, 12, 140
Galileo, 54, 199, 210, 215
Gates, J.A., 10
Genesis, 29, 61, 90
Genetic determination of human
    behavior, 223
Genetic drift, 133
Genetic epistemology, 15, 201–213, 221,
    223
Geological evolution, 221
Ghost in the machine, 149
God, 5, 8, 9, 30, 35, 37, 38, 59, 62,
    67–71, 76, 90, 109, 112, 152,
    165–169, 193, 220, 251
Gödel, K., 10
Gospels, 66
Graves (Burials), 20
Greece, 2, 5
Grelling, K., 9

Hamilton, W., 222
Hammurabi, 32
Hart, H.L.A., 95
Hegel, G.F.H., 121
Heiberg, P.A., 1
Heisenberg, W., 243
Héloïse, 71
Heredity and Intelligence, 227, 229
Heterological words, 9
Hilbert, D., 10
Hippo, 71

History and its Dynamics, 120–121
    Alexander, Tsar, 121
    Carlyle, T., 121
    "Great Man" theory, 121
    Hegel, G.F.H., 121
    Linear and non-linear dynamics, 120
    Mandelbrot, B., 120
    Napoleon (Bonaparte), 120–121
    Prediction of future events and retro-
        diction of past events, 120
    Tolstoy, L.N., 120–21
    War and Peace, 120
Hitler, A., 4
Hobbes, T., 114
Høffding, H., 234
Homo sapiens, 5, 15, 79, 84, 87, 216, 217,
    218, 253
Hook, S., 3
Hopi Indians, 185, 227
Horus, 23
Hugo, V., 100
Human social behavior, genetic
    determination of, 223
Hume, D., 56, 100, 114–116, 208
Hunter-gatherers, 21
Huygens, C., 238
Hypothetical imperative, 55–57
Huxley, J., 218

Idealism, 6, 14, 111, 156, 171
Identity definition (of personhood),
    79–80, 84, 85, 87, 149
Immaterialists, 111–113
Incest taboo, 133
Inclusive fitness, 222
Incompatibilists, 99
Indeterminism (in quantum physics), 121
Indeterminism (or unpredictability), first
    and second stage, 118
Induction (logical), 208
Insanity, 84, 102–104
Intelligible world, 14
Interactionism, 150–152
Isis, 23, 28
Israel (nation), 33–39
Israelites, 27, 37

Jacob (alias 'Israel'), 33

Natural law, 109
Natural/amoral realm, 14
Naturalistic fallacy, 219, 220
Natural selection, 15, 173, 218, 219
Needham, J., 54
Neurophilosophy, 13
Newton, I., 14, 110, 158, 208, 238
Nicomachean Ethics, 45, 47, 130–131
Nietzsche, F., 76, 255
Nile, Valley, 22, 28
Nirvana, 49
Noble eightfold path, 49
Non-natural/moral realm, 15
Noumena, 14, 158, 159
Novum Organon, 215

O'Connor, D., 11, 114
Ontology, 41
Original position, 57
Osiris, 23, 28, 35

Pais, A., 254
Palestine, 33
Pangea, 222
Parable of the Cave, 43
Paradoxes, 7, 10
Paradoxes of Quantum Physics, 237–238
Paul, St., 62
Peel, Sir Robert, 103
Persons
    Actual and potential, 91–92
    Identity definition, 79–80
    Psychological definition, 80
    Second-order volitions definition, 81
    Slaves, natural, 85
    Uniqueness of, 85–86
Pharaoh, 23
Pharisees, 62
Phenomena, 14, 158
Photoelectric effect, discovery of the
    photon, 242
Physicalist statements, 12
Piaget, J., genetic epistemology, 15,
    201–212
    Accommodation, 203
    Assimilation, 202
    Cardinal numbers, 205
    Concrete operational stage, 205

Equilibrium, 202
Formal operational stage, 206
operational stage, 204
Sensorimotor stage, 204
Time and space, 206
Planck's constant, 241
Planck's distribution formula, 241
Planck, Marga, 260
Planck, Max, 241–242, 260–261
Plato, 5, 12, 43, 44, 57, 79, 111, 232
Plutarch, 88
Polis, 46
Popper, K.G., 151
Praiseworthiness, 2
Predestination, 111
Predictability, 117
Prehistoric mankind, 19
Prince Electors (at Worms), 128
Protestant Christian Fundamentalists,
    220
Ptolemies, 27
Pure practical reason, 4, 15, 160, 161,
    162, 166, 167, 173, 175, 176, 181,
    211, 213, 216, 237, 253, 254, 261
Pure reason, 159, 161, 164, 194, 223
Pure theoretical reason, 15, 161, 162,
    165, 166, 173, 196, 197, 199, 211,
    213, 216, 237, 253, 254, 255, 260,
    261
Pyramid texts, 23
Pythagoras, 88

Quantized Bohr atom, 243
Quantum physics, 121, 237–242

Radner, D. and M. Radner, 88
Rank, O., 2, 34
Ranke, L. von, 128
Rawls, J., 57
Rayleigh's distribution formula, 239
Re (Egyptian god), 23
Reagan, President Ronald, 226
Red in tooth and claw, 218
Relativity theory, 197–198
Religion and Science, 260–261
Ren, 24
Res cogitans, 142
Res extensa, 142